CultureShock!

A Survival Guide to Customs and Etiquette

China

Angie Eagan
Rebecca Weiner

Marshall Cavendish
Editions

This 2nd edition published in 2011 by:
Marshall Cavendish Corporation
99 White Plains Road
Tarrytown, NY 10591-9001
www.marshallcavendish.us

First published in 2007 by Marshall Cavendish International (Asia) Private Limited
Copyright © 2007, 2011 Marshall Cavendish International (Asia) Private Limited
All rights reserved

Other Marshall Cavendish Offices:
Marshall Cavendish International (Asia) Private Limited. 1 New Industrial Road,
Singapore 536196 ■ Marshall Cavendish International. PO Box 65829, London
EC1P 1NY, UK ■ Marshall Cavendish International (Thailand) Co Ltd. 253 Asoke,
12th Flr, Sukhumvit 21 Road, Klongtoey Nua, Wattana, Bangkok 10110, Thailand
■ Marshall Cavendish (Malaysia) Sdn Bhd, Times Subang, Lot 46, Subang Hi-Tech
Industrial Park, Batu Tiga, 40000 Shah Alam, Selangor Darul Ehsan, Malaysia

Marshall Cavendish is a trademark of Times Publishing Limited

ISBN 13: 978-0-7614-6052-7

Please contact the publisher for the Library of Congress catalogue number

Printed in Singapore by Times Printers Pte Ltd

Photo Credits:
All black and white photos by Attila Balogh and Angie Eagan.
All colour photos from Photolibrary ■ Cover photo: Photolibrary

All illustrations by TRIGG

ABOUT THE SERIES

Culture shock is a state of disorientation that can come over anyone who has been thrust into unknown surroundings, away from one's comfort zone. *CultureShock!* is a series of trusted and reputed guides which has, for decades, been helping expatriates and long-term visitors to cushion the impact of culture shock whenever they move to a new country.

Written by people who have lived in the country and experienced culture shock themselves, the authors share all the information necessary for anyone to cope with these feelings of disorientation more effectively. The guides are written in a style that is easy to read and covers a range of topics that will arm readers with enough advice, hints and tips to make their lives as normal as possible again.

Each book is structured in the same manner. It begins with the first impressions that visitors will have of that city or country. To understand a culture, one must first understand the people—where they came from, who they are, the values and traditions they live by, as well as their customs and etiquette. This is covered in the first half of the book.

Then on with the practical aspects—how to settle in with the greatest of ease. Authors walk readers through topics such as how to find accommodation, get the utilities and telecommunications up and running, enrol the children in school and keep in the pink of health. But that's not all. Once the essentials are out of the way, venture out and try the food, enjoy more of the culture and travel to other areas. Then be immersed in the language of the country before discovering more about the business side of things.

To round off, snippets of basic information are offered before readers are 'tested' on customs and etiquette of the country. Useful words and phrases, a comprehensive resource guide and list of books for further research are also included for easy reference.

CONTENTS

FOREWORD

As soon as you walk out of the airport gates, China hits you: the sounds, the smells, but mostly the incredible density of people. Within minutes, you become aware that your first challenge will be making yourself understood. You had felt so confident on the airplane after your three months of intensive language study. The fact that you cannot recognise a word being spoken around you is a bit of a worry. The indulgent smile of the official-looking security guard you try to ask where to catch a taxi and then non-coherent response make your stomach do a quick flip. How in the world are you going to navigate China without understanding the language?

Some are drawn to the exotic nature of the country, some terrified by it. The aim of *CultureShock! China* is to demystify the Oriental mystique enough to make it easy to navigate, but still a wonderful adventure.

This book is organised into ten chapters, ending with useful facts, suggested reading and contact details for important resources. The authors begin the book by providing China context. Chapter Two moves you through 5,000 years in just 23 pages, giving you enough knowledge of where they have come from to better understand who the people of China now are. Chapter Three delves into the psyche of modern-day mainland Chinese, detailing the influences and aspirations of their lives.

Chapter Four prepares you to dive into Chinese society, providing useful tips on social mores to enable you to navigate through your first person-to-person interactions as you begin to move more deeply into your China adventure.

The biggest practical challenges to making China your home are addressed in Chapter Five. The authors cover everything from securing the proper legal status to stay in China to navigating your new home city.

Most Chinese share one common passion—food. You can't know China without experiencing the diversity and personality of her cuisine. Chapter Six takes you on a culinary trip across China, delineating the differences among regional cuisines and suggesting signature dishes for you to sample as you eat your way to your own list of favourites.

Chapter Seven provides an orientation of festivals, holidays, entertainment and destinations that take your China adventure, and related understanding of the country and her people, to the next level. This is made all the easier through tips related to learning the Chinese language provided in Chapter Eight.

Advice on the most effective way to work in China are provided in Chapter Nine. The chapter provides useful insights on how to operate effectively in China's professional environment, as well as suggests organisations that may provide valuable business networks. The chapter concludes with an overview of charities that may benefit from you / your company's support.

If this has only whet your appetite for further reading on China, the authors have provided a list of their favourite books for you to continue learning more about China.

ACKNOWLEDGEMENTS

All who contributed to this book met in China in 1995, when she was fondly referred to as the 'Wild, Wild East'. It was a time of limited Internet access, limited basic staples (no coffee, no cheese, one kind of bread), limited bars and restaurants and unlimited adventure.

We were a family of circumstance. We were pioneers in our fields. We adapted in unimaginable ways: we tested the limits of the adage that fondly describes China, 'nothing is possible and everything is possible', and crafted our own way forward.

The knowledge that shaped this book could not have been accumulated without the experiences acquired with our family of circumstance, all China pioneers in their own right. This book is fondly attributed to each of them and honours the strong bond of lifetime friendship that is forged through shared experience.

From this group, two direct contributors to *CultureShock! China* are American Clancey Houston and Hungarian Attila Balogh. Clancey wrote the chapter on the history of China. A China scholar and well-regarded business advisor, Clancey's knowledge of and passion for China shines through her writing.

Attila's photos illuminate the book. His eye for the absurd, his sense of grace, his humour, and his compassion toward people, are all clear throughout the book.

We would also like to acknowledge the support of those who generously understood when we carved extra time out of days and nights to write this book, while having already-full professional and family lives.

Finally, our thanks goes to the two Crystals, Chan and Ouyang, as well as Melvin Neo and the rest of the staff at Marshall Cavendish International (Asia) Private Limited, for their support in publishing this book and the two previous ones. The book has been made stronger by their comments and contributions.

This book is dedicated to those
who have loved us with their arms
open wide enough to let us take in the World.

MAP OF CHINA

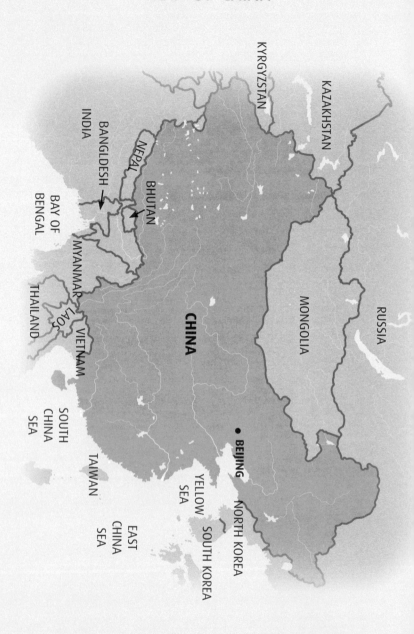

FIRST IMPRESSIONS

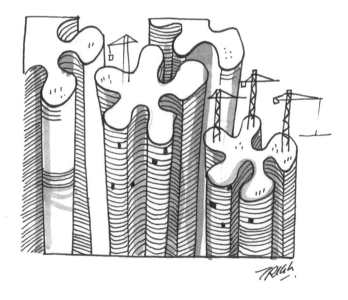

' "What's the name of that song of yours? I'm asking you what its called," (the village headman) snapped. "Mozart is thinking of Chairman Mao," Luo broke in... the headman's menacing look softened. He crinkled up his eyes in a wide beatific smile. "Mozart thinks of Mao all the time," he said. This was the first taste of our re-education.'
—Dai Sijie, *Balzac and the Little Chinese Seamstress*

WILD WILD EAST

Imagine living in a city where if you forget to pick up your dry cleaning for just a week, you run the risk of losing it forever because the block the Laundromat is located on is slated that week for demolition. In 1995, that was the risk that you ran of forgetting your dry cleaning for more than a few days in Shanghai. Twenty-five per cent of the construction cranes in the world were in Shanghai.

Imagine living in a city where the day you arrived, the place known as Pudong was a single-standing TV tower, grandiosely called 'The Pearl of the Orient', which looked like a cross between a Jetson's space home and a series of onions skewered on a stick, standing amid farmland and rundown wood shacks. A mere six years later, that same TV tower was surrounded by a shining city of iconic architecture, inhabited by millions, which hosted leaders from around the world attending the 2001 Asia-Pacific Economic Cooperation (APEC) meetings. Global news broadcasts from the APEC meetings made that skyline, which didn't exist six years before, the new image of modern China.

Each week, city blocks were moving parts of a giant puzzle, whose complete picture would be the modern day, world-class city that will host the World Expo in 2010.

When we arrived in China in 1995, it was like living in the wild, wild east. Nothing was possible and everything was possible. You were coated each day with the construction dust

Heavy traffic conditions and tall skyscrapers are a common sight in many major cities in China.

of change happening around you minute by minute. It was clearly the most exciting place to live and do business in the entire world. The one single truism was that nothing would ever be boring in China. That truism still holds.

The single question people ask when they hear that you have lived in China for ten plus years is "When will you leave?" The answer is always "When it stops being exciting."

OVERVIEW AND HISTORY

CHAPTER 2

'...4,350 years have passed from the first year of the
Yellow Emperor to the present, and three hundred and one
emperors are listed as having reigned.'
—Final edict of K'ang-hsi,
second Qing Dynasty emperor, 1722

FIVE THOUSAND YEARS OF HISTORY

Ever wonder why the Great Wall was built? Or how grand European architecture ended up watching over the traffic along the Huangpu River in Shanghai? Or how Chinese characters developed?

The answers to all of these questions—and many more —can be found buried within the more than 5,000 years of history behind the China we know today. Now, 5,000 years is a lot of time to plough through, so we're here to bring you the highlights—Chinese history 'lite', a quick march around the names, places, personalities and passions that inspired great creations like the Great Wall, Forbidden City, Beijing Opera and the Bund.

Many Firsts

Without a doubt, the sheer length of China's long cultural and national history is one of the most striking aspects of this nation of more than 1 billion people—though the fact that so many people are living within her borders is itself an astounding fact. The reality is, China represents the world's longest shared culture of any group of people, at any time, anywhere.

That culture was farming and raising livestock as early as 5,000 to 6,000 years ago; developed a writing system almost 4,000 years ago; and by 220 BC had instituted a distinct form of government—the imperial dynastic system—that shaped government for centuries.

The Beginning

How did it begin? Legends abound about China's earliest years, many of them involving wild animals, fortune-telling, and lots of flying. Then there are 'the men'—'Yuanmou Man' and his descendant 'Peking Man', who are believed to have inhabited China 1.7 million and 500,000 years ago, respectively. Not much is known about either of them, however, as an apparent preference for staying shrouded in mystery seems to have been the order of the day.

The Neolithic Age that followed Peking Man's time is represented primarily by the Longshan and Yangshao cultures, both village groups in the Northern areas of today's China. They are distinguished by their pottery, smooth and black for the Longshan, and red with black swirls for the Yangshao.

Xia (2070–1600 BC)

Perhaps best known for being the precursor to the Shang, the Xia also represents the beginning of China's dynastic history. With the Xia, China made the first turn on a wheel of unity, collapse, chaos and reunification that would characterise her development for centuries to come. This dynasty also marked a shift in the life of China's people, from primitive to slave society, under the watchful eyes of new Xia leaders.

Shang (1600–1046 BC)

Taking over from the Xia in 1600 BC, after conflict among warlords led to that dynasty's decline, Shang rulers oversaw a flourishing of important developments during their period of post-conflict calm: the earliest and most complete examples of Chinese writing on shamanistic oracle bones; an ability to use iron tools and the skills to smelt bronze, giving China the most advanced bronze-making techniques in the world at that time; white and glazed pottery; and the beauty of silk and innovative weaving techniques with which to work it.

On the very practical side, the Shang put their mark on the hierarchy and class stratification introduced by the Xia. Society was comprised of a king, nobles, commoners and slaves, each with a place and a purpose. For the last group,

Some scholars reportedly believe that the Xia, Shang and Zhou actually all resided around the Yellow River valley at the same time, eventually coming to blows and conquering each other in (relatively) rapid succession.

unfortunately, their place was often alongside a Shang king or nobleman in his final resting place—the Shang engaged in regular human sacrifice, along the lines of the famous terracotta army in Xi'an, though without the terracotta involved.

After a little more than 500 years, the Shang's highly organised armies and their fancy horse-drawn chariots failed them, and they were conquered from the outside by the Zhou in 1046 BC.

Zhou (1046–221 BC)

Stretching from 1046 to 256 BC with two distinct periods—the Spring & Autumn Period and the Warring States—the Zhou can be described as a study in extremes, between strict rule and harsh conditions and an unprecedented flourishing of philosophies and schools of thought that still influence the average man on the street today.

Actually the most powerful principality among many rather than the ruling power of a united empire, the Zhou served as a regional hegemon. The Zhou state's location in the centre of all the others gave rise to a turn of phrase—the 'Middle Kingdom'—that would infuse China's approach to foreign relations when contact with countries beyond her borders became frequent.

From this centre point, the Zhou maintained a certain peace for several hundred years before being attacked in 771 BC by 'barbarians', the common term for anyone outside of China's borders. As the invaders came in from the West, the reign of the 'Western Zhou' ended as the population moved east to establish a new capital and begin again as the 'Eastern Zhou'.

By about 481 BC, the Zhou's mandate was slowly slipping, and the Spring & Autumn period gave way to the Warring States period. Though small battles were fought regularly during the Spring & Autumn period, the Warring States was as it sounds—ongoing war between the many states that collectively were governed by the Zhou.

Eventually, the Qin, the strongest state of the seven or so remaining by the 4th century BC, fought its way to the forefront and reunited China under their own banner.

The Spring and Autumn Period

During the Spring & Autumn Period, names like Lao-zi, Meng-zi, Zhuang-zi, and Kong-zi were among those whose world (and other-worldly) views floated among the 'Hundred Schools of Thought' that battled to capture the minds of the people and their rulers at the time.

From this era of free-ranging thinking emerged three important world views—Confucianism, Daoism and Legalism—outlined in Confucius' *5 Classics*, in Lao-zi's *Tao de ching* and in various writings from Xun-zi. Collectively, these sage men of old, and many others like them, gave us the ideas of filial piety, *yin* and *yang* and the *Tao*, among many others.

In his development of the codes and ways of behaving that he believed necessary to attain certain virtue, Confucius also codified the concept of the 'Mandate of Heaven'. During a time when the success of a hunt or a crop cycle was supposedly dictated by Heaven and the gods inhabiting Heaven and Earth, it was not a large leap to put the king in the position of supreme placator. He and the dynasty he represented held power only as long as Heaven was placated; and they lost it—for whatever reason—when it was not.

Qin (221–206 BC)

The chaos of the later Zhou created the perfect vacuum of power to allow the aggressive Qin rulers to rise to the top (that and a prevalence of weaponry created from stocks of iron far greater than the other states around them).

The Qin rulers were firm believers in the logic of Legalism, which was first espoused by Confucius' disciple, Xun-zi, during the Spring & Autumn period. Legalism had at its roots a belief in man as inherently focused on his own good, and therefore basically evil. The only way to ensure control over a society of essentially selfish and self-serving individuals was institution of a set of draconian laws and corresponding

Qin Shi Huang unified the states by linking together the city walls of the individual principalities that comprised his empire. Though made of packed earth rather than masonry, this early 'great wall' was the precursor to the Ming dynasty's construction of the Great Wall we still see today.

punishments for breaking them. From 221 to 206 BC, these laws were used to maintain order against a constant backdrop of battles with the barbarians on the Qin's borders.

Supreme among the ruling class was King Ying Zheng, who upon unification took the name 'Qin Shi Huang', meaning First Emperor of the Qin, thereby establishing China's imperial system of rule. During his time on the throne, standardisation was his main focus—weights and measures, currency and a common script were among the things that became consistent across and among the various states.

Finally, Qin Shi Huang also advanced the Shang practice of burying slaves with their dead ruler, choosing to have his tomb filled with the life-size terracotta army that now attracts swarms of visitors to present-day Xi'an each year.

As was to be expected, Qin Shi Huang's mandate eventually ended, this time with a peasant leader named Liu Bang and his general friend Xiang Yu, delivering the news of Heaven's displeasure. Liu Bang then turned on Xiang Yu, and, in AD 206 proclaimed the great empire of the Han.

Han (206 BC–AD 220)

Much like the Zhou before it, the Han is divided into Western (or Earlier Han) and Eastern (or Later Han) periods, with a brief interlude between the two called the 'Wang Mang' period, during which a member of the Han court (named, of course, Wang Mang), ruled rather than the imperial family.

The Han is described by many as 400 years of glory days. Pride in this time gave the dominant ethnic group of early China its name—Han Chinese, a moniker used even today. These days of glory saw respect for scholars restored to pre-Qin levels, and the ideas put forward by Confucius during the Qin at last became a full-fledged school of thought. Confucianism eventually rose to the level of official state doctrine, governing the imperial court and through it, society.

Within the government, the Han chose its officials based on merit. Dealing with the conniving eunuchs, imperial courtesans and their scheming family members at the time surely tested any official's mettle. Exploration beyond China's existing borders, designed to expand the fledgling nation, often led to heated battles for territory and control with the tribes inhabiting those lands as well, testing the Han from the outside at the same time. A battle on two fronts was brewing.

Within her borders, the sheer size of China's territory and growing population was a growing challenge. When the Han dynasty was founded in 206 BC, China reportedly stretched from modern Shenyang (some 500 km north of Beijing) in the north to around Guilin in the south; from the Pacific in the east to the region around Chongqing in the west. It was the largest country in the world. And with a population of approximately 60 million, it was also the most populous.

Efficiency and control of a land this size, for at least a few centuries, was attempted through the further development of the bureaucracy started by the Qin: centralised control of distinct administrative regions, a form of government every successive dynasty would copy, and one quite similar to the provincial system we still see today. The proper behaviour and loyalty to the emperor codified in Confucian thought helped the court maintain its rule.

We know about this and many other aspects of Han life thanks to Mr Sima Qian, the Han's Grand Historian, who created the standard format for recording Chinese history used by all other dynasties. *Historical Records* took Sima ten years to complete, and even then it wasn't finished—the Grand Historians who came after him were tasked with picking up where Sima left off.

What the records also show is that the Han were no more immune to the effects of the dynastic cycle than those that came before them. Han society was well developed in terms of

The most famous of the Han's border battles is their defeat of the Xiongnu, a nomadic tribe, which opened the way for a special envoy of the court, Zhang Qian, to head west, pioneering what we call today the 'Silk Road' between the Han's capital city of Chang'an (now Xi'an), through Xinjiang and on to the Mediterranean Sea.

agriculture and handicrafts, culture and commerce—during this time period, the Chinese invented compasses, sundials and water clocks, and devised the lunar calendar.

However, population shifts from the Yellow River in the North to the Yangtze River in the south of the kingdom, combined with the increasing frequency of border raids by tribes in the North (a key reason behind the migration to the south) pushed yet another dynastic government to the limit of its ability to control the provinces from the centre. China witnessed another dynasty collapsed, and again, conflict and chaos ensued—350 years of it.

CHAOS AND DISUNITY

Chaos and disunity reigned from AD 220 through to AD 581, known most often as the 'Three Kingdoms' period. Barbarians from the north once again invaded the emperor's domain, assimilating themselves into the society left behind by the many Han Chinese moving south.

The Three Kingdoms

The three kingdoms of the first half of this period of disunity were Wei, Shu and Wu, each with an elder statesman at its helm. The most famous of these was Zhuge Liang (181–234), prime minister of the State of Shu. To this day, even among the hip-hop Chinese youths in the big cities, Zhuge Liang is a name that prompts one to 'give one's all' to a task, reflective of Zhuge Liang's own intense dedication to 'bending himself to the task and exerting himself to the utmost till his dying days'.

The Three Kingdoms Period was followed by the Jin (265–420), the Southern and Northern dynasties (420–589), and then eventually the Sui dynasty (581–618).

Despite the turmoil of these centuries, two important developments occurred: Buddhism took root, and one of China's most well-known pieces of literature was created—*The Romance of the Three Kingdoms*, a story that romanticises the intrigue and eventual fall of a fictional imperial court.

Buddhism had most likely already been a subject of Chinese philosophical discussion around the middle of the first century, but with the fall of the Han, it began to catch on amid an increasingly eclectic mix of thinking.

Sui (AD 581–618)
At last, unity came again, this time thanks to the sword of a strong general from the North-west, who conquered the warring tribes around him and proclaimed the establishment of a new emperor. As far as dynasties go, the Sui was a short one. But it did serve to unify China once again and provide a foundation upon which the 'Golden Age' of its successor, the Tang, could flourish.

Tang (AD 618–907)
The Tang dynasty was founded in 618, after the assassination of the last Sui Emperor in an army coup. Despite its violent beginnings (hardly a new means of dynastic succession), the Tang is revered among Chinese dynasties, second only to the Han.

During the Tang dynasty, the borders of China stretched from the area of Mongolia, Manchuria and Korea in the North to what is now Vietnam in the South; from Tibet and Central Asia in the West to the Pacific in the East. And the Silk Road meandered through it into what is today Afghanistan. Developments in land and water transportation meant that China was exploring well beyond its borders, establishing trade and cultural relations with countries throughout the region, including Japan, Persia, India and Arabia, among others.

These ventures to far-flung lands were supported by a prosperous economy. Land and economic reforms instituting equal allocation of taxes and specified values for key commodities had created an agricultural surplus that paved the way for tremendous commercial growth and the urbanisation of key parts of the empire. China can also trace much of its fame for new inventions to the Tang —papermaking, powder and fireworks.

Though plagued, as most dynasties were, by court intrigue, restless armies, and ambitious viceroys in the provinces, the time of the Tang was one of geographical expansion, a renaissance of arts and culture, ongoing invention and creation, and the flowering of even more schools of thought.

The An Lu Shan Rebellion

Though still a feudal society, the Tang dynasty was a prosperous one for much of its first century of rule. It was the An Lu Shan Rebellion that marked the beginning of the end and China's rapid descent into, yet again, chaos and confusion.

An Lu Shan was a general who commanded territory in the Northwest. Leveraging power gained during the tenure of Empress Wu (the only woman to hold the title Emperor officially), An Lu Shan eventually rose in rebellion, starting a series of battles that continued from AD 755 to 763, shattering the Tang's central control and ultimately causing the downfall of the dynasty.

Total collapse took more than another century but come it did, to be followed by another period of (yes, again) disunity—the Five Dynasties and Ten Kingdoms period (AD 907–960)—during which multiple rulers vied for penultimate control.

Song (AD 960–1279)

Not for another 50 years after the official end of the Tang was China united again, this time by a mutiny with General Zhao Kuangyin in the lead. The reign of the Song line from 960 to 1279 (again, with a movement of capital from North to South in the 1100s to escape invading barbarians) was marked by steady advancement.

China's 'Four Great Inventions'—paper-making, printing, the compass and gunpowder—were developed further; and handicraft, industry and domestic and foreign trade also boomed, with a steady stream of merchants and travellers coming from abroad, typically to coastal cities like Canton, which were rapidly becoming major ports.

Agricultural technology played a big part in China's growth under the Song by making her fully self-sustaining—there was actually an abundance of food and labour. The tremendous security that came with this led to a flourishing of the economy, and subsequently the arts and culture, all of which set the stage for much of the rest of the imperial era.

In the view of some, the comfortable situation of the Song precluded an early industrial revolution as China did not have a pressing need to mechanise in order to feed its people. What they did have a pressing need for was protection, for in the 13th century, the Great Wall that was constructed to protect China from the barbarians to the North had its first major failure. The Mongols, led by Kublai Khan, the grandson of Genghis, crossed into China's territory, establishing the new capital of the Mongol empire in Beijing and, by 1276, overtaking the Southern Song capital in Hangzhou.

Yuan (AD 1206–1368)

Proclaiming the reign of the Yuan dynasty in 1271—Yuan meaning 'first' to symbolise the first stage in a long tenure of Mongol rule—Kublai Khan became the first non-Han emperor to rule China.

Resented for their continued use of Mongol customs and language and a determined focus on foreign rather than Chinese officials to govern, the era of Mongol rule nonetheless contributed a number of significant things to China's development. The lack of roles for Chinese within the government led to a peak in all things cultural, including the creation of the Beijing Opera art form. Kublai Khan is also responsible for the construction of the Grand Canal.

Marco Polo's book about his travels in Asia provides a first-hand account of both the achievements and inner workings of the Yuan court, writing from first-hand experience as an official to the Mongol court who quickly became a favourite advisor to Kublai Khan himself.

But foreign rule grated continuously against the Chinese, making it none too hard to find parties interested in sending the Mongols packing.

Ming (AD 1368–1644)

Perhaps looking to history for inspiration, in the 1350s a group of rebels called the Red Turbans did just that. Led by Zhu Yuanzhang, they took advantage of the weakened state of control that existed after the death of Kublai Khan, capturing first the area surrounding the old capital of Nanjing and eventually the Mongol capital of Beijing. In 1368, Zhu proclaimed the Ming dynasty, which lasted till 1644. Focused intently on reorganisation and restoration of a 'local' government, Ming emperors prioritised reaffirming central government control and the edicts of Confucianism over discovery and exploration.

Copper coins with a square hole in the middle, used during the Yuan and Ming dynasties.

Power became increasingly centralised in the emperor himself, who eventually moved the capital from Nanjing to Beijing. It was at this time that the Imperial Palace (also known as the Forbidden City) was constructed and the Great Wall, as we know it today, completed.

The enforcement of a strict adherence to Confucianism under the Ming led many to label the philosophy of that day 'Neo-Confucianism'. The government rigorously applied the centuries old examination system to select officials for the central bureaucracy. Based on the works of Confucius and Zhu Xi, the examination system was expanded during the Ming to include the 'eight-legged' essay, a special style unique to this period and especially demanding for scholars taking the imperial exam.

Despite a focus on things internal, engagement with cultures outside China's borders didn't come to halt. Between approximately 1405 and 1433, seven major maritime excursions took place, led by the eunuch Zheng He. Able to boast possibly the world's largest seagoing fleet at the time, the Ming rulers sent Zheng He and his ships throughout the oceans of the world, reaching as far west as eastern Africa and as far south as Java and Sumatra. Despite the wealth of experience and exposure that Zheng He brought back to China, however, the excursions suddenly stopped and China began to slowly turn inwards. Naval exploits were replaced by a spate of navel-gazing.

Though looking increasingly inward, Chinese society at the time included a growing number of Europeans. Macau had been leased to Portugal as a trading outpost; the Jesuits arrived in vast numbers, Matteo Ricci being one of the most well-known among them; and other nationalities interested in uncovering the secrets of the Orient arrived as well.

A manageable balance was created between these mixing cultures, but by the late Ming, successive emperors presided over a government that was notoriously corrupt, at both the central and provincial levels. Greedy provincial leaders and eunuchs were managing taxation and distribution of funds to their own advantage, rapidly weakening the ability of the court to actually govern.

The timing of this decline in government authority coincided with an increase in pirates on the east coat and a rise in the strength of the Manchus to China's north. In the end, it was a last-ditch attempt to save Korea from invading Japanese troops that depleted the reserves of the government to a level beyond that which they could recover from. The dynasty was now easy prey for a sweeping invasion by the Manchus that meant the end of the Ming and the beginning of the Qing.

The Qing Dynasty (1616–1911)

Though a foreign power, the Manchus differed from the Mongols in one important way—they involved Chinese officials in governing and attempted to preserve many of the institutions and governing philosophies of the time. Their determined attempt at preservation, however, often resulted in such strictness of approach that made them even more inflexible than their predecessors.

This became most apparent in the area of foreign policy. During the Qing dynasty, firm belief in the emperor as the 'Son of Heaven' ruling with the 'Mandate of Heaven' did not allow room for the presence of other countries existing at the same level of importance as China herself; there was China, and there was everyone else. Demands for tribute were levelled at any envoy of a foreign power that visited the early Qing imperial court, limiting China's friends, but creating the beautiful collection of treasures currently housed in the Forbidden City.

Nonetheless, until the 1840s, the arts flourished and culture boomed, particularly during the reigns of the two most famous emperors of the Qing dynasty, Emperor Kangxi (r. 1661–1772) and Emperor Qianlong (r. 1735–1796). The best example of literature at this time is the classic Chinese novel *A Dream of the Red Chamber*, a tale of the activities and intrigue, and then slow decline of a prosperous aristocratic family of the time.

The 'times of prosperity' under these two emperors eventually dwindled and by the late 19th century, the dynasty was plagued by the typical maladies—rampant corruption, a steady decentralisation of power and the loss of control on too many fronts at the same time, including an important new one, an influx of Europeans in large numbers. Internal rebellions—the Tai'ping and Boxer Rebellions being the most well known—coupled by ongoing and increasingly significant challenges, both militarily and culturally, by foreign parties eventually led to a challenging state of constantly changing battlegrounds.

A stark example of the clashing of wills common between China and the West at the time are the two Opium Wars fought from 1839 to 1842 between China and Britain, and then from 1856 to 1860 (also known as the Arrow War) involving China, Britain and France. While linked to opium, the foreigners were actually fighting for free trading rights in Canton and ports all along the coast of China. With the conclusion of this conflict came the Treaty of Nanjing in 1842, the first in a series of what came to be known as the 'Unequal Treaties'.

These treaties created a China segmented by the presence of numerous foreign concessions; without the authority to deal with foreigners who broke Chinese law ('extraterritoriality' allowed them to be tried by their own country's China-based courts); and beset by foreign navies sailing unobstructed up and down her rivers and waterways.

Strangely enough, this intensive intrusion by foreign powers was balanced by ad hoc support from these same nations for the ailing dynasty, such as the crushing of the Boxer Rebellion by US troops in 1900. The foreign concession holders realised that their cushy positions would only last as long as the Qing itself did.

And last it did not. That end came at the beginning of 1912, with the abdication of the last Qing emperor (who was actually only six years old at the time), and two millennia of dynastic rule in China came to a close.

THE REPUBLIC OF CHINA (1912–1949)

In contrast to the falls of previous dynasties, at the close of the Qing, the reigns of government were quickly taken up by a group that had been agitating for revolution for many years. The nominal head of this movement was a man named Sun Yat-sen, the universally-regarded father of modern China.

Sun Yat-sen's rise to president of the Republic of China (ROC) began when he was actually living in exile in the United States. A group of rebels in Wuhan staged a rebellion on 10 October 1911, inspiring similar uprisings in neighbouring provinces.

After seizing control of their areas from the Manchus, the leaders of this newly independent section of China chose Sun Yat-sen as their leader, establishing him as the head of the new Republic of China's government in Nanjing. The negotiations with the Manchus that ensued resulted in the formal abdication of the last emperor of China, and the formal establishment of the ROC as the 'dynasty' of the future.

Sun did not serve as president of the ROC for long—in March 1912, he was forced to resign according to the terms of the settlement agreed with the Manchus, and hand over the reigns to his elected successor, Yuan Shikai.

Despite pledges to the contrary, after initial efforts to

Intent on restoring China to Chinese rule for years prior to the end of the Qing dynasty, Sun Yat-sen espoused three basic principles: nationalism (a China free from foreign control), democracy (the Manchus replaced by a democratic political system) and people's livelihood.

draft a constitution and democratise the political system—which did include the formation of the Kuomintang (or KMT)—Yuan did not govern with Sun Yat-sen's three basic principles in mind. Instead, he focused on expanding his own power base, purportedly with the goal of re-establishing the imperial system with himself as the newest emperor.

Yuan's efforts to return China to the bad old days of imperial-style rule were thwarted by internal opposition, and just in time, as the war waging in Europe was finally being felt as far away as China. China threw her support to the Allies in 1917, having been promised the return of all foreign concession land at the close of the war. That promise became yet another of the many unfulfilled. The response to this bad taste of betrayal came in the form of a massive popular protest in Beijing on 4 May 1919, involving thousands of students from the numerous universities in the capital.

This event was the beginning of the May Fourth Movement, widely seen as China's first truly populist national movement. Students, workers, merchants and scholars pushed for reforms that would restore China's independence and pride. A split among its leaders eventually led to the end of the movement, with its various causes taken up alternatively by the KMT led by Sun Yat-sen, and a fledgling Communist Party of China, which had held its first party congress in Shanghai in 1921. At that meeting, a new recruit—the young and ambitious Mao Zedong—surfaced.

By 1920, the Comintern (Communist International) was already actively engaged in recruitment and education in China, and when the Soviet Union cast about for political support, the more promising partner was Sun Yat-sen. Having been rebuffed by both the United States and Great Britain in his search for support, the approach by the Comintern was a timely one for Sun.

Sun's buddying up to the Soviet Union led to a strange arrangement: official recognition of the KMT as the party in charge, but with China's communists admitted as members. Soviet aid then poured in, helping to create a KMT army to defeat the warlords in control of much of northern China. Among those trained in Moscow was a young military officer named Chiang Kai-shek, who returned to China and assumed the leadership of the Whampoa Military Academy.

Unfortunately, Sun Yat-sen died of cancer in 1925, before he could see his dream of a united China realised. The leadership of the KMT passed on to the younger Chiang Kai-shek, who embarked on a 'Northern Expedition' from Guangzhou to Shanghai in July 1926, to root out opposition and recapture territory. By April of the following year, Chiang and his troops had reached the lower Yangtze and were preparing to move on Shanghai. Despite the inclusion of communists among KMT party ranks, Chiang's move on Shanghai included a massacre of communists that marked a firm break with much of the rest of the KMT. The Communist Party members thus fled to the countryside in droves to escape further crackdowns by KMT troops, which pressed on to Beijing in a similar frame of mind, reaching their destination in 1928 and formally unifying the country.

The Lead up to the Long March

With recognition of the Nationalist (KMT) government by international powers and the funding that came with it, a path was paved for the swift development of a prosperous, independent China, ruled by Chinese. But the all-too-familiar issues of corruption, internal discord and interference by foreign powers (this time the Japanese) kept Chiang Kai-shek's attention splintered and distracted from the immediate need to improve the lives of the people.

While Chiang carried out a determined effort to eliminate these issues, the communists, under the leadership of Mao Zedong, focused on winning over the hearts and minds of those in the countryside with the agrarian reforms that Chiang was neglecting.

Yet the KMT would not give up their hunt for the communists, leading to a massive siege in Jiangxi in 1934, that prompted The Long March. The communists' escape from behind the KMT lines set them on their trek from Jiangxi to Shaanxi Province, a colossal effort that began with more than 100,000 men and women, but ended one year and 6,000 miles later with less than 10,000 people. It was at their new base in Yan'an that Mao consolidated his position as the sole leader of the revolution.

While the KMT and Communist Party were fighting and hiding, the Japanese were busy invading Manchuria, creating the puppet state of Manchukuo in 1932. Eventually, recognising that they risked losing everything to yet another foreign power, the KMT and Communist Party agreed to form a united front in an effort to defeat this latest invader (though only after Chiang's own generals kidnapped him and forced from him an oath that he would fight to defeat the Japanese before battling his own countrymen).

The alliance could not have come at a better time, as war with the Japanese broke out on 7 July 1937. A battle between Chinese and Japanese troops at the Marco Polo Bridge near Beijing started it, but the fighting spread rapidly, with Japanese forces occupying first Beijing and then cities along the coast with amazing speed. By 1939, most of China's coastal cities, from Shanghai to Guangzhou, had been overrun by the invading forces.

From 1939 to 1943, the KMT desperately lobbied for US intervention while the Japanese pulled the strings of puppet governments, first in Beijing and then in Nanjing. The communists were powerless to impact the situation as Chiang Kai-shek had them blockaded in north-west China, despite their supposed united front.

By the time of the Japanese surrender to the Allies in August 1945, US aid to the KMT had been squandered or misused, and China's two parties quickly resumed their civil war. A brief cease-fire went into effect in January 1946, negotiated by US General George C Marshall. But after the Communist Party's proposal for a coalition government was rejected outright by the KMT, civil war erupted yet again.

At this point, the Nationalists of the KMT were seen as corrupt, saddled with a huge debt incurred during the war, and poor economic managers. Hyperinflation, caused primarily by the overprinting of currency in order to pay off KMT debt, worsened the lot of an already war-torn populace.

The Communist Party, in contrast, was seen as a force working for the people, their land reform measures having had real impact on the lives of those in the countryside over the years. A slow shift in the mood of the populace was palpable, and the Communists took advantage of it. Mobilising their rural base, by the fall of 1949, the Communists had taken control of all mainland territory except Tibet.

Chiang Kai-shek and his followers (along with numerous crates of national treasures) quickly fled to the island of Taiwan. From high above Tiananmen Square, Mao Zedong formally established the People's Republic of China on 1 October 1949.

THE PEOPLE'S REPUBLIC OF CHINA

As Chairman of the People's Republic, Mao Zedong was finally in a position to make his version of Marxism—eventually enshrined as the 'Marxism–Leninism–Mao Zedong Thought'—the guiding philosophy behind the party and the country's new government.

Creating striking similarities to the dynastic systems that came before him, Mao built a system of bureaucracy able to efficiently and tightly control and lead society at all levels. Essentially, the Party set policy, which was implemented by government officials from the central down to the village township level, all of whom were also members of the CCP. The end result was a government operating as an organ of the Party.

Aside from a brief interlude in 1950, when China intervened in the Korean War to save the North Koreans from being wiped off the map, Mao's focus was on furthering the reforms begun by the Communist Party during its years of wielding power from amongst the farmers in China's vast countryside.

These reforms were accelerated with propaganda never seen before—in 1958, Mao launched the Great Leap Forward. China was to achieve a massive increase in crop production in lightening speed through the immediate collectivisation of China's farmlands. Collectivisation would in turn free up oodles of labour that then could be put to work producing steel, thereby building China's industrial might virtually overnight. The reality was quite different from the vision. In the three years that the policies of the Great Leap Forward were implemented, 30 million people are estimated to have starved to death in what many consider to be the greatest man-made famine in history.

China slowly began to recover from the devastation wrought by the Great Leap Forward, though with little help

A statue of Mao Zedong, the charismatic Communist Party leader of the People's Republic of China .

from her neighbours. Following closely on the heels of Mao's experiment came a decisive break with (and closure of the money tap from) the Soviet Union in 1962. The return to stability and productivity following such a massive disruption of the country's economy was not swift, nor without political consequences for Mao. Primary among them was a visible retreat from some of his more aggressive policies, in an attempt to appease his increasingly vocal opponents.

But as with rulers before him, the possibility that his position as the supreme ruler was under threat galvanised Mao into action, and in 1966 Mao's next major campaign, the Great Proletarian Cultural Revolution, got underway. For a full decade, China can best be described as existing in a state of general anarchy. The very fabric of society—the hierarchy that those centuries of dynastic rule had virtually perfected—was torn to shreds, with Mao and his followers exhorting China's youth to question, rebel and defend against the renewal of authority. And respond they did, as students-turned-Red Guards believing Mao's exhortation that 'red is best' ruled the streets, each one working to prove that he was redder than the rest.

During the ten years that the Cultural Revolution ran its course, universities and schools were closed, historical sites, artefacts, documents and any symbols of the West —along with the people connected with these things—were summarily destroyed, devastating China's record of the last 5,000 years of her history.

By 1969, growing weary of the fighting and with little left to destroy or overturn, the political turmoil caused by the movement eased, though the disruptions did not completely abate until Mao's death in 1976. The 'cult of Mao' that formed during these years reflects a remarkable ability on the part of a tremendous leader to tap into the fears, needs and motivations of a significant population. He had help—in the form of his sidekick, the confidant Lin Biao, a general in the People's Liberation Army—but he also had his own recipe of powerfully potent charisma.

Mao's personality cult persisted until his death. His heir apparent Lin Biao then disappeared in a mysterious (and some say directed) plane crash in 1971. Mao's death left China with no one at the helm, resulting in a brief but significant power struggle among the highest ranks of the Party.

The battle was between the hard-liners, more moderate reformers and the radicals. It was won by a well-known name, Mr Deng Xiaoping, and his supporters. The year 1978 marked Deng's third return to prominence, having lost favour twice before.

The story of his remarkable opening of China to foreign investment and establishment of a 'socialist market economy' is well known, and perhaps best encapsulated in his classic quote: 'It doesn't matter if a cat is black or white, as long as it catches mice.' This acknowledgment of the power for positive change that the accumulation of wealth can provide is a mantra that still guides many of the white-collar professionals working the halls of any one of the international businesses in China today.

From a legacy of cyclical struggle, unification, collapse and regular periods of complete chaos, China has emerged as one unified country, with 1 billion people living collectively on 9,326,410 sq km of land, contributing daily to a GDP that rivals that of the world's most developed nations.

Adaptation and change, advancing on the foundations created by the previous dynasty, ruler or philosopher, has been built into the fabric of the country's political and social system for centuries, providing an intensity of purpose, an ability to look beyond roadblocks, and a determination to advance that is unfailing.

Despite the many pressures dealt by a large population, a growing gap between urban and rural areas, and between the rich and the poor, China continues down her path of development, creation and innovation, affording more and more opportunities and an increasing variety of adventures to her own people and to those who choose to be her guests, for a day, a month, or possibly a few years.

THE CHINESE

CHAPTER 3

'The Han Chinese didn't get to be the all-time world
champion ethnic group by being nice guys...'
—Neal Stephenson, in *Wired* magazine, February 1994

THE PEOPLE OF THE 'PEOPLE'S REPUBLIC'

With some 1.31 billion people by official count (up to 1.5 billion by some estimates), China remains today the world's most populous country (although India is an increasingly close runner-up). Despite runaway global population growth (the UN estimates that there are now nearly 6.5 billion humans worldwide) and strong Chinese family planning programmes, it is still true that nearly one out of every five humans on earth lives in China.

China's population numbers are in some sense incomprehensible, especially for people coming from some Western countries where under-population is considered a problem. In China, a metropolis of half-a-million people may well be called a 'village'. Medium-size Chinese towns are often larger than all but the largest US or European cities.

In China, to be considered a big city, it has to have a population of at least 5 million people. China has 10 cities with a population over 5 million, compared to 2 in the US. Shanghai, with some 16.6 million people is among one of the world's most heavily populated metropolitan areas. Beijing with 12.4 million people, Chongqing with 9.4 million and Shenzhen with 9 million all rank among some of the largest cities worldwide.

Many quips and quotes attest to attempts to bend minds around the vastness of China's population. "You know," one old saying goes, "if you really, truly, are a 'one-in-a-million' kind of guy, in China there are 1,300 other guys just like you."

THE CHINESE PEOPLE

First off, it's important to recognise the complexity of definitions. 'Who is Chinese?' is easily (though perhaps less obviously to outsiders) as complex and fraught a question as 'What makes an American?' or 'Who is a Jew?'

Does 'Chineseness' refer to citizenship in the People's Republic of China (PRC)? If so, that includes 56 official (and probably many unofficial) minority ethnicities living primarily in border regions annexed by China over the centuries, some of whom (such as the separatists among the Tibetans and the Muslim Uighurs of North-west China) refuse to acknowledge Chinese sovereignty over them as valid.

Collectively, all of China's minority ethnicities make up approximately 8.5 per cent of the total population, making China far less of a melting pot than many nations of Europe or the Americas.

China's Ten Largest Minority Ethnic Groups by Population

Name of Group	Approximate Population	Native Region (note: most groups now have nationwide distribution)
Zhuang	16,178,811	Guangxi, parts of Yunnan, Guizhou, Hunan
Manchu	10,682,263	Throughout North-east and North-central China
Hui	9,816,802	North-west China, especially Ningxia and Gansu
Miao	8,940,116	South-west China, especially Yunnan, Guangxi, Guizhou
Uighur	8,399,393	North-west China, especially Xinjiang
Tujia	8,028,133	Hubei and Hunan

Name of Group	Approximate Population	Native Region (note: most groups now have nationwide distribution)
Yi	7,762,286	Sichuan, Yunnan, Guangxi, Guizhou
Mongolian	5,813,947	Mongolia, and parts of Xinjiang, Heilongjiang
Tibetan	5,416,021	Tibet, Qinghai, and parts of Sichuan and Yunnan
Buyi	2,971,460	Guizhou

Source: http://www.china.org.cn/e-groups/shaoshu/

Alternately, is 'Chineseness' an ethnicity? If so, is being Chinese identical to being a member of the Han people group? The Han is the majority ethnicity in China, named after the Han dynasty, which united the core of what is now China starting in about 221 BC. If so, where does this leave the non-Han minorities; are they Chinese or not?

What about ethnically non-Chinese people who have immigrated to China (there are increasingly many as China's economic opportunities grow)? What about the emigrants, the 'overseas Chinese', an estimated 35 million people of mostly Han ethnicity now living outside China? Many such overseas families haven't visited mainland China for generations. Does it make a difference if they live in what is often called 'Greater China' (which includes Hong Kong, Macau and Taiwan) as opposed to in New York, Vancouver or Paris? What about children of mixed marriages? Or ethnically non-Chinese children adopted by Chinese couples?

There is even the traditional north-south division within the Han. Archaeological records show, for instance, that bronzes, oracle bones and other ancient Chinese technologies were adopted more widely, earlier on the Yellow River than along the Yangtze River plains. Does that make the people of North-central China 'more Chinese' than the rest of the Han?

These and similar questions, as with 'what makes an American' or 'who is a Jew', are freighted with emotional sensitivities and political consequences. People tend to hold very strong opinions, some of them at times self-contradictory. Chinese visa officials, for instance, will generally grant special 'visiting your relatives' visas to 'half-Chinese' children of mixed marriages, but may deny those visas to 'one-quarter Chinese' grandchildren of such marriages—even as China in many ways tries to court anyone with any degree of Chinese ancestry to come 'contribute to the homeland' as teachers, investors, and so on.

About all one can say for sure is that the question is complex. Again, beware of easy generalities. For purposes of this book, except where noted otherwise, we focus predominantly on citizens of the PRC—but we are well aware that other definitions exist.

'Blue Ants' No More

One thing for sure, the Chinese, however one defines them, are definitely not homogenous. In truth, of course, they never were, but the totalitarian controls of the Maoist years imposed an external sameness on all those living in the People's Republic.

During the Maoist years, the mainland Chinese were almost all universally born in state hospitals or helped by state-funded midwives, attended state schools and lived out their lives in small, simple apartments or rural villages assigned by the state.

They worked in jobs assigned by the state, used towels, clothes, washbasins and dishware manufactured by the state in a narrow range of utilitarian designs, and slept under the same state-assigned quilts. They sold through state-run stores, read newspapers published by the state, saw news and entertainment funded and controlled by the state, were married by the state and in the end, cremated and buried by the state. Thus, it's small wonder they appeared to be the same to outsiders.

In Mao's time, more than any other clothing, the Chinese wore cheap blue cotton outfits which Westerners label 'Mao

Suits'. The Chinese call them the 'Zhong-shan-fu' or 'Sun Yat-sen suits', since Sun, the father of Modern China, first advocated wearing simple traditional peasant designs as a classless national uniform. This led to the Chinese being called 'Blue Ants' by many Westerners, seen as faceless masses working together for the common good. Some scholars saw this as 'natural', declaring China's rapid adoption of Communism to be a direct outgrowth of the stratified social obligations and denial of individual passions inherent in the traditional bureaucratic and Confucian ideals of imperial China.

Of course, the truth was more complex even in Mao's day. The authors have spoken with farmers who kept tiny patches of illicit tobacco growing right through the Mao years for extra income and some sense of independence. We've met children raised in the Mao years by aunts and grandparents, effectively 'hostages' held at home to ensure Communist Party loyalty while their diplomat parents, selected in part for language skills, worked abroad (such children, unsurprisingly, often grew up with mixed feelings about the Party). We've also met some 'Young Princes'—children and grandchildren of top Party leaders of the Mao era—who saw first-hand the corrupt cynicism that pervaded much of the top ranks and reacted variously by growing up as neo-idealist reformers,

While China's economic reform has not yet led to wholesale political transformation (and may never lead to a Western-style democracy), it has vastly expanded the space in China for popular and non-traditional culture, and for the 'marketplace of ideas'.

as politically uninvolved artists or scientists, or as the most corrupt of power-brokers in China today.

Since economic reform began in China in 1979, accelerating through the 1980s and since, Chinese have become more free than ever to pursue and express individual desires and dreams, at least to the extent their individual economic means have expanded to match 'New China's' economic opportunities. As a result, the obvious, on-the-surface complexity of mainland Chinese society today is far more similar to that of the US or Europe than it is to China of the Mao era.

Today there are religious Chinese and hedonistic bar-hopping Chinese, fashion-conscious Chinese wearing the latest from Gucci and Chinese who stick to Mao Suits due to poverty or political convictions. There are Chinese sports fans and opera fans, traditional sword dancers and hip-hop break-dancers, techno-nerds and drag queens, drag-racing fans and pseudo-intellectuals dragging on their Gauloises, and everything in-between.

Increasingly, there are rich Chinese and poor Chinese, which brings a host of social ills: crime and unrest that marks the grinding poverty of a potentially permanent underclass. Yet China today also has a middle class that the World Bank estimates at 300 million people and growing, placing China, famously, among the world's top market, as well as being the world's top producer of consumer goods of all kinds.

THERE'S CHINESE AND CHINESE

There are, in short, almost as many ways to describe the Chinese people as there are individual Chinese. That said, to help create some order out of the complexity, we offer the following categories as one way to think about some of the broad divisions within mainland Chinese society today:

The Forgotten Farmers

In all the hype about rapid industrialisation, moving up the manufacturing value chain and becoming 'workshop to the world', it is easy to forget that China today is still predominantly rural.

It is true that China has experienced an urban population explosion the likes of which the world has never seen, from an estimated 72 million urbanites in 1952 to an estimated 540 million in 2004, a migration of nearly half a billion people. Current UN estimates foresee 900 million Chinese living in cities by 2020. That said, as of today, some 750 to 800 million people, which is between six or seven out of every ten Chinese, still live in the countryside.

Some 150 million of these villagers now work for 'township and village enterprises', often at the dirtiest and most dangerous of industrial jobs. The rest are still largely subsistence-level farmers, struggling with everything from erosion and falling water tables, to fixed grain prices and corrupt tax collectors, to disappearing rural healthcare networks.

Because little foreign investment takes place in rural areas, and because most Chinese villagers are too poor to appear on the marketing radar screens of global companies, foreign

businesspeople may go through entire China assignments never meeting and hardly ever thinking about any of them. But it is worth remembering that villagers are still the majority in China, and that their ongoing struggles with poverty are a major and growing source of unrest. China's current leadership, heirs afterall to a revolution that started among the peasants, is acutely aware of, and worried by, that fact.

Marooned State Workers and the Xiagang

Similarly, while the headlines have tended to go to the deservedly praised economic miracles of Shanghai and Guangzhou, in poorer parts of China, over 250 million Chinese still live in the twilight limbo of the faltering state-owned sector.

Here we do not include workers at the relatively few state-owned enterprises (SOEs) or state-invested enterprises (SIEs) which have successfully transitioned into competitive modern enterprises, the Lenovos and China Telecoms which have carried out global IPOs and are poised for growth into China-based MNCs. Rather, we are talking about hulking, faltering SOE steel, power and weapons plants, and banks still propped up by government subsidies because they are seen as too important to national security to allow to be controlled by foreigners, and/or as 'too big to fail'.

These SOEs are notoriously inefficient; a 2005 US Congressional study estimated that SOEs still accounted for some 62 per cent of China's urban employment nationwide, but less than 48 per cent of her urban GDP. In fact, many workers at these plants have been cut back to half or even quarter time, kept on only nominally to provide some semblance of stability and avoid contributing to the unemployment statistics.

There are also tens of millions of *xiagang*, the laid-off SOE workers officially 'awaiting reassignment', though everyone knows the reassignment will almost certainly never come. Such workers, who may or may not still receive health coverage or other benefits from their former employers, throng the day-labour markets which have become features of so many poorer Chinese cities.

The *xiagang* and partly-idled state workers largely explain the difference between China's official unemployment estimates, which still hover around 4 to 5 per cent, and the much larger estimates (15 to 20 per cent) of many international observers. When thinking about those numbers, by the way, it is also worth bearing in mind that during the Great Depression in the United States, US unemployment was approximately 23 per cent.

As many economists have observed, the irony is that the more heavy state investment cities got in the Maoist years to build an economy dependent on SOEs, the harder a time those cities have had readjusting to a market economy since 1979. All these millions of idled and semi-idled worker are another major source of current and potential unrest, and of worry for the government.

Again most foreign businesspeople, active in China's booming south-east and central coastal regions, will find the *xiagang* and semi-idled state workers far off their daily radar screens. But it is worth remembering that China has an enormous 'rust-belt' running from the once-proud industrial centres of Manchuria in the North-east, through to cities like Taiyuan, Wuhan and Chongqing.

The Floating Population

What most foreign businesspeople will see up close is China's 'floating population', the estimated 140 million or so rural Chinese who have left their villages and crowded into the coastal boom towns searching for higher-paying jobs.

China's restrictions on personal mobility have lightened considerably in recent years, but 'floating population' migrants still live without *hukou*, the residence permits that ensure access to schools, healthcare benefits, housing subsidies and other urban amenities for official residents.

As a result, 'floaters', even those who may have lived in wealthy coastal areas for years and have relatively stable jobs, often live in shantytowns on the edge of garbage dumps and along filthy canals which provide their only running water. These are the people who sweep the streets, shine the shoes, do the dirty work on construction projects, and take the toughest 'no one else wants them' factory jobs in China's boomtowns.

If, like most businesspeople assigned to China, you have an *ayi* (cleaning lady and/or nanny), live in an apartment complex with tended grounds and gardens, and work in an office building where cleaning crews scrub the bathrooms and sweep the halls, you will see some of the floating population around you every day. If you speak a little Chinese, you may find their stories fascinating. Many are, for instance, more educated than meets the eye. They may have been schoolteachers or nurses in their home villages, but may earn more for their families scrubbing toilets for ten months in Shanghai than they could for several years at home.

Interestingly, there is also a slowly growing awareness among the floating population of their rights as workers; some of the most notorious sweatshops in Guangzhou have had to start cleaning up their acts to be able to keep attracting workers. Of course, some of them have also started closing their doors in China, and setting up shop in countries like Bangladesh, where there are poorer and more desperate

workers than China's floating population, but that aspect of globalisation is another story...

The New Working Class

Meantime in China's boomtowns, while the floating population handles bottom-tier jobs, official residents are moving quickly up the value chain in job skills and quality of life. In offices and factories owned by foreign-invested enterprises and by the better-run SOEs and private Chinese-owned companies, new generation Chinese workers are learning skills their forebears never dreamed of. Many (especially among office workers) are fluent in English, German or Japanese. Many are computer whizzes, or expert technicians, or are familiar with every nuance of ISO 140001 environmental quality controls.

Increasingly, these skills are commanding salaries their forebears never dreamed of either. This is the bulk of that 300-million-strong middle class the UN writes about. Most live in decent apartments, with heaters, running hot water and other amenities their parents rarely and their grandparents never experienced. Ever-increasing numbers aspire to own their own apartments and cars. The following table, following a local penchant for numbering systems, outlines what the Chinese working class have, with more than a grain of truth, called:

The Three Most Desired Items in Decades of Chinese Daydreams			
1970s	**1980s**	**1990s**	**2000s**
Sewing machine	Colour TV	Private apartment	Luxury home
Rice cooker	Refrigerator	Car	Sports car
Bicycle	Washing machine	Computer	Home entertainment system

Struggles still abound—even in the best-run companies in China's wealthiest cities, most workers still commute very long distances (sometimes hours each way) on public transportation, and work very long hours for salaries generous by Chinese standards, but still just a fraction of those of global peers. But compared to the floating population, the *xiagang*, the villagers, or indeed their own parents, these workers by and large have opportunities undreamt of, and their future looks as boundless as that of China as a whole.

Managers and Technocrats

Leading these offices and factories are a considerably more select group. These are the Chinese workers who have mastered not only technical and language skills, but also some of the 'softer' arts of business, from managing teams and negotiating deals to handling cross-cultural issues.

Many of these are 'returnees', Chinese who have done stints of study or work abroad and are bringing their experience home. Others have worked their way up the ranks within Chinese or foreign-invested companies, learning first-hand how global business works. Many have also received coveted international assignments from previous employers and have a good sense of living standards abroad, which they seek to adopt at home.

Such experienced managers are increasingly in short supply in China as more and more foreign companies crowd in, seeking the guidance of managers with both deep local knowledge and serious global exposure. As a result, middle-to-senior Chinese managers often command salaries much closer to those of their global peers than to salaries of other Chinese. They tend to have lifestyles that combine some of the best of the global and the local. And they tend to be very savvy in terms of managing their careers and planning for their children.

Paralleling this successful managerial class in the business world are growing ranks of thoughtful administrators within the government, academia and the growing numbers of think-tanks in China. While China's government is still far larger and more heavily staffed than those of most developed nations, it is continuing to shrink and becoming more efficient over time. And increasingly, it is staffed by sophisticated technocrats far less concerned than their forebears with issues of Party loyalty, and far more with performance that make China (and thus, yes, the Party) succeed.

Leaders, Entrepreneurs and Stars

At the top tier of Chinese society is a variegated group that, again, more resembles the multi-layered elite of developed societies than it does the uniformly careful 'senior cadres' who ruled the roost in China past. Today, China has sports, films and theatre stars whose antics, while still tame compared with those of their US counterparts, are enough to fill increasingly popular society tabloids.

There are also rich entrepreneurs who have created business empires and now enjoy the fruits—and limelight— success brings. Aside from that, there are top government officials and leaders of top SOEs, some risen through the ranks via merit, others via patronage and perhaps corruption (how many fall into each class is a subject of much debate in China).

Increasingly, Chinese elites are similar to wealthy jet-setters of any society. They may maintain apartments in Shanghai or Beijing, and country homes near a golf course or fishing region. They may vacation in Hawaii or Paris or the beaches of Thailand. They may travel frequently on business trips to New York, Tokyo or Frankfurt. They may have impeccably old-money sorts of tastes, or they may favour bright colours and gilding reminiscent of the last emperors, and laugh at any who call them nouveau-riche.

What these elites have in common is money—in the form of salaries and bonuses, and/or in the form of perks and benefits, and expense accounts. And in China, as in any modern economy, this translates into options in terms of lifestyle, and potential to control one's own fate.

Retirees in the Parks

Step out early any morning to any public park virtually anywhere in China and you will see some of the liveliest use of communal space. The parks are thronged with people in the morning—all ages, from children, but especially retirees —dancing, singing, practising martial arts or *tai chi*, climbing hills, swinging from trees (believed in traditional Chinese medicine to help strengthen the lungs as well as the arms), strolling, or just gossiping.

Life after work is still very much a central part of Chinese society, and most Chinese look forward to a physically and socially active retirement full of community involvement. In addition to the public parks, there are also community centres and chess clubs, neighbourhood associations and volunteering, part-time job opportunities and of course grandchildren to look forward to, family planning policies or not.

In China's poorest areas, of course, there is no retirement, just a struggle for subsistence that lasts till people drop. But increasingly, in most of China and especially in the booming coastal regions, growing national wealth has allowed the beginnings of social safety nets. Maintaining community services and public spaces for retirees tends to be a relatively high priority among these, and the benefits of that are clear to see.

A group of women practicing *tai chi,* a popular form of morning exercise, in the park.

Drop-Outs and Druggies, Artists and the Avant-Garde

As with any modern nation, China has many people living at the fringe of mainstream society not necessarily due to poverty (some are children from well-to-do families) but rather due to dedication to one or another alternative lifestyle. Given how out of character these groups seem to be relative to traditional images of China, they have grabbed more than their share of media coverage.

Images of Chinese transvestites, fetus-eating Chinese 'performance artists', artists in communal colonies, Ecstasy parties and rockers pounding out the rhythms of China's ever-more furious nightlife have captured the imagination of many writers and expatriates. Based on how some expatriates spend their time, they may in fact believe the nocturnal denizens of the 'bar streets' of Beijing, Shanghai and Guangzhou are the truest representatives of the modern Chinese.

Certainly, these various fringe groups do represent some interesting trends in modern China. With the lifting of totalitarian political controls, the seamier side of life has returned to China along with the better access to travel, books and global performances. There is a flourishing drug trade

in many Chinese cities today, and prostitution has returned with a vengeance. As in other nations, those 'sin trades' as practised in high society evoke sumptuous night-clubs, well-dressed escorts and genteel whiffs of extremely expensive powders, while the lower-heeled versions involve a lot of dirty needles and exposure to AIDS.

China's more freewheeling atmosphere today also allows far more experimentation than in the past in virtually every musical and artistic genre, and every form of lifestyle choice. Enjoying some of the cultural fruits of these experiments is an exciting part of life in China today. But when thinking about what they do and do not represent about China as a whole, it's worth keeping in mind that they are still very much a fringe phenomenon, even in that cutting-edge fringe of China that is the wealthy coast.

Summing Up

The above categories are obviously based on general employment and social status. We could offer many other ways of breaking down China's population—by age, gender, political views and so on—each of which would likely paint a different picture of China, all no doubt valid. Again, China's is an enormous, complex and rapidly changing society. We offer the above merely as one way of thinking about the problem.

WHAT CHINESE WANT?

Marketing firms spend enormous sums trying to pinpoint the needs and desires, values and aspirations of the various groups within Chinese society—at least those groups potentially able to afford the marketer's client's products. The question of Chinese values is thus at once a philosophical, psychological and economic concern. We do not pretend in this brief chapter to explore all aspects of these complex questions, but do offer here a brief overview of some of the ways they are often discussed.

From a philosophical standpoint, many have observed the long persistence of many traditional Chinese values despite all the meanders of modern Chinese history. The village farmers working hard on the land despite slumping returns, the floating population struggling to send home earnings to give their children a better life, the *xiagang* looking to the state they once depended on as a source of authority (even as they prowl labour markets for odd jobs to feed their children), the 'new workers' striving to pull themselves and their family up the social ladder, all attest to a host of traditional values permeating Chinese society that centre on family, work ethics, education and hopes for a better future.

Psychologically and economically, China today is in some ways a perfect illustration of the psychologist Abraham Maslow's famed 'hierarchy of needs'. Among the poorest, survival is paramount. China's subsistence farmers, *xiagang* day-labourers and floating population urban hunter-gatherers mostly want clean water to drink, shelter to keep them warm and dry, enough food to avoid starvation, a bit of secure income, and perhaps the ability to see a doctor if they get sick. In Maslow's terms, they spend their days at the bottom of the pyramid, dealing with physical survival and personal safety and security. These groups tend to buy as little as possible, and most of that unprocessed staples.

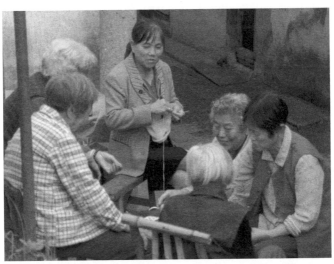

Although their country has changed greatly in the past few decades, many Chinese continue to observe traditional values and customs.

Of course, even the poorest aspire to more than mere survival. They still dream and hope, and appreciate beauty ('Even beggars can look at the moon' goes one traditional Chinese saying). They fall in love and have children, seek self-respect and the respect of others.

Among the poor are much of the floating population, who support their family back in the villages out of their meagre urban wages. Many *xiagang* workers, many of them middle-aged or older, after sweating all day in the labour markets and caring for their family in the evening, still struggle in night-schools to learn English, or how to use computers, so they too can join the ranks of more sophisticated workers. And more villagers leave the farms and join the floating population every day.

From the perspective of Western businesspeople, it is worth appreciating the dignity of the struggles of China's poorest. Many effective corporate philanthropy or corporate social responsibility (CSR) activities in China are aimed at helping to ease those struggles. Building schools and hospitals in rural areas, supporting educational programmes, providing scholarships, funding worker retraining programmes and the like can help China's poor in meaningful ways, and also help position companies as partners of choice for China, more likely than others to receive coveted permits or project selection preferences.

Even from a marketing perspective, China's poorest should not be wholly forgotten. Consumer products firms, for instance, do very well selling shiny little single-use foil packs of shampoos or face creams in China. These 'affordable luxuries' have become popular gifts among China's poorest when they want to offer each other a special-occasion alternative to hand-made lye soaps. Similarly, banks wanting to offer Rmb savings services have gotten a foot in the door offering low-cost ways for floating population migrants in the cities to safely transfer funds to their families back home. Pharmaceutical firms have gotten permits to sell higher-end medications in China's boomtowns only after agreeing to sell more basic or near-generic products at-cost in the countryside. Similar examples abound. Even China's poorest seek to be part of the new economy, and to bring its advantages to themselves and their families. Companies seen as helping them can 'do well by doing good'.

For China's middle class, survival and basic personal security are pretty well given. They spend their days largely in the middle of Maslow's pyramid, dealing with family and children, self-esteem and the esteem of others. This, of course, makes them perfect targets for marketing campaigns based on family happiness, health and closeness, as well as on individual and social esteem. Spend any time watching successful advertisements on Chinese television and you will see a range of familiar images from similar advertisements in the US: happy couples, smiling children, nice homes, or chic youngsters with chic friends. These basic messages reflect a similar reality: most target consumers in China, like most target consumers in the US, want to feel loved, close to their families, and respected by themselves and their peers.

At the highest levels of Chinese society, these values play out as well—hence the markets for luxury cars, nice villas, expensive family vacations and private schools. But the higher levels of Chinese society are also most likely to be concerned with the self-actualisation at the top of Maslow's pyramid: creativity, spontaneity, knowledge and acceptance of the world and so on. Thus in China as in many societies, the artists, musicians and poets are most often children of the middle-to-upper classes, as are the scientists, entrepreneurs, government leaders and others who lead China's growth.

A recent study, by advertising giant Young & Rubicam, found that the two core motivators for many Chinese youth today are the urge to live a materially better life than their parents, and the urge to contribute to their families and society—a combination of goals different in several nuances from those that motivate the average young American today.

Of course, there are more complexities in the desires and psychological or emotional drivers of Chinese people today than the above simple overview can encompass. Some observers have pointed out other complexities, such as the role China's strict criminal and security laws (for good or bad) play in a personal sense of security for the average Chinese, and the role changing healthcare delivery systems is playing in breaking down senses of community and personal security.

Nevertheless, there is a clear sense that China's middle class and elite audiences today, from a marketing perspective, are more than less similar to their Western counterparts. This represents a shift from earlier times, when Maslow's hierarchy was seen as to some degree reversed in China. In the late 1970s and early 1980s, for instance, psychologist Edwin C Nevis did research in China suggesting that China's intense group-orientation at the time (the tail-end of the Blue Ant era) meant that self-esteem for Chinese came not from individual but from group recognition. Even then, however, Nevis predicted that economic reform might shift China closer to the US in that regard, and that shift seems in fact to have largely taken place.

Of course, beneath all these psychological and marketing complexities are an even more fundamental layer of values and philosophical ideals handed down from China's very long and complex past.

SOME CHINESE TRADITIONS AND THEIR MODERN FATE

Despite the centuries of war, revolution, economic reform and other transformations and dislocations that have changed so much about China, many traditional Chinese values still persist. This is unsurprising, of course; deep cultural values tend to be resilient.

Both ancient Chinese traditions like Confucianism and Buddhism, and more modern traditions like socialist ethics, behave within China in similar ways to the Judeo-Christian tradition in Western societies.

Some people are true believers, purposely organising their lives around these traditions. Others are 'lapsed', or perhaps never really believed at all. Still, these values affect most Chinese to some degree, just as Judeo-Christian values affect most Americans (including Muslim and Pagan Americans). They may believe, they may scoff, they may accept or not, but they are affected, for these values are part of the air they grow up breathing.

The following are some key traditional Chinese values with persistent modern echoes.

Confucianism

As early as 1958, historian Joseph R Levenson, in the classic *Confucian China and its Modern Fate,* explored the degree to which the intellectual and political ideals of traditional Confucian China were transformed by Maoism (despite the Chairman's penchant for quoting from Confucian classics). Levenson is still well worth reading; boiling down his thick volumes to a paragraph is impossible. Suffice it to say that Levenson and many since have observed that Confucian stress on the importance of calm, social order, strong leadership, clear hierarchies and moral example continue to affect Chinese culture, despite many transformations in the understanding of those concepts.

Some believe that the tendency to revere tradition and authority in Confucian values precludes Western-style democracy in China; many have noted that relatively authoritarian governments prevail throughout the Confucian-influenced world, from Korea to Singapore and beyond. Taiwan's flamboyant and sometimes troubled democracy may be the exception that proves this observation.

From a business standpoint, it is worth remembering that a cultural tendency to authoritarian leadership (and parenting) styles means most Chinese have grown up expecting to be told what to do, micromanaged, and discouraged from criticising superiors. If you don't actively and thoughtfully encourage Chinese team members to take initiative and offer opinions, they most likely won't. Efforts to boost China's innovative capacity by shifting toward educational systems that encourage critical thinking are starting to change this among young Chinese, but such change comes slowly.

> As a manager, you may enjoy the quiet and seeming respect with which Chinese employees allow you to hold forth at meetings, but you will likely be more effective if you find ways to mobilise their talent and local knowledge. For more on this, see Chapter Nine, on doing business in China.

Focus on Education

One aspect of Confucian values which continues to have a very strong and largely very positive effect on Chinese culture is the traditional Confucian reverence for learning. This is a large factor behind China's literacy rates, among the highest in the developing world (and in urban areas among the highest in the world), and behind her growing prowess in engineering, math and science. It is also, by the way, one of the central factors in the complex 'model minority' status that overseas Chinese tend to have in the US and other countries, for good or bad.

Respect for teachers remains strong in China; anyone who has taught courses there can speak to the pleasure of teaching in an environment where students are generally not only eager to learn and hardworking but actually still compete to carry bags for and otherwise support the teacher. In fact, this respect extends to anyone who takes on a teaching role, which is part of why, from a business perspective, it is so important for expatriates to take on training and mentoring responsibilities, and why outreach to local universities can be such effective corporate positioning. See Chapter Nine on business for more details.

Buddhism and Daoism

Many have commented on the ways that Chinese interpretations of Buddhism and local Chinese traditions of Daoism both encourage a culture of self-restraint and distrust of passion. Historian Orville Schell writes of the Chinese concept of *ping*, which is often translated as 'peace', but literally means 'flatness'. The famously 'inscrutable' Chinese face is really a reflection of this ideal of calm self-restraint.

China's Daoist and Buddhist 'hermit' traditions have their modern counterparts also, not just in revived (and growing) monasteries and nunneries throughout China, but in such fringe groups as artist's colonies.

Once you have been in China for some time, you'll find that Chinese faces are as readable as Western faces, but the cues are subtler. For more on this, see the section on non-verbal communication in Chapter Eight on language.

Family Values

American watchdog groups who advocate strong family ties might well look to China for what truly strong family ties mean. Growing out of Confucian ideals and other Chinese traditions, China places a centrality on the importance of family obligations that surpasses anything most Americans are familiar with. Most Chinese parents and children grow up as a matter of course eating almost all meals together, sharing free time together, supporting each other at times of stress, and sharing resources remarkably freely from a Western perspective. The busy American family, leaving each other Post-It notes on their way to conflicting sports events, meetings, and so on, is largely incomprehensible to most Chinese.

However much Westerners admire the upside of Chinese family closeness, the downsides of it can cause friction and misunderstandings. Even in adulthood, Chinese family members tend to involve themselves in each other's

The family is the centre of focus for the Chinese, and children are brought up to be filial and close to their families.

An American friend of ours living with a Chinese man was amazed when the Chinese man wanted to turn over much of their joint savings to a needy cousin starting a business. The Chinese man, in turn, was amazed that his Western partner could possibly hesitate to share savings with family.

lives (from choices of clothes and appliances to choices of a spouse and job) to a degree most Americans would find uncomfortable.

These intense ties to family affect most Chinese in many, many ways, and are important for businesspeople to be aware of. For instance, your Chinese employees will unlikely value work deadlines over significant family issues, so it is well to deal generously with employees who are caring for sick parents or otherwise dealing with strong family obligations. Similarly, Western concepts of nepotism simply had no traditional counterpart in China; helping family members was simply more important than some sterile concept of 'business ethics'. While that is beginning to shift, it is still an important conversation to have with Chinese employees on an ongoing basis, particularly those with hiring and procurement responsibilities.

In-group and Out-group

In part as an extension of these strong family ties, Chinese people tend to view the world in terms of those to whom they do and don't have connections and commitments. The philosopher Joseph Needham called this China's 'courtyard view of the world'. The Chinese, Needham observed, take meticulous care of their homes and of the inner courtyards viewed as interior to their homes, but think nothing of dumping garbage in the alley immediately outside.

A similar mentality affects human relations. Those 'inside the courtyard'—family, close friends, classmates, close colleagues—tend to be very close and to have stronger claims on each other than their counterparts in the US. This shows up in everything from readiness of personal loans and assistance in job-finding, to introduction of potential spouses, to the famous 'connections' (*guanxi*) that still characterise much of Chinese business. While not generally as strong as family ties, the other 'courtyards' within

Chinese people's lives remain powerful, which can bring both advantage and disadvantage from the perspective of a foreign employer.

At the same time, from a Western perspective, there is generally remarkably little regard among Chinese people for those 'outside the courtyard'. Such phrases as *wailairen* ('outsider', often used to refer to newcomers, whether to a city or to a place of work) and *waiguoren* ('foreigner', but literally 'person from an outside country') attest to this 'us-and-them' sensibility. As many have observed, this has set a low bar in terms of expected treatment of strangers. Chinese people pushing and shoving their ways onto buses, ignoring people who might appreciate having a door held for them, and so on are partly results of China's overpopulation and scarce resources, but also partly cultural. Most Chinese lacks any traditional phrase equivalent to the English expression 'common courtesy', though of course that idea has been translated into modern Chinese.

With exposure to new ideas, such traditional 'us-them' attitudes are starting to shift in China. As present, though, from the Western perspective, Chinese people are a little over-involved and meddling in their relations with family and friends, and surprisingly rude to strangers. Of course, from the Chinese perspective, in a commonly repeated phrase, Westerners 'treat strangers like friends and their family like strangers'.

There is no doubt some truth to both perspectives. There is also some degree of 'When in Rome, do as Romans do'. If you ever hope to get into a crowded subway or elevator in China, you too may need to learn to sharpen elbows—and then may find yourself needing to tone down your behaviour again once you arrive back home!

These are a few values from classical Chinese culture that persist in some form. Another set of ideas, ideals and worldviews emerged from the century of struggle against foreign domination that forged modern China. These again form part of the cultural background that shapes modern Chinese thinking:

Nationalism and Internationalism

As any Chinese 101 student knows, the Chinese call China 'Zhongguo', literally the 'Middle Kingdom', centre of the ancient world. China had a few periods (such as the glory years of the Tang dynasty) of cosmopolitan attitudes toward trade and cultural exchange. But largely, in the days of the Mandarins, China was seen as totally self-sufficient, and the outside world as having nothing to offer. As shown from Chinese history, this set of attitudes, leading to strong Chinese exports of silks and teas and many other goods unbalanced by any imports due to government bans, helped create some of the pressures that eventually exploded into the Opium Wars.

Mao's China made a strong break with that insular past. In his earlier years, Mao deliberately sought to position China as the leader of the developing world and to build global ties. Yet in his later years, he too retreated to a more Mandarinate position, and his Cultural Revolution cut China off from the outside world as effectively as any imperial edict.

Chinese families visit relatives and close friends during the Lunar New Year or Spring Festival. Many of them wear the traditional Chinese dress, which is typically made of silk.

The Forbidden City was the Chinese Imperial Palace from the Ming Dynasty to the end of the Qing Dynasty. This beautiful example of traditional Chinese architecture now houses the Palace Museum.

A lion dance performed during the Spring Festival. Drums and cymbals accompany the performance and create loud, noisy beats which are believed to scare away evil spirits and bring good luck.

Street shopping in China can be a rewarding experience for visitors. Stalls offer a variety of items whose prices can be further bargained down.

China wowed the world with its majestic opening ceremony at the 2008 Summer Olympic Games. The event was held at the Beijing National Stadium, colloquially termed the Bird's Nest Stadium.

Duck is a favourite meat with each ethnic group developing its own style of cooking. One such dish is roast duck rice (featured here). However, Beijing's Peking Duck remains the most popular, having a history that dates back to imperial times.

Today, these traditions—the nationalist and the internationalist—continue to coexist in creative tension in China. As an internationalist nation, China is extremely concerned with how many global bodies it joins and deliberates in, in every field from sports to science to trade to law. As a nationalist nation, China tends to send formal, politically connected national-level representatives to these global bodies, and to be very frustrated with countries and groups that operate more flexibly.

As an internationalist nation, China claims full support for global initiatives such as the Kyoto Protocol on greenhouse gasses. As a nationalist nation, China resists outside attempts to dictate its environmental and other policies. As internationalists, young Chinese are leading users of the Internet, immersed in games and music and other aspects of global pop culture. As nationalists, young Chinese tend to be deeply suspicious of perceived attempts to 'contain' China, and generally more supportive than their own parents of military and other growth for China.

> What should be clear, from this simple overview, is that China today is a fascinatingly complex society: layers of Confucianism peek through a rip-roaring market mentality, robber barons work cheek-by-jowl with both hold-out Maoist ideologues and bright-eyed young idealists reminiscent of 1960s America

This combination can be awkward for businesses to negotiate. In trade negotiations, for instance, over information technology security standards, China attempted to spur greater support for China's home-grown WAPI standard by contrasting support for WAPI from the Standards Association of China, a national-level representative to the relevant global standards-setting body (the ISO-IEC), with support for the competing WiFi standard from the IEEE, an industry association without national-level status. This argument, put forward very seriously by China, was generally ignored within the ISO-IEC, causing great resentment and acrimony in China.

Pride in Personal and Gender Equality
One of the great ideals of the Mao era was for greater equality for all than in China's peasants-and-Mandarins past. This was

Women in modern China enjoy greater gender equality and independence, and many successfully juggle family life and a busy career.

to include an economically classless society, created via land reform and restructuring of the economy and educational systems, and also a society free of gender bias in which, in Mao's famous phrase, 'women hold up half the sky'.

Of course, even in Mao's time, there were Chinese Communist Party (CCP) leaders with comfortable lives and peasants who starved (discussing the class significance of access to automobiles in Mao's day, Simon Leys spoke of 'the riding classes and the walking classes'). And while women made great strides in education and employment, they still fell far short of equality, even in Mao's time.

Economic reform has pushed equality largely off the agenda as an official goal for China. A culture of feminine beauty has returned to China, diluting the focus of young women on education and careers. A class of nouveau riche don't mind sporting the latest designer clothes and driving imported luxury cars.

Still, Maoist ethics have not wholly gone. Most Chinese remain uncomfortable with conspicuous consumption. A friend who once worked for Sotheby's in China observed that he could tell who was able to bid highest at auction by who wore the blandest old sweater.

The ways the goal of equality still persists as an ideal can be seen to some degree in the jauntiness of Chinese cab-drivers, and among her bow-to-no-one farmers, and in the popularity of Hu Jintao's efforts to redirect wealth inland and to the poorest Chinese.

Neither has the 'women hold up half the sky' ideal wholly disappeared. There is far more room for strong female leaders in today's Chinese society than in many other cultures, including more traditional cultures within Greater China. Many expatriate women find this to be a refreshing advantage to doing business in China.

Pride in Personal Initiative

Many have observed that perhaps Mao's most positive legacy is breaking the tradition whereby only copying and learning from the past was highly valued. Those sent to the countryside, imprisoned and denied education in the

Cultural Revolution years were forced to think of other ways to construct their lives, and have since become some of the greatest entrepreneurs and thinkers of the post-Mao era.

Of course, the above is, again, the merest overview of an extremely complex set of topics. Levenson perhaps best summed up this complexity: 'China's past will be kept in mind, and fragments from its world of values valued. No radical westernisation will put an end to the historical significance of China.... Their modern revolution, against the world to join the world, against their past to keep it theirs, but past—was a long striving to make their own accounting with history.'

There is an active and creative tension between the needs of family and the individual, between getting ahead and getting along, between China's nationalist and internationalist urges. Seeing how all that plays out among individual Chinese one befriends, and watching how it all plays out for China as a nation over time, are among the most fascinating aspects of having that front-row seat to history that an assignment to China provides.

SOCIALISING

CHAPTER 4

'In China, the sharp divide of insider and outsider
dominates other distinctions. The insider, no matter
how he fails, is accepted and welcomed in the fold.
The outsider, regardless of character or achievement,
is not to be trusted.'
—Seth Faison, *South of the Clouds*

SOCIALISING WITH THE LOCALS

In 1997, one of the author's colleagues was making his first trip to the United States. In preparing to depart, one of his questions was, "How much does it cost to get mugged in New York?" After carefully explaining that there was no fixed or negotiated price involved with being mugged, it was strongly suggested that he avoid going to places that he was likely to be mugged. Pirated movies had strongly influenced his view of crime, sexuality and lifestyle in the United States.

Upon returning from the same trip, it was none of these three that had created a profound impact; the one that had an impact was that no one knew that he was a foreigner in the United States. His sense of heritage and belonging was so strongly affiliated with China that it was staggering to him that anyone would think he was from anywhere else.

Stranger yet was a place where people's citizenship wasn't dictated by their ethnicity. In China, it is clear when you are a foreigner. Unless you are born Chinese, you can never become Chinese. Blood is the defining factor that makes you Chinese.

The expression used for foreigners in China is *laowai*. Alternated with 'hullo', it is the most common greeting and exclamation of surprise when you are sighted in less worldly parts of the country. *Laowai* is a combination of two words that mean 'old' and 'outsider'. Together they are a polite word for foreigner.

Hairy Arms

Chinese view foreigners with open interest. Recently, a Chinese lady was heard making comment about the arm hair of a male Australian colleague. The commentary, without any malice intended, went something like this. She said, "Foreigners have very hairy arms, Chinese don't. We think they have hairy arms because they are less evolved and more closely related to apes." There is the pride, authority and superiority of 5,000 years of continual civilisation behind that comment.

Chinese hold a strong sense of national pride. In part because they are well-taught in school to do so, and in part because both ancient and modern China have made an indelible mark on the world. To the Chinese, China losing her first Olympic bid wasn't just a defeat, it was an embarrassment. It was a vote of no confidence by the rest of the world.

When China won both the bids for the 2008 Olympics and the 2010 World Expo in one fell swoop, citizen confidence skyrocketed. Immediately after the World Expo bid was secured, a senior Chinese professional at an international business roundtable was overheard commenting that she now felt confident enough in China's future so she was going to purchase real estate. China had now taken its rightful place on the world stage.

All of that expectation comes with great expense. The future of China rests on the shoulders of the current working generation. This generation has more earning potential and more responsibility than any other has had. Because of mandatory early retirement to trim excess employment cost off of Chinese state-run companies, a 30 to 45-year-old breadwinner is usually supporting up to four generations of his or her family, as well as aunts, uncles and cousins that may need financial support. It is likely that they are making more money than any other generation of their family ever has.

This was highlighted during research to develop the brand positioning of a leading Chinese insurance company. One of the surprising findings about Chinese men that emerged is that they were as concerned about health and fitness as their American counterparts. When probing more deeply as to the reason for this, it emerged that they were concerned that if their health deteriorated, they would not be able to care for their families. Not just their immediate family, but also their parents and extended family.

Interestingly enough, in Young & Rubicam's Brand Asset Valuator study published in 2005, Chinese youths were more aspirational than their Japanese or American counterparts, but they continued to hold the traditional value of filial piety just as strongly as their ancestors had. This is the generation that will drive China into poll position in the 21st century.

In China, there is one sure way to get ahead and that is through education. The government has done an excellent job identifying the best and the brightest, no matter what remote part of China they were born and raised in. The system identifies and separates them out of the masses, putting them into the top universities in the country.

Excellent performance in university assures a shot at a top job. It also provides an opportunity for future education, increasingly overseas.

A strategy shared by two female MBA students who are married is to become pregnant when they are departing for their MBA so that their child can be born overseas. This assures their child an overseas passport and guarantees more opportunity for their future, which directly translates to more opportunity for the entire family to be successful.

THE POWER OF *GUANXI*

The second way to get ahead is to know someone who can help provide a better opportunity. Throughout the advent of Communism the best way to create an opportunity for yourself was to know someone in a position of power willing to help you. This is called *guanxi* and is a very important concept.

There is a well-known Chinese expression that says 'the nail that stands out gets hammered down'. We can add unless that nail is made of the Chinese equivalent of kryptonite—personal power.

Power comes from the implied authority of position. Most senior ranking government officials have a great deal of power. Their positions do not net them high salaries, but they do net them privilege. With the position comes nicer homes, nicer cars, overseas education opportunities for children, preferred jobs for family members, and if the cards are played right during your career, a well-funded retirement posting that you can leverage into a personal business opportunity.

Power also comes from the respect and trust of those that know you. People of authority who make good decisions, offer good advice and help others when they are able are also revered. As they help people around them to achieve greater personal success, those that they help make sure they are taken care of. This is the kind of power that a university professor, doctor or senior businessman can have. They are in a position to help people improve their lives, in return they win life-long loyalty and reciprocation when needed.

In this vein, there is one other term that is important to have a conceptual grasp of when interacting with Chinese, this is the word *mianzi*, which roughly translates into self-respect or pride, but when spoken of in English is literally called 'face'. When you embarrass, put down, insult or demean a Chinese, especially in front of another person, you have made them lose face. Although they smile through it, thank you for pointing out their error, or never change their facial expression, it is a sore that will fester. It will not be forgotten.

There is a fine line to be walked in offering criticism or advice in China without making the other person lose face. The first step is to assure that you have a substantial build-up of goodwill and trust with the other person. The second is to be very clear as to the benefit of the criticism to the other person. The third, make sure you give feedback in a private place where no others will be privy to the comments.

Before giving the feedback or making an accusation, ask questions to clarify any points that you may have missed that led you to judge the situation unfairly. Finally, make your statement and follow quickly by asking what the other person thinks of the comments that you made. Ask them to speak frankly.

Chinese are so sensitive to 'face' that they will not make you lose it without cause. If you do find yourself in a situation where you feel verbally attacked by a Chinese person that you have a social or professional relationship with, pay close attention to what is being said and find out as quickly as possible what is behind it.

LOCAL FRIENDSHIPS

Chinese people are open and friendly. They welcome an opportunity to better understand you and your culture. A gracious generosity toward others is deeply embedded in their culture. Street-level, limited resource with too many people to vie for it has demolished this grace, but it can be experienced one-on-one as you make friends in China.

In Chinese society, a friendship means more than knowing one another, it means that your lives and personal well-being have become intertwined. It is expected that if you have it within your means to help a friend achieve an aim, you will, while they will go out of their way to do the same for you. There is a subtle give and take that goes on, creating a mutual bond between friends in China. You are not truly a friend until you demonstrate an understanding of that. This is not something that is overtly requested or anticipated, but seems to be the flow of social fabric. Once you have reached a friendship on this level in China, it is for life.

Sensitive Topics Not to Discuss:

- The Japanese
- Tibet
- Politics and government
- Tiananmen
- Religion

Meals

Probably the most popular way for family and friends to spend time together in China is around a banquet table. A Chinese meal is as much about socialising as it is about food. An important and easy way to stay in touch with past colleagues, schoolmates and childhood friends is to invite them to meals.

Enjoying a meal together is the most common way for family, friends and colleagues to get together.

A meal involves a great deal of celebration. Mid-way through shouts of *gombei* will begin as people start to challenge one another to drinking matches. It is thought to be inhospitable to let the glass of the person next to you go empty. Accompanied with the drinking is laughing, joking, story-telling and teasing.

At the end of the meal, it is a point of pride to wrestle the bill from the waiter and pay it. Winning the right to pay the bill demonstrates your goodwill and affection toward the people that shared the meal with you.

Visiting Someone's Home

It is a great honour to be invited to someone's home in China. Most Chinese entertain in restaurants rather than at home. This stems from the fact that until recently, many homes were small government-issued flats, oftentimes sectioned off from larger houses and shared by multiple families. It is only in the last ten years, with a government focused on transitioning people to modern housing, and with the ability to purchase better space to live in afforded by an increase in discretionary income, that Chinese people have had homes that they were proud to share with guests.

The Chinese Hospitality

The author remembers being incredibly humbled by her first invitation to dinner in a Chinese home. The family of three adults had been assigned the attic of an old house. The door to the attic took up one-third of the floor space. Beds around the outside of the room took up the remainder of the space. It was only after the attic door was closed that the small table could be moved into the middle of the room to serve the meal on. In contrast to the space, the meal that was served was fit for a palace. The effort, relative cost and intent behind the meal has made it one of the best consumed by the author anywhere in the world.

When invited to a home, be sure and bring a small gift, usually a bottle of wine, some fruit or chocolates are adequate to show your appreciation. Be punctual, when told dinner will start at 7:00 pm, that means the food will be ready to eat at that time. After the meal, stay alert to signals that the visit is over. Most Chinese come, eat and leave with precision.

Giving and Receiving Gifts

Chinese are very generous toward people that they aim to build relationships with. It is customary for people who first meet you in a business setting to give you a small gift, as a token of their good intent. People who view you as a mentor or seek your support will also give you a gift. For example, in China when someone receives a promotion, a raise or a significant business win, they invite the people that played a role in that success out to a meal.

Gifts are typically given to guests at meetings, receptions and banquets. Usually, they are given in a bag with other materials. If you are presented a gift in person, receive the gift from the giver with two hands. It is not mandatory that you open the gift in front of them, although they will be delighted if you do so and express your joy and appreciation.

Oftentimes if you are a business VIP, you may be expected to take a photo with the gift and the giver. Position the gift between the two of you so that you are both holding it, or are shaking hands as if it was just exchanged, while looking directly at the camera.

It is common to give gifts during different holidays and special occasions. During Chinese New Year, you should give red envelopes with a token amount of money to children, as well as to people who provide you service and support throughout the year, like your housekeeper, driver or doorman. During Mid-Autumn Festival, it is customary to give moon cakes. When someone has a new house, a fruit basket signifies wishes for good luck.

Group Fun

Chinese love to socialise in groups and there is no better way to do this than an outing. Popular outing destinations are karaoke bars, sports halls with badminton nets or ping pong tables and bowling alleys. Groups of friends will often take day trips to nearby parks or tourist destinations for hikes, sightseeing or shopping expeditions. An important ingredient to any outing that requires travel is snacks. Almost immediately after getting on a train or bus in China, you will see everyone around you start unpacking and nibbling through an unending quantity of snack food.

Most companies have annual outings. These are typically day trips to nearby destinations where a combination of skill building and sightseeing is undertaken. Companies that

have had financial success will even take their entire office on longer trips, some as far away as Thailand.

WOMEN

There is a strong sense of balance between men and women in China. There is a lovely Chinese expression that says that women hold up half the sky. Traditionally, Chinese are respectful and courteous toward woman. One of the most powerful figures in Chinese government is a woman, Madam Wu Yi.

There are parts of China where women hold dominant social position. In Shanghai, the man is the better housekeeper and cook, while the woman manages the money. There is even a functioning matriarchal village in Yunnan, where the women own all possessions and men stay with them at their wish, or return to the house of their mother.

That said, there is a strong sense of gender roles between men and women in China. It is sincerely thought that they balance one another out with gender-specific characteristics. At one point when a row of women were sitting together in work cubicles and new male employees were joining, the women insisted that the man sit in between them as alternating male and female is 'strengthening the flower, like a rose blossoming between thorns'.

Foreign woman are unlikely to be harassed or badly treated in most of China. Muslim customs in Xinjaing create some sensitivities toward dress, especially in mosques. Women travelling in this region should be aware and dress accordingly.

RACISM

Although Chinese profess to not be racist, discrimination exists on many levels. The Chinese are proud people—proud of 5,000 years of continual civilisation, proud of the purity of Han blood, and proud of the role their country has played in world civilisation. The Chinese believe that their country sits directly in the middle of the map of the world.

Given this reference point, there are a number of biases that emerge. Anyone that does not have pure Han blood

Karaoke bars are great places for friends and colleagues to relax after a hard week of work, or just to meet up and have fun.

Opinions of people from other countries are run through a filter of relative prosperity. When asked what he thought of black people, a Shanghai professional commented that most Chinese typically think of blacks as poorer than they are.

is not considered ethnically Chinese. This means that people of mixed Chinese and foreign heritage are not allowed to claim Chinese citizenship. This also means that minority groups are viewed as inferior. Dig a bit deeper and there is bias of one region against the other, people from Beijing look down upon people from Shanghai, and vice versa.

Because of a history of bilateral issues between China and Japan, the Chinese often have an ingrained dislike of Japanese people. Insulted enough by the past Japanese occupation of China, memory of the massacres that took place in Nanjing remain a raw wound in the minds of many Chinese.

ALTERNATIVE LIFESTYLES

There is a large gay community in China, comprising both locals and expats. The view of the government toward gays and lesbians varies. Although overtly gay bars are tolerated in major cities, it is within acceptable interpretation of laws on 'social order' to imprison gays. There have been reports from international watch groups of sentences up to five years for 'disturbance against social order'.

China has been known to treat homosexuality as a psychological disease with electric shock therapy. Books and movies addressing the subject of homosexuality are routinely banned in China. Gay and lesbian bars are discreetly listed as 'alternative' in lifestyle publications.

Despite its popularity, drug usage is prohibited in China. Foreigners in China caught in possession of or using drugs are subject to harsh punishment, typically local imprisonment.

COURTSHIP AND STARTING A FAMILY

Because Chinese families are extremely close, even through adulthood, many singles live with their parents until they are married. Parents are very protective of daughters, even fully adult daughters. They expect a slow courtship, which the boy will earn their trust and respect as he does their daughter's, and are oftentimes strict about curfews and intimacy.

Many foreign men dating Chinese girls do not understand the strong ties between the parent and daughter, and sometimes encourage independence and rebellion against parental control. This is completely contrary to the way that a Chinese suitor would approach the family, and only tends to create a wedge between the parents and daughter.

Oftentimes a girl will not tell her parents she is seriously dating someone until she believes he is accomplished enough to win her parents' respect. In one case, a Chinese friend had been dating a man for 12 years before she introduced him to her parents. This was only after they had agreed to get married and she had little choice. Her concerns were well-founded. She spent the next year negotiating with her parents over his suitability to be her husband.

Weddings

There are usually three stages involved in getting married in China: legal registration, photo-taking and the wedding banquet. The legal registration is an administrative process that is done without recognition or celebration. It is basically receiving the Chinese government's approval to be married. The real festivities start with an elaborate series of photos that the couple commissions to be taken.

Wedding photography has become a huge money-making industry in China. Couples spend entire days dressing up in various rented costumes, having their hair and makeup done, and posing in front of natural and artificial backdrops.

On any given auspicious date, parks will be full of couples lined up to have their photo taken. There is a park in Hangzhou, a popular wedding photo destination, that has an entire section of props for wedding photos, from traditional fake-flower covered archways to *Gone With the Wind*-style porch swings. The most popular wedding photo pose has the bride beautifully coiffed and looking demurely into the camera, while the groom is staring up at her with eyes full of adoration and longing. After hours of this, the couple ends up with a professional album, long before the actual day of the wedding celebration.

A modern Chinese couple celebrating their marriage at a wedding banquet with friends and family.

Friends and family celebrate the marriage of a couple at their wedding banquet. Chinese wedding banquets have become a blend of Western customs like saying vows, exchanging rings and pouring champagne, with truly Chinese customs like changing clothes four to five times, rounds of *gombei* toasts at individual tables, and a game where the bride attempts to light cigarettes for the guests while people playfully blow out the flame before she can accomplish her task. The wedding banquet is an elaborate multi-course dinner theatre that lasts for hours.

If you are invited to be a guest at a Chinese wedding, a preferred gift is a red envelope with money inside. If the person being married is an employee, you should give them a generous portion of crisp 100 Rmb notes, preferably adding up to a number that signifies good luck, like eight. At a lavish banquet, it could be upwards of 1,000 Rmb. Check with local friends to confirm what would be expected in the city of the wedding.

Do not be surprised if you are asked on the spot to give a speech or make a toast. It is still considered a bit of a novelty and an honor to have foreigners at the wedding. Foreigners living in more rural areas have been invited to weddings of virtual strangers only to find that they are the guest of honor at the wedding, expected to give speeches and make drinking rounds with the bride and groom.

When you first enter the restaurant, there will be a guest book to sign at a reception table. Usually sometime after that, you will be asked to take photos with the bride and groom, which is when you give them the red envelope. After photos are taken, you should be escorted to an assigned seat at the table. The host and hostess are usually very thoughtful about making you feel at ease and will try to seat you with people that you can speak with or that may have something in common with you, like being foreigners.

At the end of the evening, a group of friends will accompany the bride and groom to their hotel room and orchestrate a number of mildly naughty games to cajole and embarrass the newlyweds. They are then left alone to start their new life together.

That doesn't last for long though, most young couples end up living with their parents until they can afford to purchase a house of their own. It is not unusual for multiple generations of family to live together in China. Oftentimes, should a couple afford to buy a house of their own and live independently, it is only a short time until they have a child and need their parents close by to care for the child while they work.

Pregnancy and Childbirth

In China, a woman is only allowed to give birth to one child, so pregnancy is a very careful time for Chinese women. If she works in an office, she will immediately begin wearing

Children are treasured and doted on in China, and family life often centres around the development of the child.

a maternity apron to protect the child from any harmful radiation that may emit from computers of other business machines. That apron will become her work uniform all the way through her pregnancy.

The Chinese government allows 90 days of maternity leave for a mother after the birth of a child, and three days of paternity leave for men. If the woman has had a difficult birth or is older than 23 years, she is allowed extra days. Many women are encouraged to schedule a cesarean birth, rather than deliver the child naturally. Because of the population size of major cities, maternity wards use scheduled births as a way to create some predictability in the doctor's work schedule. Because of this, many Chinese women know in advance when they will give birth and can be clear about their work schedule.

The 'Seated Month'

Traditionally, Chinese women rest and eat healing foods immediately after a baby is born. This time is called *zuoyuezi*, which literally means the 'seated month'. For the purists, this time allows no bathing, no exposure to fresh air, and no movement or effort. Families gather around and care for mother and child. A baby will not normally be allowed to leave the house during the first three to six months. It is fine to visit the new mother or child at home during this time. Bring a small gift for the child and a token of congratulations for the new parents when you first meet the new baby.

RETIREMENT—THE GOLDEN YEARS

To better manage the profitability of state-run companies, China lowered its retirement ages. A man is meant to retire when he is 60 years old (55 if in a blue-collar position), a woman when she is 55 years old (50 if in a blue-collar position). Retirement is funded by pensions and personal savings; China does not yet have a cohesive social security system.

Some people who are viewed as indispensable in their skills are not forced to retire—usually these people are leaders in their specialised field and can work well into their 80s. While they continue working, they are not subject to the same demands of others, and quite often are treated deferentially.

Elderly retirees playing cards under the shade of trees in the park.

In some cases, people come to their homes to consult with them and seek advice rather than require them to go to the workplace on a regular basis.

Most Chinese people look forward to retirement. Chinese are very active retirees, it is a newly won badge of aging honour and commands further respect. It is a time to pursue hobbies, spend time with grandchildren and play a stronger role in community.

FUNERALS

Ancestor worship is an important part of Chinese heritage, in more traditional households, you can still occasionally see ancestor shrines honouring the dead. The Chinese view toward death relates to whether it is in synch with the cycles of life. If early and unexpected, it is an immense loss to the family, especially in a time where the law allows only one child and the social welfare of the family depends upon the success and well-being of its breadwinners.

It is more easily accepted with old age. Death at the end of a long life, with multiple generations of a happy, thriving family to carry the name forward, is viewed as having lived a fulfilling life within Chinese society. The dead can be sure that their graves will be tended lovingly each

By law, all bodies in China must be cremated to save land that would otherwise go to gravesites. The exception to this rule are ethnic minorities, like the Tibetans, who are allowed to follow their traditional customs.

year, and they will be honoured and remembered through future generations.

It is traditional in China to wear a black band around the upper arm when someone in the family dies. The Chinese government provides three days off work as bereavement leave for working members of the deceased's family.

Funerals are usually not religious and usually involve family and friends gathering in a function room at the local crematorium to show appreciation for the deceased's life and console bereaved family members.

If asked to attend a funeral, be sure and check with the person that invited you whether you will play any role. There may be an expectation, even if you do not know the person, that you will say a few words in their honor.

Some Chinese believe that the more people to send someone off into the next life, the stronger their chance of getting there quickly. Because of this, a recent law has had to be enacted banning the hire of 'extras' at a funeral. It had become a trend to hire students to attend funerals to provide the extra support needed to give a strong launch into the next life.

SETTLING IN

CHAPTER 5

'The most difficult things for me were the things I needed
to do often, like ordering water, finding food I liked,
telling taxi drivers where I wanted to go. I found simple
solutions to most of these issues not long after I got here,
but the first few weeks were difficult.'
—101010 Newcomer, *China Daily blogsite Survival Tips*

LIVING IN CHINA

The discussions are over, the soul searching done, and the contract signed—it is decided that China is your new home. The first step to becoming a full-fledged resident of China is issuing the proper paperwork.

It is important that you check with your local China embassy or consulate about specific requirements for people from your country when planning a visit to China. Some countries have negotiated special deals that allow their citizens to visit China for a limited time without visas.

The governing body for all China visa matters is the Entry & Exit Administration under the Public Security Bureau (PSB). Their regulations are published online at http://www.shangahi.gov.cn.

China Visas

- Z Visa is issued for people working in China.
- X Visa is for long-term students.
- G Visa is for transit.
- D Visa is for residents.
- F Visa is for visiting business people or students who do not intend to stay longer than six months.
- L Visa is for tourism.

When applying for a working visa, you need to enter China with a Z Visa issued by a China embassy or consulate outside of China. This will be converted to a permanent Z Visa within China once you have registered with the local police station,

If you have not yet secured a job in China and are coming in to scout for potential postings, it is easiest to enter on a tourist visa. Should you require an invitation letter, most agents who specialise in China travel have a counterpart in country that will issue one for you.

had a resident's permit issued, obtained a physical from a locally designated China hospital and filed appropriate supporting paperwork.

The supporting paperwork required is your resume, a copy of your employment contract and a letter from your company confirming that you are filling a role that cannot be filled by a Chinese national. You will need a number of small passport-size photos to accompany the paperwork: some will be used for the resident's permit, some for the work permit and some for the records office.

Confirm with the administrator's office before submitting your paperwork. Policies vary slightly from city to city. This typically needs to be finished within 30 days so you should begin the process soon after you arrive.

It is very important that you are registered with the police station in the district you are staying once you arrive. If you are staying in a hotel, the hotel automatically takes care of this. Most cities penalise you with hefty fines if you have stayed in a residential area for more than a few days without registering with the local police.

If you do not enter China on a Z Visa, you will need to leave China and re-enter with one. This can typically be done within two working days in Hong Kong or Singapore. A spousal visa can be converted to a work visa without leaving China.

Once all of the paperwork has been filed, it normally takes two to three working weeks to have it processed. During some of that time, they will need to keep your passport. Carefully coordinate with the passport office on the timing if you need to travel. They can issue a temporary paper to travel with domestically should it be an issue.

A ROOF OVER YOUR HEAD

Once you are legally allowed to stay in China, the next challenge is to choose your home. Long gone are the days when foreigners were relegated to a couple of hotels or apartment compounds. Living options in China have never been more exciting, from skyscrapers to renovated factories to golf villas, you can find a home that suites your personality and budget.

Fast and Easy: Serviced Apartments

If you have adequate budget, the option with the greatest convenience is a serviced apartment. In the early days of opening, a few hotel chains made an accurate assessment of the difficulty that setting up a China presence would involve and set up an 'instant solution'. In every major city are a few five-star hotels that provide serviced apartments to live in, have authorised office towers attached, and have enough restaurants, shops and nightlife that you seldom need to leave.

These serviced apartments provide fully furnished homes with housekeeping services, laundry, shoe repair, health clubs, massage services, food delivery and a hairdresser. Many also have delis, grocery stores and a variety of restaurants nearby to choose from.

Some also provide butler service as needed for entertaining. Because the hotel-owned serviced apartments are expensive, most who reside in them are senior level executives on solid expat packages.

On the other hand, there are a growing number of residential compounds that offer serviced apartments at the less-serviced end of the scale. Private companies are buying up blocks in newer compounds and some offer short-term leases that include basic furnishings, laundry and housekeeping service. These are usually occupied by people working on short-term contract in China who would prefer to

Although serviced apartments provide an easy launch pad for expats to transit into living in China, in some respects it is too easy, and many who opt for this life live in an expat oasis, removed from the everyday hustle bustle, haggle and humour of the real China.

There are many modern and luxurious apartments in the major cities in China.

stay in an apartment rather than a hotel, either because of personal preference or financial restraint.

Prices for serviced apartments range from US$ 1,400 per month for a short-term lease in a reasonably new apartment building, to upwards of US$ 10,000 per month in a five-star hotel-run compound.

DIY: Non-serviced Apartments

The real estate boom in China has made standard apartment options far more attractive than they once were. Newer compounds are nicely renovated with elegant foyers and lift lobbies, they have new elevators that whiz up and down the building, the plumbing and electricity are modern so you can flush tissue down the toilet and can run more than four appliances at a time, water pressure is reasonable, and they have regulations that restrict your neighbours from hanging their laundry on poles out the window. The rubbish bins are cleared twice daily by building maintenance, the gardens are manicured and they have health clubs and community rooms. They also have excellent security facilities, and professional companies manage these.

Older locally developed apartment compounds are built in the Soviet style. They are entirely cement blocks which have limited insulation. If they are eight stories or less, they do not have an elevator; if they have more than eight stories, most have an elevator and may have a dedicated elevator attendant who sits in the elevator pushing the buttons.

Typically these buildings are inhabited by people who have been assigned there by the government, or have purchased their first home there. Quite often their lives spill over into the common area—bikes are parked in the hallway, children and grandparents are the VIPs, maintenance pops in and out of your apartment as they wish and old ladies will carefully watch how you are managing your life, often stopping you to make comment on your electricity usage and when you should close your curtains. Living in these compounds is full immersion into life as most Chinese live it.

A majority of people coming to China will live in a non-serviced apartment. Rent in the older local compounds outside of city centre can be as little as US$ 400 a month, while newly developed modern compounds in the city centre can cost US$ 1,500 monthly and up. These prices are relative to which city you are living in, for example, Beijing is clearly more expensive than Wuhan.

There are a few critical things to look for when inspecting a non-serviced apartment. The obvious are to check water pressure and whether there is adequate electricity flow to run multiple appliances. The less obvious is the amount of noise around the apartment: Is there a wet market that sets up outside at 4:00 am every day? Is the place close to noisy rush hour traffic? Is it next to a school that blares its exercise music at 7:00 am every day?

Next is to check the ventilation in the kitchen. Most vents are shared between apartments. If done poorly, your apartment will end up being at the exhaust end, and you can smell your neighbour frying fish (or other strong smelling food) every evening.

The third is to look at construction activity nearby. Even a person with the steadiest nerves in the world can be reduced to blithering mush after two weeks of non-stop drilling or pounding which has left them sleepless for nights on end.

Construction sites are a major source of noise pollution. Check if there are any near your apartment.

Walk the exterior of the building and see if there is any construction going on nearby.

It is also critical to understand if there are any unfinished apartments in the block you are looking at, and if so, when they intend to renovate them. The sound of drilling and hammering in cement buildings carries many floors each way. Typically the construction crew is from the countryside and lives in the apartment while they are renovating it. They get paid by the job and want to hurry through it. Regardless of building regulations, they will start tapping away as soon as the sun comes up and they are awake, and if under time pressure to finish, will do the same in the middle of the night.

Many cities have adopted regulations for renovations to assure reasonable coexistence during it by neighbours. If there is renovation that will be going on in your building, you must feel confident that the building management will police it properly. If they are not diligent, the situation quickly deteriorates into you having to take matters into your own hands and do battle with poor peasant farmers who have no reason to listen to you. It is a no-win situation on both sides at that point.

Apartments in China typically come either partially or fully furnished. When viewing apartments, keep in mind that they can be changed. You can negotiate new furniture or appliances into the rental price of the apartment. If it has not yet been furnished, a landlord may provide you a furniture allowance. The same is true of appliances. Usually this means a refrigerator and a washer or dryer. Ovens and dishwashers are not standard in China. They require additional negotiation.

The landlord will usually provide you with a list of items to be purchased and a budget limit. Remember to stay within the budget to avoid dispute. If you decide to purchase different items to those on the list, amend the list and get it signed off before spending the money.

When selecting appliances, it is best to select the brand and model of the appliances you want and have the landlord purchase them for you. It keeps them responsible for the repair and maintenance. Ask the landlord where they normally purchase appliances to make sure that you are looking at the same models they will consider purchasing. Landlords with multiple properties usually have preferred relationships. If your landlord cannot suggest a place, look at either Carrefour or at Gome. Both are reasonably priced, and provide delivery and standard warranties.

It is very important to keep an accurate record of the items that were provided by the landlord when you move in. You should go through the entire apartment and create a detailed list, all the way down to lamps, curtains and remote controls. Have both parties sign the list. It is useful to take photos of each room for your own records, just as backup. This prevents any misunderstanding when you are moving out.

Housing Allowance and Contracts

If you have a company-paid housing allowance, it is important that you confirm your landlord will provide you with an official tax receipt. Depending upon the city, there is about a 5 per cent tax that the landlord will have to pay each month to receive an officially-recognised receipt. Your company will need this receipt for its records and must have it if being audited. Paying taxes is still viewed as an inconvenience rather than a responsibility in China, and many landlords will attempt to increase the rental rate if they need to include an official tax receipt. Make sure that it is included from the start rather than having to renegotiate later.

Contracts are only valid in China if they are in Chinese. You may request your landlord provide you with both English and Chinese. Only the Chinese is valid so make sure that you have someone fluent in both languages review the contract to assure the Chinese version has the same terms and conditions as the English version.

When your landlord offers to provide you satellite or cable television, be sure and ask whether this is a legally provided service. China still has media control and oftentimes a compound is not allowed to have service. Many get around this by purchasing individual satellite dishes. You can see them mounted to apartment balconies. There are two problems with having a rogue satellite dish, the first is that the card has to be changed frequently as the service changes its coding to keep from being pirated. The second is that occasionally the police decide to crack down and do a sweep of a compound, confiscating all of the satellite dishes.

Villas and Suburbia

Many people electing a quieter lifestyle will chose to live in villa compounds outside of the hustle and bustle of downtown. Villa compounds are usually built near international schools or around recreational areas like golf or tennis clubs. They provide a safe and secure area for children to play outdoors. They are the closest things to a freestanding house that you can find in China if you are yearning for a backyard and slow, unhindered sunset strolls around the neighbourhood.

The suburbs are also pet friendly, many cities in China have regulations that are far stricter for pets kept downtown than those living in the suburbs. In Shanghai, it is actually illegal to walk your dog on the street during the day inside the ring

Suburbs usually have more lenient laws regarding pets. Here, a pet-owner gives her dog a blow-dry after its bath.

road. Some police will tell you that it is illegal to walk your dog outside at any time in downtown Shanghai; different districts apply the law differently. Your pet is far more vulnerable to crackdowns in the city centre that it is in the suburbs. During SARS, the police in Beijing targeted large dogs.

Electing to live in the suburbs has its pros and cons. Oftentimes you are living in an oasis surrounded by farmland, and restaurant and shopping options are limited. Public transportation is sparse and you are reliant upon your own car (and driver) or the compound shuttle service. On the positive side, the suburbs are normally more green, clean and traffic-free than downtown. Many find them a far more positive environment to raise kids.

Unique Space
If going the traditional route doesn't exactly seem your style, there are more exciting new options available to foreigners living in China than ever before. Would you prefer a refurbished factory floor along Suzhou Creek in Shanghai? How about a traditional house complete with your own courtyard in the Beijing *hutongs*?

Most expat families like to relax and entertain their friends in the gardens of their villas.

Boutique realty companies have begun emerging in China that cater to some of her more discerning new residents. You can find them listed in lifestyle publications like *That's Beijing* or *That's Shanghai* in the real estate section. A good example of the kind of offerings they provide can be found at http://www.space.sh.cn, the website of boutique agency Space.

ADDING YOUR OWN TOUCH

One of the joys of China being the manufacturing hub of the world is that many beautiful pieces of furniture and interior decoration items originate here. With the big shift that has taken place in private home ownership, every white collar Chinese worker has already gone through one round of home decoration 101 from a concrete shell out.

Big global DIY shops like B&Q and IKEA entered the country, providing the template for local companies to gear up for similar services. Some of the high-end items started staying behind for domestic consumption. For people who like to roll up their sleeves and put their own touch on their home, China is a gigantic playland.

Whether you have your landlord's money to spend or you want to put a few touches on the place to make it more yours, there are a few routes to follow. For an instant solution on a budget, IKEA is the tried and true standby. If you want to dig into the community a bit more, each city has a few concentrated blocks of local furniture and home decoration stores. In this respect, China is logical; stores tend to collect in areas so you can wander from one to the other selecting light bulbs, appliances and sofas all in one go. Even IKEA has become a nucleus: paint shops, kitchen stores and drapery shops seem to spring up in a four radius block around it a few months after opening.

If you are the type that religiously subscribes to *Wallpaper* and *Interior Design* and wouldn't imagine touching your home without consulting a designer, there are a number of individuals and companies that offer the service. A good resource for the best of these is high-end hotels and restaurants as they typically scour the market when setting up to find accent pieces and often use local celebrity designers. Some of the boutique lifestyle shops also have solid connections into the design community. Have a quick chat with the manager for a referral.

Fusion Pieces and Antiques

If you were clever when negotiating your contract, you have a very comfortable budget for repatriation. One of the best ways to add value to that homebound container is to collect beautifully crafted pieces of antique Chinese or Tibetan furniture. After ten years, there are far fewer originals to select from, but you can still purchase in China for a fraction of the price you would pay in the US, Europe, Hong Kong or Singapore.

Chinese and foreign perception of antique furniture is completely different. To them, the old pieces were what you were stuck with when you couldn't afford to buy anything better. On the whole, Chinese tastes run to the new, modern and elaborate. In the last five years, a group of

The search for antiques can become a wonderful hobby during your China stay. Some of the best antique pieces I have seen have been negotiated away from 70-year-old mahjong players in a small alley who are thrilled that a foreigner wants that old piece of junk sitting in the corner.

collectors has started to develop among the more elite of Chinese society.

Each large city in China has an antique market, especially those cities on the tourist route. Antiques can also be found in some of the larger street markets. Buy with high caution because many of those just out of the grave Tang dynasty pieces are younger than your toddler. The knock-off antique business is robust in China. Look for the more discreet stores where its owner coddles each piece. If it is a deal too good to be true, it is definitely not real.

More on Antiques

There are well-loved antique furniture stores like Hu & Hu Antiques in Shanghai, where the religious make pilgrimages a weekend a month to scour for new arrivals. *That's* lifestyle magazines have furniture and decoration sections in their listings. There are additional websites and magazines that are resources for the shops more frequented by expats listed in the Resource Guide at the end of this book.

Purchasing Necessities

Major staples, cleaning supplies and other necessities can be purchased in one marathon spree at French retail chain Carrefour, German warehouse store Metro, or the American equivalent Wal-Mart and Sam's Clubs. All of these chain stores carry both domestically produced and imported food products and household goods.

The shelves are lined with products from global manufacturers like Unilever, Proctor & Gamble and Johnson & Johnson, as well as major domestic and Asian labels. Carrefour has an extensive fresh food section, catering to both domestic and foreign habits. You can find everything from 20 varieties of mushrooms to pre-cooked roast chicken to fresh baked breads. Its wine section is probably the best value for money buying imported wines as they are able to buy in bulk and pass the savings through to shoppers.

There are a number of Chinese and Japanese bakeries in larger cities. The Marco Polo chain is well established and it bakes fresh bread daily. A number of delis are making meats, salads and cheeses more readily available. Most major hotel chains have delis with a selection of imported items and fresh baked breads.

Major cities also have chains of stores that cater to foreign tastes with a broad choice of imported items. In Beijing, the mainstay for imported food items is Jenny Lou's; in Shanghai, it is City Shopping. Both have a number of branches, usually in a central location near expat compounds. The 'food from home' that you can purchase at these stores comes premium priced. Import food still carries heavy tariffs; a box of cereal sets you back about US$ 8, and a small jar of Dijon mustard is US$ 6.

It is still hard to find some spices, packaged foods, sauces and seasonings in China. Most long-standing expats still allocate a portion of their luggage on returning from home leave to bringing back the things from home that are still hard to come by in China.

The most cost efficient way to live in China is to adopt local eating habits. When you delegate the kitchen to the *ayi* (local housekeeper), shopping magically happens within neighbourhood markets and grocery stores. After a few weeks of new delights each night as she demonstrates the breadth of her regional cuisine, you can agree on your favourite dishes of her cooking repertoire. From then on, there is a lovely luxury of finding a table full of steaming hot food at the end of a long workday.

CHINA OR BUST!

A whole service industry has sprung up in China around relocation. The lack of transparency, coupled with the exoticness of the destination, has made it a profitable business. A good relocation company makes the whole process relatively painless. It packs, ships, insures, tracks and unpacks, providing full door-to-door service. It knows how to get the family pet into the country with the least amount of stress to family and Fido. It supports during scouting trips to look at home and school options. Once on the ground, it provides orientation, cultural sensitivity training, helps you

You should plan at least three months from the time you decide to move to China to when you receive the shipment of goods at your door. Pay particular attention to Chinese holidays. During Spring Festival, the first week of May and the first week of October, China shuts down. If your goods are meant to arrive during that time, anticipate that there will be at least a two-week delay in receiving them as many workers from the countryside take extra time off to go home to visit family.

find an *ayi*, and points you in the right direction to build a social network of the like-minded.

When choosing an agency to support you in your move to China, it is important to look at two criteria. The first is whether they are fully licensed with a registered China office or affiliate. This will dictate whether they are capable of clearing Customs on their own, or whether they need to work through another company. The more parties involved in the process, the more likelihood that accountability and quality will deteriorate.

The second criterion is the quality and professionalism of their staff. It is better to have a relocation company that utilises full-time employees through each step of the process. The level of care they take of your household items is directly related to the amount of training, supervision and experience they have. Companies like Sino Santa Fe and Crown Relocations have more than ten years experience moving professionals in and out of China.

Make sure to do proper due diligence on the company your company recommends you use. Investigate their China track record, the depth and breadth of their China presence, ask about their registration and whether they use partners or do the work themselves, ask to see the resumes of managers and key employees that will be involved in your move, ask for references of families that have used their services recently and touch base with them to understand their level of satisfaction with the service provided.

Most people use a combination of airfreight, express shipment and ocean freight to move their furnitures and goods. Depending on the level of service you request, airfreight and express shipment take less than two weeks but are very expensive. People typically use these services for day-to-day necessities and small high-value items requiring additional insurance.

When managing your move, whether with a professional relocation agency or on your own, it is critical that you pay great attention to the detail of the paperwork. To remind yourself of items being shipped and the condition that they are in, it is useful to create a photo inventory. This will provide backup to make a case should they become damaged or lost in the shipping process.

Make sure that you have the full documented value of your household goods itemised on the insurance sheets. Although at the time you are packing you feel confident that you know each unique piece, months and miles later, it is difficult to recall exactly which four small cabinets you were referring to if you have not gone into sufficient detail. Be on hand when the moving company is packing and moving boxes to assure that each box is sequentially numbered and makes it out the door. On your copy of the packing sheet, mark which boxes important items go into that you will need as soon as the shipment is unloaded at your new home. It is handy to know where hammers, measuring tape, garbage bags and other items are as you organise your new home.

There are some items that are either not cost effective or are illegal to bring to China. Wine, liquor, cigarettes and electronic appliances command high import duties and are readily available in China. It is better to purchase them in China than pay a premium to bring them in. The import duty on furniture is much lower and is nil on personal effects.

Customs may confiscate CDs, DVDs and videotapes. Sensitivities around pirating have led to liberal removal of these items from shipments into China. You are unlikely to have them returned and if you are able to get them returned, the amount of administrative hassle and badgering will taint your first few weeks in China.

Do not attempt to bring in pornography or sensitive books. At best they will be confiscated, at worst they could seriously limit your time in China.

Be mindful that there are three items that are particularly hard to take out of China when you move onto your next assignment. They are pets, DVDs and CDs and antiques. Make sure that your pet's vaccinations stay current and that

they are properly registered as is required by your city of residence. Antiques must be properly certified and fumigated before leaving the country. Any qualified dealer will assist you in preparation for export. You will always run the risk of DVDs and CDs being confiscated because of piracy in China. It is best to transfer them to a digital device before you leave. Otherwise, it is a lottery as to whether they will get through.

BRINGING THE FAMILY

An expat assignment can be one of the most life-enriching experiences a small child can have. Their ability to absorb language allows them to be proficient long before their parents. Making friends with children from other countries and cultures gives a global perspective that will shape their lifeview well into adulthood.

One of the critical factors of this experience is the school that they will transfer into when they arrive in China. In each major city in China, there are a number of international schools tied to their home country curriculum, such as the American School, the French School, the German School, the British School and the Singapore International School. In

Students of an international school doing morning exercise in the courtyard.

addition, there are high caliber locally-founded schools that follow international curriculum like the Western Academy of Beijing or Yew Cheng Shanghai International School.

Most international schools are newly built and employ teachers and administrators on expatriate packages. This cost gets passed on through tuition, which ranges from several thousand US dollars for part-time preschoolers to as high as US$ 18,000 per year for older children. On top of this are bus fees, books, uniforms, food and fees for extracurricular activities. This puts the cost of a year of school in China about equivalent to the cost of a private international university.

Documents Needed to Enrol in Overseas Schools
- Passport
- Copy of birth certificate
- Transcripts from prior schools
- Health certificate / vaccination records

Many international schools cater to parents who are on full expatriate packages which include schooling. For those that are not, there are Chinese schools that offer an international curriculum that may be a reasonably priced alternative. Some parents have opted for these schools, choosing to take advantage of their time in China to give their children full exposure to the culture and language. Students enrolled in Chinese schools typically end up ahead of their peers at home in Mandarin, science and math.

Caring for Children

One of the joys of having a family in Shanghai is the care and affection that the Chinese lavish upon children. At local restaurants, wait staff will whisk your child away to look at fish or take a few spins around the room to explore. Old people will sit on a park bench and hold long, delighted conversations with a toddler.

Blonde haired, blue eyed babies are a special attraction. Chinese have no qualms about walking up and planting a kiss on a chubby hand, or even pick up or hold your child. Some children in their twos and threes begin to feel threatened by the amount of attention they receive on the street in China. If you prefer strangers to not touch your child, you will need to devise a polite way of discouraging it. The Chinese do not intend any harm with the attention. A natural affinity toward

Most Chinese women have a lot of affection for babies and are able to take good care of them.

children, coupled with limits set by the one child policy, has made a child a treasure in China.

Because of the talent and affection that Chinese have for children, many families end up employing a full-time nanny who takes care of the children at home. Many women with teaching degrees offer themselves as nannies and make wonderful caregivers for small children.

The only drawback to this solution is that it limits your child interaction with others his or her age. There are part-time daycare centres and schools that are available for children three or older. Playgroups are also a good opportunity for both children and mothers to make new friends. Most expatriate publications and bulletin boards advertise groups.

Employing an Ayi

One of the most important members of your household when you move to China is your *ayi*. The world *ayi* literally means 'auntie' and is a form of respect that a person uses to address an older woman. Becoming an instant member of your household is bound to drive some culture shock on both sides.

When choosing the right person to become your *ayi*, it is important to look at employment history and references. Included in this should be conversations with past employers where you can closely question disciplinary standards, levels of responsibility and ethics of past behaviour. For those who find the culture gap too wide between Chinese *ayi*s and how they would prefer their homes run, there are an increasing number of Filipinos in China seeking domestic employment.

Many expats who hire nannies, particularly for young children, pay for a physical exam before they begin employment. They also pay for the nanny to take a first aid course in Chinese for domestic helpers to better prepare the nanny to identify and handle medical emergencies that may arise in your absence.

Many *ayi*s do not have household appliances in their own homes, have only used them while employed to care for other people's houses, and will need to be trained in proper

Because Chinese who lived through the Cultural Revolution were reprimanded for thinking on their own, it is very important to set clear guidelines on duties and expectations. Older *ayis* will rarely take action without being asked; they prefer to have a set routine that they repeat on a weekly basis.

use. The biggest issue always arises with the clothes washing machine. It is very important to create a clear system for the *ayi* to identify which clothes can be washed in the machine and which cannot. You also need to teach her to separate the loads so that she gains a clear understanding of what can be combined in the wash. Educating on use of vacuum cleaner, iron, dryer, dishwasher and most small kitchen appliances will ensure proper use and maintenance. Taking these steps early will alleviate heartache on both sides later on.

Give the *ayi* clear guidelines translated into Chinese on what children may and may not do, what they may and may not eat, and where they may and may not go. Chinese views toward discipline are much different to Western views and an *ayi* may focus more on the happiness of her charges than the rules that they are meant to follow.

Wages for *ayi*s vary between cities and are influenced by the level of responsibility that the *ayi* takes in the household. Typical monthly salaries range from 500 to 2,000 Rmb. *Ayi*s should also be given a 13-month salary and compensated for working holidays.

SHOPPING STRATEGIES

If they made shopping into an Olympic sport, the Chinese would take the gold every time. If there is one thing most Chinese have a passion for, it is getting a good deal. If shopping was the sport, negotiation would be the finesse that would win the gold. Chinese negotiate for the pure joy of it.

Foreigners often mistake negotiation as conflict or a struggle, rather than as a passionate pursuit. In many instances, if you forgo the negotiation and cave into an initial ask price, you would have taken the fun out of the job for the seller. If a seller is able to charge you an exorbitant amount without a quibble from your side, he would assume that you are far more stupid than you look, rather than a person of

China is a shopper's paradise, as anything can be found in its sparkling malls and quaint little shops, and often at good prices too.

high moral fiber. Forget once shame on you, twice shame on me. In China, integrity falls on the side of the person who negotiates the best deal.

China is no longer the poor cousin of Hong Kong, Tokyo or Singapore when it comes to shopping. Major cities have beautiful malls housing a collection of the world's leading luxury brands. It is rumoured that the bulk of Louis Vuitton's global revenue growth in the last few years has come from China. Shanghai has become the trendy launch pad for new designer clothing collections. The occasional Bentley and Ferrari have been seen doing an elegant crawl down Beijing's wide boulevards.

Fashion Brands

International brands are congregated in high-end shopping malls and near five-star hotels. China's importance to these brands has risen to the point that seasonal releases are in line with other top cities around the world. Historically, sizing was an issue and some international brands do not cater to the petite Chinese figure with sizes running from 2 to 10. New entrants like Zara are turning that logic on its head and have come into China with a full range of sizes at good value. This strategy has made them a fast fashion favourite for both locals and expatriates.

Fakes

With badge consciousness has come a booming business for fake luxury items. It is impossible to walk down any major shopping street or through any clothing market without having a man sidle up to you shaking a sheaf of glossy magazine pages in your face and ask, "Rolex watches? Gucci bags? ...cheap cheap..."

Hard core shoppers come from around the world to shop at China's fake markets. There are regular shopping tours from Thailand and Hong Kong that scour the stalls and shops looking for high quality knock-offs to go head to head with the real thing in a fashion face-off at parties, society balls and business meetings.

Many expat bargain hunters make staking out the best shops a full-time job. Even the fake shops have adequate fakes for the average person and a special section in the

A large variety of food can be bought conveniently at neighbourhood shops.

back for connoisseurs. Because selling fakes is illegal, most are located down a small alley, up rickety stairs, through someone's kitchen, and in a well-lit back room with shelves jam-packed with luxury badges.

Shanghai's famous Xiang Yang market has been disbanded and re-emerged in smaller clusters of shops throughout the city. Beijing has its Silk Market and the Russian market. The best way to identify the current location of these shops is to ask at the concierge desk of any of the main five-star hotels or to scan any of the lifestyle websites listed in the Resource Guide at the back of this book.

Local Designers and Custom Tailoring

Shanghai Tang has made its mark in red silk on the fashion industry. It is a precursor to the original designs that we will see coming from China in the next ten years. In the streets, alleys, artists blocks and funky small malls, China's designers are experimenting with lines and fabric that are beginning to catch the attention of the world.

One of the luxuries enjoyed by China visitors and residents alike is the quality custom tailoring that can be had for a reasonable price. There are tailor shops in many hotel compounds frequented by expats, like the JW Marriott and Portman Ritz Carlton in Shanghai, and the Kempinski Hotel and Holiday Inn Lido in Beijing. Listings of tailors that offer English-language service are also listed in local lifestyle magazines. Qualified tailors can also be found at local fabric markets and fabric chains like Silk King.

At the tailors, allow adequate time for fitting and alterations. A good tailor will measure you the first time you visit and then have you back at least twice for an initial and final fitting.

The safest bet in having new clothes made is to take your favourite jacket and skirt in to be copied in new fabric. A good tailor will be able to measure and design a suit according to a photo or your style guidance.

Children

There are three choices in shopping for children. The first are traditional stores located in shopping malls or along main shopping streets. Most international name brand children's stores are in China's main cities. You can shop at either their branded retail outlet or at department stores like Isetan that feature the same brands in the children's section.

Secondly, many large international brands manufacture in China and have outlet stores that are featured in lifestyle magazines that welcome independent shoppers during fixed times. Finally, each major city in China has a children's clothing market where you can find both domestic and international labels on the clothing. Much of the international brand clothing found in the market has either been rejected because of quality defects or 'fell off the back of the truck' on the way out of the country. Check seams, buttons and pattern matching carefully when purchasing.

Toys

China's little emperors can now have all of the play options that their peers overseas have. Lego Learning Centers, Gymboree and Toys R Us have all firmly established their presence in China. Every market or small shopping mall has retail space dedicated to children's toys. When Ebay dealers

A street shop in a Chinese suburb offers affordable toys for the children in the neighbourhood.

had snatched up every Cars figurine in the United States and held them for ransom, you could easily find a complete set in a small shop next to a massage parlor in Suzhou.

One caution to buying children's toys in China are potential safety and IPR risks. Be careful when buying local toys as some Chinese toymakers ignore global safety standards. Any Game Boy with a price too good to be true probably isn't the real thing. Fake equipment and games are rife through the market. You run the risk of them being confiscated when travelling home for holiday or repatriating.

IKEA has an extensive children's sections and are a good source of furniture, colourful storage units, block toys, art supplies and such. Sports equipment is available at Carrefour or Decathalon stores throughout China.

HEALTH CARE IN CHINA

One of the biggest concerns of people moving to China is the level of health care accessible should they become ill or seriously injured. Major cities like Beijing, Shanghai and Guangzhou now have modern medical facilities, with well-educated doctors using modern equipment. Regulatory changes have opened the field for private medicine and dental care in China. Local hospitals have imported more medical equipment, and some specialty clinics in the larger cities have care equal to their counterparts elsewhere in the world.

Medical Clinics, Hospitals and Emergency Service

There are three types of medical facilities that are available in China. The first is a foreign-managed facility with expatriate and local physicians. The second is local hospitals that have special units for foreigners and VIPs. The third is a standard local hospital. Some standard local hospitals have specialties. For example, most cities have hospitals solely dedicated to the care of children.

Foreign-managed Hospitals

Foreign-managed facilities adhere to global standards, offering medical care that is on par with what would be offered in a developed country. Most of their physicians are foreign or Chinese who have practised medicine overseas and returned. The nurses and administrative staff are local. The clinics may lack some of the laboratory facilities, equipment and emergency capability of their international counterparts. If this is the case, they typically rely upon labs in Hong Kong to do analysis and feedback results. They also rely on relationships with local hospitals to access equipment and emergency services that they don't have in their own facilities.

It is prudent to check with your closest consulate to map hospitals and evacuation services in advance of needing them. International SOS has a call center staffed 24-hours a day with expatriate physicians who are trained in remote medicine; they offer member telephone consultation services and medical evacuation services in case of an emergency.

The advantage of a foreign-managed facility is that you can trust the doctors speak your language, are educated in health care in a standard that you are accustomed to, and have the experience required to be properly licensed. They also have pharmacies attached that offer internationally manufactured medicines that align with your home country prescriptions. The disadvantage is that they are generalists and lack the equipment and facilities to make timely diagnosis in some cases.

The United Family Hospitals have facilities in both Shanghai and Beijing. World Link Medical and Dental Centers are also in Shanghai. There are an increasing number of foreign-managed hospitals in both cities.

These hospitals will accept most major medical plans or take credit cards and cash. They are more expensive than local hospitals—an initial consultation can easily cost up to US$ 100. But they offer memberships which provide services at a discount.

Foreigner Units of Local Hospitals

Several local hospitals have foreigners or VIP units that offer higher standards than normal Chinese hospitals and have local staff that are English speaking. These hospitals can vary widely in how well they meet foreigners' expectations for sanitation and health care standards.

Payment policies are different than the foreign-managed hospitals. You may be required to pay a deposit of at least US$ 1,300 just to be admitted. Still, the cost of an examination in a local hospital's foreigner unit is less than US$ 50, usually at least half that of the foreign-managed hospitals.

Cultural differences toward health care can also create stress when a foreigner is being cared for in a Chinese hospital. Chinese people are usually passive participants in health care and faithfully follow doctor's orders. Chinese doctors unaccustomed to foreigners may find the questions, discussion and talkativeness of Western patients unsettling. A foreign patient must be persistent and tactful to get the information needed to feel comfortable.

It may also be difficult to secure medical charts when leaving the hospital. Do not assume medical records will be provided. If you need them for your home physician to review, it is best to be proactive in securing them.

Chinese approach to medical practices also differ from those in the West in that Chinese prefer aggressive treatment. It is standard to put someone feeling under the weather straight onto an IV drip. Antibiotics are often given for just a common cold.

Local Hospitals

Staff in a local hospital rarely speak English, so foreigners who use them must speak Mandarin or bring a friend to translate. Local hospitals are for the masses. In going to them, you will experience long lines, bureaucratic processes and no say over which doctor you'll see or when it happens. There are few private wards and if admitted for an overnight stay, you will be put into a room full of people with similar health issues. There are also usually no support facilities for family or friends to stay with you.

Although some people have received quality care in these kinds of facilities, the US consulate cautions that 'there is more than anecdotal evidence that foreign residents regularly encounter medical care quality problems in China'.

The one advantage to a truly local hospital is the cost. A district hospital charges about US$ 1, a better hospital double that.

Health Insurance

Having adequate insurance coverage in China requires that your provider cover medical care received abroad. There are companies and policies that specialise in this type of coverage. Aetna Global Benefits and BUPA International are among the most common. If you are covered under your company policy, assure that it is adequate for China. If you arrive in China without health insurance, contact your local Chamber of Commerce to ask about group policies that they have organised as a member benefit.

Foreign-managed hospitals usually have direct billing with major insurers, which allows you to utilise services without paying out of pocket. If your insurer is not registered with them, you may have to pay first and then file with your insurer for reimbursement.

Purchasing additional emergency evacuation insurance through a provider like International SOS is prudent in China. This type of coverage will arrange for transport to the nearest qualified hospital or your home country in case of a medical emergency. Without this coverage, medical evacuation can cost from US$ 5,000 and higher. Consulates are not able to help with this type of service for uninsured people; you are left to hope for the best care possible from local facilities.

Other Health Concerns

Before coming to China, you should check with your doctor to understand your country's immunisation recommendations for China. At a minimum, you should be current with courses of diphtheria and tetanus, hepatitis A, hepatitis B, Japanese B encephalitis and polio.

The major health issue encountered by expatriates in China is food poisoning. Although food preparation standards are improving in major cities, the sanitary condition of Chinese kitchens and hygienic training of its staff is dismal by global standards. Unless you are at a trusted restaurant, it is best to assure that all vegetables and meats are well cooked, to drink boiled water or open bottled water yourself and to avoid eating the rinds or skins of fruit.

Given the prevalence of hepatitis and China's rapid spread of AIDS, it is important to practise safe sex. Awareness is still low as to how these diseases are spread among the bulk of the population.

MONEY AND BANKING

China is still a cash society. It is normal to see people bringing significant amounts of money to banks and government offices by the bagful. Use of personal checks is relatively unheard of. ATMs are abundant although not interconnected and inter-bank fund transfers are used regularly. Credit cards are a new concept but accepted in some restaurants and department stores. Debit cards have been around a little over five years and are more widely used.

Local Currency

China's local currency is called Renminbi (RMB), which literally means 'the people's money'. The basic unit is the *yuan*, also called the *kuai*. One *yuan* = 100 *fen* = 10 *jiao*, which is also referred to as *mao*. Notes come in 2 *mao*, 5 *mao*, and in 1, 2, 5, 10, 20, 50 and 100 *yuan* denominations.

It is very easy to open a bank account in China, all that is required is your passport and a small amount for initial deposit. Since full implementation of WTO, your choice of bank has expanded dramatically. Foreign banks like HSBC, Standard Chartered and Citibank have established a credible national presence. You can open multiple currency accounts in foreign banks, which is a convenience in moving money between countries.

The Bank of China still has the largest national presence and can provide the broadest range of services. If you need a cash advance from your credit card or to cash a personal check using an American Express credit card as backup, you have to go to the Bank of China.

If you have an ATM card that is part of the international networks, you can use it at Bank of China ATMs or those of any of the foreign banks. It is the easiest way of drawing cash out of your foreign bank account. Most banks charge a small fee for this transaction. Domestic banks issue ATM cards and debit cards. Some have just begun issuing Rmb credit cards.

It is better to use the banks to change money than the black market moneychangers. There is an abundance of fake currency circulating in China. Banks are meticulous about checking currency. You are far less likely to end up with fake Rmb from a bank than you are from a black market moneychanger.

GETTING AROUND

Ask people in the 1980s who came to China what their initial impression was and they will say dark streets, no Coca Cola and bicycles everywhere. In 20 years, China has come a long way in transportation. It is the fastest growing car market in the world. There are now more Volkswagons, Buicks and Citroens on the road than there are bicycles.

China has nearly 500 airports, a train system that is the backbone of travel in the country, as well as buses, taxis, subways, light rail and private cars. The government has made heavy investment in the highway system, and paved roads connect every provincial capital in China.

A majority of Chinese travel by train or bus long distance. They use the more affordable buses and subways within cities. But an increasing number of Chinese now own private cars. Guangzhou, Shanghai and Beijing match their American and European counterparts in traffic congestion. During rush hour, it can take up to an hour to get across any of these cities, more than that for Beijing.

Most businesspeople in China use a combination of taxis, subways, company cars and walking to move around the city from office to meeting to home. A good assistant proves invaluable in estimating departure time for meetings to avoid being late for or missing appointments.

In order to control traffic, many cities have implemented licence plate bans during peak hours through tunnels or inside the central ring road. It is important to understand these limitations in advance of using public transportation.

Taxis

The easiest way to get around Chinese cities is by taxi. In China, you can identify available taxis by a red oval that appears in the front window. When a taxi is occupied the oval is down.

Taxi companies are well regulated. Most taxis are clean, the drivers are courteous, and there are clear regulations written in English to help you understand acceptable behaviour. There is a complaint number to call should you have an issue. The base taxi fare varies from city to city, but you can generally expect a starting fare of 12 to 16 Rmb. Cost goes up according to distance driven and the amount of time spent in the taxi. The taxi driver should have a clearly displayed meter and give you a receipt at the end of the trip. If a taxi driver refuses to use the meter, get another taxi.

To flag a taxi in China, stand on the side of a street and wave your hand with the palm down, using a motion like bouncing a basketball. Taxis cannot stop at intersections. In most cities, the rear door behind the driver is locked and you must enter and

Taxi drivers are a wealth of information in China. They spend the day putting forth opinions on everything from politics to sports teams. Many have begun studying English in anticipation of world events in China like the Olympics and the World Expo. If your driver seems willing, enjoy a chance of getting a slice of China through a good conversation with them.

exit from the back right hand door. It is locked to prevent people from opening the door on the traffic side of the car. You may either sit in the front seat or the back seat of a taxi. In extreme hot or cold weather, your best strategy is to sit in the front to get full impact of the heating or air conditioning.

On occasion, opportunistic taxi drivers have attempted to charge China neophytes hundreds of US dollars for a fare that should only be about US$ 10. Typically, the fare from the airport to downtown that takes about 45 minutes to an hour should be no more than US$ 20, or 160 Rmb. If you believe that you are being taken advantage of, stop a taxi at a five-star hotel and ask the concierge to help you determine whether you are being fairly charged. If you still have issues, either call the taxi company or have the concierge call the local police. They should have a foreign-speaking police officer that can help you sort things out.

The two biggest scams that taxi drivers pull are to say their meter is broken or to put the meter down before you get in the car. Insist that they use the meter. If they won't or can't and you have no other transportation option, clearly agree on a price before they depart.

The best way to ensure you end up at the proper destination is to have a Chinese friend write the name and address, including the nearest cross street, in Chinese. If it is a restaurant, business or hotel, it is also valuable to write the phone number. All taxi drivers have mobile phones and can call for directions if they are unfamiliar with the address.

Subways and Buses

Many Chinese cities have established and are rapidly expanding subway systems. They are well used by locals, which makes them crowded at peak hours. If you purchase a good map, subway routes are clearly marked. Fares are a few *yuan* a ride.

Most people commute by bus. Buses are increasingly clean and convenient but are usually more crowded than the subway and prone to being slowed by heavy traffic. Buses cost a few *yuan*. You pay the bus driver when you enter the bus. If you are unsure of your stop, stay near the front and ask the driver to tell you when you are at your destination.

Most petty theft occurs on buses. If you are riding a public bus, be sure to keep your wallet and other important personal items in a secure place. A number of people have had rear pockets and backpacks slit with a knife and possessions lifted.

Hiring a Private Car

Many new residents, especially those with children, opt to lease a car and driver while living in China. With your own car and driver, you are more in control of your schedule, and are unlikely to face the situation of being 30 minutes late arriving at work or meetings because of a taxi shortage caused by rain or rush hour.

Long-term car hires are less expensive than purchasing your own car. The leasing company will take care of insurance, maintenance and any traffic issues that arise, which takes a significant administrative burden off of you.

You can lease a full-sized luxury car like a Buick or Passat for about 8,000 to 11,000 Rmb per month. A driver typically costs less than 1,000 Rmb per month. You need to pay additional for overtime.

Drivers rarely speak English—you will need to employ the same technique of written direction and pre-trip briefings by your assistant to assure you arrive at the proper destination in a timely manner.

Driving on Your Own

Although the police are attempting to put more order into China's streets, driving in China is still one of the highest risk adventures you can undertake. In China, every person that drives will be in a minor traffic accident at least twice a year. Even if you are a very safe and experienced driver, you are closely surrounded by people who did not grow up in a car culture. Most people driving in China have only been licensed within the last ten years. Many drive a car as if it were the same as riding a bicycle.

That said, a number of expats are steadfast in their desire for freedom of movement. This can only be addressed by securing a local driver's licence. China does not accept any international licences; you are required to have a PRC-issued licence to drive a car in China. If you are caught driving a car without a licence, you may be jailed.

Getting a Driver's Licence

If you hold a valid licence from your home country, the process for securing a licence in China is to pass a written test and a physical examination. The actual driving test is waived in most cities if you already have a driver's licence. Many cities now offer the tests in English. They will provide you a study guide in advance. The questions are in multiple choices and the test must be taken in a supervised environment at the city's designated government office.

There are services that assist in the process. Any that offer you a licence without having to take a test are not aboveboard. China is getting more strict about licensing. A bogus licence from a small city in central China cannot be converted into a licence in any of the major cities anymore.

Once you have secured a licence, you can buy or lease a car. You may lease a car for personal use from the same agencies that provide cars and drivers. Many opt to have a driver during the week and then drive themselves on the weekends.

Bicycles

One of the best ways to get out and experience China at its own pace is by bicycle. Still the main form of transportation used for commuting, delivery and running errands, most major thoroughfares have bicycle lanes. In most cities, bicycles need to be registered with the police. A small plate is issued to signify registration. It is critical when parking a bicycle that it is in a designated zone and well secured. Police do regular sweeps to remove illegally parked bikes. Thieves do regular sweeps to knick poorly secured bikes. Most people in China have had at least one bicycle stolen.

All major buildings have bicycle parking lots. Many of them are supervised by attendants. In apartment towers and office blocks, bicycle parking is usually either in a basement

If you know how to cycle, getting around on a bicycle is a great way to experience the sights and sounds of China.

or on a side lane. Ask the security guards if you are unsure where to park.

STAYING CONNECTED

Within the last ten years, China has become one of the easiest places to stay connected to the world. The mobile phone network is phenomenal. You can get phone service almost anywhere—the entire length of the Three Gorges Dam river cruise, along the first stretch of the Karakorum Highway, the highway on the rooftop of the world, on the beaches of Sanya, and at monasteries in Shangri-la. This, coupled with the cheap service that IP provides, allows you to have a daily chat with your mother the same way you did when you lived five blocks away back home. Services like Skype and IP phone cards make staying connected to your friends and family easy.

Telecommunication options in China's cities now match what is found in other parts of the world. Each home comes equipped with a traditional landline. There are two mobile phone systems in China, GSM (European standard) and CDMA (American standard). Newer buildings come pre-wired for broadband. Blackberry service began at the end of 2006. You can even purchase a modem card for your computer so that you can connect via the mobile network anywhere in China that there is mobile phone reception.

Landlines in China come standard with only domestic phone service. In order to have international service (IDD), you must go to the phone company and provide a copy of your passport as well as a deposit. They will then open the line for you to make international calls.

China Telecom is China's largest service provider. It continues to have about 80 per cent of the telecommunications market in China and spun off a mobile phone division which is called China Mobile. China Unicom is a newer service that is going head-to-head with China Mobile. Both have adopted the US sales approach of giving away phones to entice people to subscribe to its service.

Historically in China, mobile phone service is not linked to the phone. The phone and a chip are purchased separately. The phone number and service is attached to the mobile phone chip. It is one reason that phones have become such an accessory item in China. By moving the chip from one phone to the next, a person can easily change phones on a daily basis.

There are two different options for mobile phone service. The first is to register with the service provider, provide a small deposit and receive regular invoices in the mail that must be paid on a monthly basis. Using this service, you can apply for international service and are able to place calls anywhere you travel in the world, as long as your phone is compatible with the local system.

The second mobile phone service entails purchasing prepaid cards that are rechargeable. You buy the chip attached to a small credit card-sized piece of plastic. In addition, you buy prepaid cards that you activate through an automated system.

Internet connections can be made through dial-up service that is charged to your phone or through having a DSL line activated in your home. Your local phone company can provide you information on each of these options.

Many hotels, coffee shops and restaurants have installed wireless networks. There is a running tally of them on expat websites listed under the Resource Guide at the end of this book.

SAFETY AND SECURITY

Most Chinese cities are far safer than their global counterparts. The only part of China where petty crime seems to abound is south China, where reports of muggings, home theft and road piracy seem to abound.

Most crime is initiated by the desperate in China, rather than hardened criminals. Many families dream of the opportunities provided by a provincial capital and use all of their savings to relocate. Once they arrive in the cities, they are unable to secure jobs. They then resort to petty crime in order to support their families.

Places where you are prone to theft are train stations, buses, subways, hypermarkets and tourist attractions. Take care as you would with any large city and make sure your bags are closed and tightly attached to your body.

When choosing a place to live, spend time on the streets to understand the relative wealth and level of care that the people living there exhibit. Is it a community where people watch out for one another, keep their homes clean and lead comfortable lives? Be wary of living in rundown neighbourhoods. Even if your compound seems an island of luxury and modernity, if it exists in a very poor area, it may only serve to rub in the disparity of wealth and make it a target for the desperate and poor.

Most modern apartment buildings and compounds provide excellent security. If you are comfortable with the level of diligence paid to protecting your household, the only other concern you will have is from the level of trust you can place in your domestic help. When trusting your home and children

to an *ayi*, it is important to have solid references from other families that have employed her. Pay her adequately—often she has the highest earnings in her

Be discreet with money, counting it inside your bag or in a private place, as what may seem little to you is a year's worth of earnings for the poor in China.

family and will be supporting her own plus relatives. Remove temptation by keeping a safe for valuables and cash. Ask her to keep close account of the cash that you give her to manage the household. Diligence should assure accountability, which will save heartache on both sides.

EATING YOUR WAY ACROSS CHINA

'Food in China is tradition, folklore, mythology, ritual, and religious observance as well as nutrition. Nowhere else in the World is the daily table so entwined with, so much a part of, a people's national fabric.'
—Eileen Yin-Fei Lo, *Chinese Kitchen*, 1999

THE ROLE OF FOOD IN CHINA

The West is just catching on to the role that food plays in our well-being, something that has been well known to Chinese for thousands of years. Food in China is a central theme, ingrained intricately in life and language. When someone wants to politely greet you, they say, "Have you eaten?" When someone is feeling unwell, they are instructed to balance their body by eating 'hot' or 'cold' foods. Every festival, family gathering, business deal, celebration and significant event is marked by eating. Sacred alters are decorated with food offerings.

Food defines life's milestones, relationships and cadence in China. There are special foods for special occasions: mooncakes are given as gifts during the mid-Autumn festival, noodles should be eaten at birthdays to signify long life, and so on.

Chinese food is based around five different core tastes —sweet, sour, salty, hot and bitter. Cooking styles range from fast and hot searing in a wok to the slow melding of flavours of a simmering hot pot. Ingredients used provide delightful, delicate flavouring that melds to create a unique experience with each bite of food taken.

LIVING TO THE RHYTHM OF FOOD

Typically, morning begins with a quick stop at a streetside stall before beginning the tasks of the day. Here you can pick

Delicious food can be found everywhere in China. Here, a cook prepares the food for his customers at a roadside eatery.

up a vegetable bun, a meat dumpling or a steaming cup of soya milk and a long doughnut stick to dip into it. The same stalls also serve lunchtime noodles, and will provide a small stool so customers can sit and quickly slurp down a bowl of noodles. The meal will end with a grand finale of tipping back the bowl and shovelling the last juice and noodle remnants into the mouth.

Chinese are punctual about eating. At noon, chopsticks invade lunch boxes and restaurants are crowded and noisy. Tea is a constant throughout the day. A steaming cup is sitting on most desks, stashed away between seats in taxis, or tucked in a corner of the floor next to a chair. The afternoon is for snacks, savoury or sweet depending upon the person. At 6:00 pm sharp, an exodus begins toward home or restaurant in pursuit of dinner.

BEVERAGES
Tea
Tea has played a vital role in China throughout recorded history. It is an industry which generates jobs, has distinguished scholars, has been used as currency and cash, and is an important component of any meal or meeting. Through its gentle fragrant steam, many important decisions have been made in China; whether between Mao and Nixon or husband and wife, a cup of tea is always within reach.

Although there are thousands of varieties of tea grown in China, there are three main types which stand out: green, red and black. One of the most famous teas in China comes from the eastern city of Hangzhou, a place called Dragon Well that sits in the hills.

If you visit Dragon Well, you can experience the making of tea firsthand. Farmers roam the steep hills terraced with tea bushes carefully picking delicate buds, placing them in a big woven basket. Once the basket is full of tea leaves, the farmer carries it down the mountain and begins the drying process. As you stroll through the small villages, you will see large heated shallow cone-shaped vats that the tea leaves are hand dried in to make tea. Rough hands swirl the leaves around and around the rim, releasing a musty fragrance as

moisture is released from the leaves. It seals in the flavour which is released when moisture is added back as the tea leaves are seeped in hot water to make tea.

Pouring Tea

Throughout China's history, making tea has been considered a delicate art. A full tea ceremony is a show of grace. A standard teapot is a round white porcelain pot with a short spout. Different regions have variation to their teapots. When eating at restaurants whose food origin is along the silk road, they have pots that look as if they came directly from an Arabian nights story, complete with its own genie.

These pots are a direct result of vibrant trade through the ancient Silk Road. When used in a restaurant, pouring is a cross between an athletic event and an art form. There is usually one person who is the designated server of the hot water that streams from the very long spout of this pot. It is used to pout hot water into cups of *ba bao cha*, eight treasures tea. To pour, the server pumps the pot with

The signal of thanks when someone pours you a cup of tea is to tap the table lightly twice with your first two fingers. For most, this is an unconscious act—there is no need to pause conversation or draw attention to this subtle form of thanks.

a gentle rocking motion until it has enough momentum built to shoot out the spout and create a hissing hot stream into your tea cup.

After the waiter or waitress has pouted the first round of tea, the teapot is placed upon the table. It is customary to pay close attention to the cups of those sitting nearby and to pour fresh tea for them as their cups empty.

When the teapot runs out of hot water, signal to the waiter or waitress to add water by placing the lid of the pot upside down and at a slight angle on top of the pot of tea. The waiting staff knows this is a signal to refill the pot. They will typically just add hot water to the pot, using the old leaves. Whether in your teacup or in a pot on the table, one batch of tea leaves is usually good for up to three rounds of tea.

Drinking Tea

Tea in China is typically served loose leaf, which means that as it is poured, you will have floating tea leaves in your cup. The trick in drinking tea with loose leaves is to wait until the leaves have settled into the bottom of your cup before trying to drink it. Gently blowing on the leaves at the top of the cup to move them away from where you are sipping is an acceptable strategy. Inevitably, you will end up consuming a few leaves and stems. If so, either swallow happily (many great dishes are made with tea leaves) or if you have little sticks of stems in your mouth, discreetly transfer them to your hand or a napkin as you would the shell of a nut.

Water

Do not drink unboiled tap water. Although many local people happily drink it, tap water in China is still a health risk. Water for tea has been boiled, and once water hits its boiling point, 99 per cent of the germs that can hurt you would have been eliminated.

Typically, if Chinese order plain water, it is hot. It is a preference but there is also hygienic logic behind this. If you want to drink room temperature or cold water, be sure to order bottled water, and in more remote places, watch them put the bottle on the table and assure that it is sealed. There are rumours that enterprising individuals collect used water bottles and refill them with tap water.

Alcohol

The Chinese expression *jiu* means alcohol. *Bai jiu* is a potent grain-based liquor. *Pi jiu* is beer. *Hong jiu* is red wine. Ingredients used in Chinese alcoholic beverages are varied, although sorghum-based *mao tai*, hop-based beers and grape-based wines are most commonly consumed.

Chinese people have a strong tradition of drinking alcohol. Most drinking is done while eating out, with family, friends or business associates. Be prepared, drinking marathons occur at formal banquets, whether a festival, a wedding or a business function. It is against Chinese tradition to drink on an empty stomach.

One of the most famous rice wines, called *Shaoxing* wine, is from Zhejiang Province which neighbours Shanghai to the south. In addition to being a favourite drinking wine,

A bartender behind the counter, pouring beer, or *pi jiu*, for customers.

Shaoxing wine is a common ingredient used to cook food in the regions of eastern China.

It is a tradition in the north to keep wines in big covered wooden vats. When frequenting a restaurant that specialises in northern cuisine, it is a treat to watch the wait staff pull off the lid of the vats and scoop fragrant cups of wine out for your consumption.

In China, *pi jiu* (beer) is a very common social drink, quantities of large bottles are consumed in small hole-in-the-wall neighbourhood restaurants to accompany three-hour dinners complete with drinking games and toasts. The Germans introduced beer brewing to their concession city of Qingdao. The tradition of brewing and drinking beer has since spread across China.

TWO CHOPSTICKS AND ONE SPOON
Eating Basics

Eating in China is all about enjoying the food and the company. The one thing that novices tend to focus on when starting their China eating adventure is their skill with chopsticks. This comsumes their attention to the point that they are oblivious to all of the other intricacies and nuances that make up a Chinese meal.

Using a spoon and your chopsticks together is perfectly acceptable in Chinese eating etiquette. Many restaurants in major cities will also have knives and forks handy should you require them.

A standard Chinese place setting includes chopsticks resting on a holder, a large plate, a small plate and a small bowl with a spoon in it. At nicer restaurants, there will be a smaller plate nested in a larger one, and a single stand that both your chopsticks and a metal spoon rest against, instead of the porcelain spoon.

In a restaurant with good service, the meal will begin with the waiter or waitress taking the paper cover off your chopsticks, tucking your napkin under your plate so that it drapes into your lap and offering you tea. There will be a rolled wet napkin to your left for you to wipe your hands before you begin eating. At some restaurants, the table setting includes a

A typical restaurant place setting which includes chopsticks, a metal serving spoon and a porcelain spoon.

large plastic pack that encloses smaller packs that contain your chopsticks, a wet cloth, a paper napkin and toothpicks.

Fancy Eating Versus Family Style

In a Chinese meal, most dishes are shared in the centre of the table. A meal typically starts with a number of small cold dishes. These are placed upon the table as you are first seated, to be nibbled at while the main dishes are being prepared. If there is a large group, a rotating glass disk (or a Lazy Susan) is placed in the centre of the table. It is turned constantly so that all the dishes are easily accessible to people sitting around the table.

When the waiter or waitress first puts a dish on the table, it is customary for them to turn the glass disk so that people around the table can see the dish being presented. Depending upon the restaurant, if in a finer dining establishment, the waiting staff will then take the dish away and place individual servings into small dishes which are then either presented to you individually or are put upon the glass disk to be individually taken.

When eating Chinese food, it is customary to take only one or two bites of food at a time, and continue taking small portions as the dish passes you. You should first put the food onto the plate before putting it into your mouth. It is acceptable to dip the food down to just touch the dish and then put it in your mouth if you are in immediate need of a bite.

During a meal, the glass disk is constantly being rotated on the table as people present dishes to each other. Chinese are customarily very considerate and polite of those around them and will give servings to people sitting on their right or left before taking food themselves. There is etiquette involved in using the rotating glass disk, which requires that before spinning the desired dish to its place in front of you, you first check to see if anyone else is taking food. You must wait until they are finished. Then you need to slowly rotate the dish you desire toward you, making sure to stop if people want to take something from one of the passing platters.

In eating 'family style', each person uses his or her own chopsticks to pick food out of a common serving dish. In a more formal environment, there are dedicated chopsticks and serving spoons that accompany each dish. You should use these to serve others and yourself, and then eat with your own chopsticks. If you would like to serve another person food using your chopsticks, the polite thing to do is to turn them over and use the end that you are not eating from to serve the other person. To show thoughtfulness to the people eating with you, especially if they are older or in a position of respect, it is usual to serve them before serving yourself.

In a formal situation, everyone will wait for the guest of honour to take the first serving before they begin eating. If the person who seems to be taking charge of the meal spins a dish toward you and offers it, you are being honoured as a guest and should take a serving so that others at the table can also begin eating. If you would like to show your respect to someone else sitting at the table, instead of putting a serving on your own plate, put it on his or her plate instead.

Rice or noodles accompany most meals, and they are usually served as one of the last dishes, eaten to 'fill the empty corners of your stomach'. Many visitors to China prefer to have rice as an accompaniment for their meals, as it allows them to enjoy the sauces and combines starch with meats and vegetables in a way that they are more accustomed to. If you would like to have rice or noodles with the main dishes, you must ask the waiter or waitress to bring the rice earlier. It will normally not come until the very end.

It is thought as good luck to have more food than you can eat. If you were trained by your parents to finish all of the food on your plate, you will be in agony by the end of the meal due to overeating. If you are with an aggressively well-mannered host or hostess, the only way to stop them from continuing to stuff food into you is to feign an inability to finish what is on your plate. You must also realise that a good Chinese meal or banquet is usually a marathon of food, rather than a sprint. Unlike the West where there may be three to five distinct courses, in China, dishes can keep coming one by one, for hours. A signal that you may be near the end of a meal or banquet is if soup is being served. Soup and rice or noodles are usually the final dishes to be served. Midway through the meal, sweeter dishes may start being served; although they are dessert, the meal isn't typically over until fruit is served.

It is usual in China for dessert to be served while the main dishes are, sometimes in the last two or three dishes. There is not as much of a separation of the main meal and dessert as a person may be accustomed to in other cultures.

How to Evaluate a Restaurant

The old adage of 'if you want to be sure of good food, go where the locals go' holds true in China. Whether expat or Chinese, the people who live in the city have suffered the bouts of food poisoning, bad service and being overcharged, giving them an informed view that is worth following. On a very basic level, that criteria involves going to restaurants where they can be sure they will not suffer ill health effects, followed by the finer points such as value for money, ambiance, food quality and service.

Some basic rules are when in Chinese restaurants, stick to dishes that their chefs have been trained to cook well, which typically means Chinese. There are good reasons that most vegetables are well cooked in China, from the way they are raised to the hygienic conditions in kitchens. One of the biggest risks that you can take is ordering a Western dish that includes raw vegetables from a Chinese kitchen.

An extension of this logic is to not be the first to try out a new Western restaurant unless it is opened by a seasoned China restauranteur, as it will take some time for them to train their kitchen staff to properly clean and store ingredients. It is best to give a new Western restaurant four to six months to get the kinks out before you can be sure that you will have a pleasant experience, both during and after the meal.

In the first-tier cities of Shanghai, Beijing and Guangzhou, there are readily available monthly magazines and websites that offer credible restaurant listings and critiques. One of the better in Shanghai and Beijing is *That's*, which also has a website listed in the Resource Guide at the end of this book.

If you are in a less mapped area, ask for recommendations from the concierge at some of the better hotels in town, track down long-time expat residents, or follow the crowds to find the better local restaurants.

Securing a Seat

The average restaurant in China will not take a booking for less than ten people. Most mid-sized restaurants will have a general seating area and then a few small private rooms. A party of six people or more will typically book a private room where they will have dedicated wait staff, a nice atmosphere to visit and relax, and if they are lucky, their own karaoke setup. When booking a private room, it is common for the restaurant to ask for a minimum charge on food and drinks to be consumed.

It is typically first come first serve, with preference given to regulars and friends of the owner or manager. You need to be fairly aggressive to secure a seat in a crowded restaurant. First you need to determine whether there is a host or hostess at reception. If there is, catch their eye and make sure that they are aware that you would like a table. Stay in front of them as much as possible to assure that you are seated when one becomes available. Others will have no qualms about taking a table that you move too slowly on. You will need to carefully track and defend your position.

DINNER ENTERTAINMENT

Eating is a common excuse to meet and enjoy friends in China. It is one of the primary ways that family and friends stay connected. Fun-loving Chinese use a meal to nourish their bodies as well as polish their sense of humour. It is very common for groups to have lengthy dinners that involve eating interspersed with stories, drinking games and feats of continual bravado.

At any banquet, you will be expected to participate as a guest. The most usual form of this is rounds of drinking. They begin with a twinkling-eyed person leaning toward you across the table, filling your glass and shouting *gan bei*, which is the Chinese equivalent of 'bottoms up'. If toasted in this manner, you are to drink the entire contents of your glass, and once finished, tip the glass toward the person that initiated the toast showing that you have consumed all contents. If you are not a hardened drinker, you can usually get away with raising your glass in toast, taking a sip and setting the partially full glass back down on the table.

Acting as Host

If you have the honoured position of being the host at a lunch or dinner, your main objective is to take extremely good care of everyone else. From the minute they enter the room, you should make sure they are guided to their seats and have something to drink.

You should take charge of ordering the food, or if you are unsure, have your assistant or someone whose judgment you trust order the food in advance. There should be a balance of cold dishes to start, a reasonable sequence of meat, fish, vegetables in the middle, followed by soup and noodles

Seating order is important—you must think in advance and make sure that the most senior or important people have the prime seats at the table and are seated next to people of equal stature. You should also try to ensure that they will find their dinner companions entertaining and engaging. Consider their language, personality, and background.

or rice at the end of the meal. Better dinners will end with fruits as the final dish.

If you are sitting next to the guests of honour, you should make sure that their cups are never empty and serve them food before filling your own plate. It is best to ask the restaurant to provide servicing spoons and chopsticks so that you are not serving them with your own chopsticks. If the restaurant does not provide these, turn your chopsticks upside down to serve food, so that the side that has touched your mouth is not touching their food.

If the teapot is empty during the meal, bring it to the waiting staff's attention. You can do this by either tipping the lid to the side, or discreetly flagging them down during the meal to refill the hot water. If you are drinking alcohol, make sure that there are always full bottles on standby.

Before you are mid-way through the meal, you should make a small speech thanking your guests for attending the dinner and offer a toast to them. Look at the most senior person or people at the table when offering the toast. If there are multiple tables in the room, go from table to table offering a toast. Typically if you cannot reach all the people's glasses to touch them in toast, you can tap the bottom of your glass on the Lazy Susan in the middle of the table, to offer a toast to all around it.

If you are hosting a dinner that requires translation, it is customary for the translators to sit beside the people they are translating for at the table, discreetly keeping them informed of what is being said at the table. If it is a very formal dinner, the translator may sit a bit behind and not eat during the meal, but focus entirely on facilitating the conversation.

It is important that you intercept the bill before it reaches the table in order to assure others that you are able to pay for it. Others will show their respect for you by being very insistent that they pay. In order to alleviate the conflict over paying the bill, it is better to either arrange to have it paid separately by your assistant or to leave the room briefly before the meal is finished and take care of the paying at the counter. Avoid having the bill for the meal brought into the room in order to keep things under control.

You are not required to tip in China. If you are at a restaurant that you go to often or have asked for special treatment, you may elect to give a small tip. Normally tips go into a common pool and they are either kept as additional income by the owner of the restaurant, or they are split among all of the staff. If you want one particular person to receive the tip, you should discreetly slip them the money.

Do not feel insulted if everyone seems to finish dinner and get up to leave at the same time. Chinese rarely linger over a formal meal. They like to eat punctually, in more traditional places this means between 6:00 and 7:00 pm. Once the meal is finished, they will leave.

Walk your most important guests to the door and accompany them to their car or taxi. Be profuse about your appreciation for them coming to the dinner. Warmly promise that you will meet again soon.

FOOD SCAMS

A word of warning to China newcomers, one of the most common scams involves restaurants. There are two things that may happen. The first is that you meet a person on the street who strikes up a friendly conversation with you and then invites you to have a meal with them, either to get to

know you better or to further improve their English. They will then take you to a restaurant and order a number of dishes. When the bill is presented, it is an extremely high amount and the owner or manager of the restaurant insists that you ate the food and must pay it. Usually, the person who brought you to the restaurant is involved in a scam with the owner or manager and gets a percentage of the money that they take from you. If you elect to put yourself in the situation of accompanying a stranger to eat, be sharp about taking a role in selecting the restaurant and pay close attention to the dishes being ordered and the cost of each dish.

The second scam involves overcharging and the wait staff blocking exit from the restaurant until you pay. If you find yourself in either of these situations, sit down and request that the owner or manager of the restaurant call the police to sort things out. Request that the police send someone that speaks your language to sort out the situation.

WHEN IN CHINA, DO AS THE CHINESE?

Table etiquette in China is vastly different from the West. Slurping, belching and spitting out the bits you don't want to eat are all acceptable table manners. Slurping and belching are a show of satisfaction with the meal.

Because they do not use knives, the Chinese are very adept at putting whole pieces of food in their mouth, bones and all, and to dissect the part you can eat from what you can't, depositing the non-eatable back on their plate or the table. When eating chicken, ribs or shellfish, it is common for Chinese to end up with a mountain of bones or shells in front of them.

At a better restaurant, the wait staff will continually clear your dirty plates, replacing them with clean ones. In a home-style restaurant, this may not happen unless you ask for new plates.

At the end of the meal, most Chinese use toothpicks to clean their teeth. The proper way to do this is to discreetly cover your mouth with a slightly cupped left hand while the right hand holds the toothpick, so that the use of the toothpick inside the mouth is not visible.

An interesting sight that you might see are these mobile stalls that go around the neighbourhood selling fruits, vegetables and other food items.

REGIONAL DIFFERENCES IN CUISINE

While Shanghai cooking mainly employs steaming, dishes from north China are usually braised or stir-fried. Ingredients in dishes prepared in north China are typically meat and root vegetables. A legacy from the Mongolian hordes that stormed north China, no northern meal is complete without noodles or dumplings.

Xinjiang food is influenced by its age-old ties to the Middle East as an ancient outpost of the Silk Road. The food in this region is typically hearty and filling, with bread, meat, rice and root vegetables frequently featured. Lamb is often a key ingredient in Xinjiang food, making it unique to the beef, pork and fish-based dishes of the east and north. Xinjiang dishes makes use of unusual spices such as cumin that are unique in Chinese cuisine.

Cantonese food is thought by some to be the most refined in China. Fresh ingredients and a tradition of small snacks, known as *dim sum*, have made Cantonese food famous worldwide. Much of what is now known as Chinese food in other parts of the world originated in Guangdong province.

Northern Dishes: Hot Food for a Cold Night

- Traditional-style bean curd with shallots (*xiao cong ban dou fu*)—Cold bean curd chunks blended with soy sauce, vinegar and sesame dressing and seasoned with chopped spring onions.
- Empress dowager's beef (*ci xi tai ho niu rou*)—Sliced preserved beef seasoned with five spices.
- Candy vinegar cabbage mound (*cu liu bai cai*)—Pickled Chinese cabbage marinated in sweet and sour sauce, and topped with spicy peppers.
- Boiled peanuts (*shui zhu hua sheng*)—Served with chopped peppers after being soaked in brine and seasoned with star anise.
- Beijing duck (*bei jing kao ya*)—Duck marinated in oil, sauce and molasses and roasted. Slices of crispy skin served with thin flour pancakes, which should be eaten with plum sauce and slivered spring onions or finely sliced cucumber.

- Stir-fried mutton with spring onion (*cong bao yang rou*)—Thinly-sliced mutton cooked till tender with sliced spring onions in a hot wok.
- Stewed chicken and mushrooms (*xiao ji dun mo gu*)—Chunks of chicken cooked slowly in a clay pot with mushrooms and potatoes. The broth is a tasty light brown sauce that goes well with rice.
- Willow of duck in a nest (*ya si yao guo*)—Slivers of duck meat sautéed with cashews, onions and peppers, served with a spicy sauce. The mixture is scooped into a nest made of deep-fried string potatoes.
- Stir-fried cabbage in sweet and sour sauce (*cu liu bai cai*)—Cabbage cooked in dark brown vinegar, lightly sweetened with sugar.
- Dumplings (*jiao zi*)—A mainstay of northern cuisine: meat and/or vegetable-filled dumplings that are eaten by dipping into a sauce of garlic, soy and vinegar.

Western Sichuan: Spicy, Hot Hot Hot!!!

- Sichuan pickled vegetables (*pao cai*)—Vegetables marinated in vinegar, soy and hot peppers. Served alone or to accent a dish.
- Shredded chicken and green bean noodles in spicy sauce (*ji si la pi*)—Chicken shreds served with sesame and chili sauce over a bed of chilled green bean noodles.
- Finely sliced pork with garlic sauce (*suan ni bai rou*)—Paper-thin slices of pork served in garlic and chili sauce.
- Cucumber slices in pepper and sesame oil (*qiang huang gua*)—Flash-fried cucumbers accented with Sichuan peppers, served with light chili oil. Very spicy!
- Beef slices boiled in a hot sauce (*shui zhu niu rou*)—Beef flash cooked in a bowl of very hot oil, chilis, onion and coriander. There are hot rocks in the bottom of the dish to keep the oil hot.
- Spicy pork ribs (*xiang la pai gu*)—Deep-fried pork ribs seasoned with a spicy coating of salt, pepper and Sichuan pepper.
- Spicy chicken with peanuts (*gong bao ji ding*)—Well-loved in the West as *kung pao* chicken: fried chicken chunks and

peanuts served in a bed of red peppers and garnished with coriander.

- Dry-fried green beans (*gan bian dao dou*)—Hot fried green beans seasoned with pickled black beans and pork mince.
- Sichuan pepper bean curd (*ma po dou fu*)—Soft bean curd chunks cooked slowly in a spicy brown sauce, seasoned with pork mince and spring onions.
- Spicy noodles (*dan dan mian*)—The most addictive Sichuan food: thin flour noodles boiled and then served with a spicy broth. Depending on the base of the sauce, it can taste nutty if the recipe uses more sesame or spicy if it uses more chili. Usually served with pickled vegetables and crushed nuts on top.
- Hot and sour soup (*suan la tang*)—Chunks of tofu, shreds of bamboo, pieces of mince pork, mushroom chunks and spring onion served in a vinegar-based broth and seasoned liberally with fine black pepper.

Eastern Seaboard: Shrimp, Crabs and Fish

- Lotus roots stuffed with glutinous rice (*gui hua tang ou*)—Lotus root stuffed with glutinous rice infused with osmanthus flowers and covered in a sugary syrup.

Spicy noodles (*dan dan mian*) is one of the most delicious and addictive Sichuan food.

- Drunken chicken (*zui ji*)—Tender pieces of parboiled chicken marinated in Shaoxing wine.
- Bean curd and mushrooms (*kao fu*)—Spongy bean curd blended with wood ears, golden rod and peanuts, marinated in a sweet brown sauce.
- Preserved bamboo shoots and soy beans (*you men sun mao dou*)—Lightly-cooked shreds of bamboo mixed with soybeans, laced with light sesame sauce.
- Home-style pork in brown sauce (*wai po hong shao rou*)—Chunks of pork that are half fat and half lean meat, cooked slowly until extremely tender in soy sauce, ginger, Shaoxing wine, sugar and star anise. Served with hard-boiled eggs and bean curd twists. A related dish of Shanghai fame is braised pork knuckles (*ti pang*), which is a whole piece of meat on bone cooked slowly in the same sauce until it is about to fall off the bone.
- Freshwater shrimp (*qing chao he xia ren*)—Another Shanghai favourite: small freshwater shrimps peeled and quickly sauteed over hot fire. Eaten by dipping in black vinegar sauce.
- Salt and pepper spare ribs (*jiao yen pai gu*)—Pork ribs marinated in wine, soy sauce, garlic and sesame oil, and

A serving of home-style pork in brown sauce, with hard-boiled eggs and bean curd twists.

deep fried. They are served with loose salt and pepper next to them.

- Boneless eight treasures stuffed duck (*ba bao jiang ya*)—An entire duck deboned and stuffed with bamboo shoots, peas, mushrooms and sticky rice.
- Shanghai hairy crabs (*shang hai xie rou*)—A delicacy in the fall, Shanghai's special hairy crabs are boiled and served dipped in a vinegar sauce.
- Greens with winter bamboo (*dong suan ta cai*)—Green vegetables stir fried with bamboo slivers.
- Pan fried scallion cakes (*cong you bing*)—A thin pancake infused with scallions and dusted with sesame seeds on the top.
- Shanghai stir-fried noodles (*shang hai chao mian*)—A lunchtime favourite: stir-fried noodles with pork shreds, mushrooms and green vegetables, laced with soy and sesame sauce.
- Steamed buns (*xiao long bao*)—Meat steamed in bite-sized buns, cooked until it has a delicate skin that melts in your mouth when you bite into it.

Refined South: Dim Sum and Dipping

- Wonton noodle soup (*yun tun tang mian*)—Meat-filled dumplings and strands of long thin noodles served in a broth and seasoned with fresh chopped spring onions.
- Shrimp dumplings (*sia jiao*)—Chunks of fresh shrimp steamed in a thin wrapper that creates a tasty juice broth inside when cooked.
- Glutinous rice with chicken (*nuo mi ji*)—A mix of glutinous rice, meat, mushrooms and salted egg yolk wrapped in a lotus leaf.
- Barbecued pork buns (*cha shao bao*)—Savoury pork cooked inside a bun.
- Baked turnip pastry (*luo bo si bing*)—Delicate flaky pastry with a savoury filling of shredded turnip and seasoned with salted ham and scallion.
- Spring rolls (*chun juan*)—The original of the Western favourite known as an egg roll: meat and vegetables deep fried in a thin wrapper.

Pork dumplings (*shao mai*) is a very popular *dim sum* dish in China.

- Pork dumplings (*shao mai*)—A mix of minced pork and shrimp, cooked in an open egg-based wrapper.
- Turnip cake (*luo bo gao*)—Steamed and mashed turnip, mixed with sausage, pork, shrimp and mushrooms, and pan fried. Tastes great when dipped into a little vinegar.
- Congee (*zhou*)—Rice cooked until it is soupy and seasoned with different meats and vegetables. This is a favourite breakfast dish in China.
- Crispy chicken (*jiao yan cui ji*)—Barbecued chicken that is crisp on the outside and tender on the inside. Served with salt, pepper and soy sauce on the side.
- Sweet and sour pork (*gu lao rou*)—Familiar at Chinese restaurants in the West: deep-fried chunks of pork served in a sweet sauce of ketchup, sugar and vinegar.
- Stir-fried beef with onion (*cong bao niu rou*)—Strips of steak stir fried in oyster sauce with onions.
- Egg custard tart (*dan ta*)—Small pastries cooked with a slightly sweet egg custard inside. A legacy of the Portuguese influence on south China.

CHAPTER 7

'It has been no hardship for me to study the Chinese,
their character, history and institutions,
for I am as keenly interested in them today as
I was when I was thrilled by my first ricksha ride,
a quarter of a century ago.'
—Carl Crow, *400 Million Customers*, 1937

PUTTING CHINESE CULTURE IN CONTEXT

Get in an argument with a Chinese person about how something is or how it should be done and they are not long to remind you that their opinion is coming from the experience of 5,000 years of history. China has one of the oldest continual civilisations in the world, which makes it culturally rich and gives it a depth that takes decades to understand properly.

In most parts of the world, we are just rediscovering lost civilisations or important cultural influences, while in a place like Xian, an average citizen can tell you that the slight bulge in the ground over there is actually a 2,000-year-old tomb of Emperor So-and-So.

China has rich record of its history, through relics, poetry, painting, pottery, music, festivals and customs that trace their roots back thousands of years. It is one of the most fascinating cultures to experience today. In one generation, China has exploded from its bound-feet, feudal past into a global force. One can still occasionally glimpse a tiny hunched grandmother hobbling down the street on miniature feet, just a few of the last. It was in the early 1980s that Wong How Man, the head of China's Exploration and Research Society, made an urgent trip north to record a discussion with China's last living Shaman before she died.

We are fortunate to be living and working in China on the cusp of its emergence as a 21st century force, enough remnants of the past still exist that we get to experience both its past and its future simultaneously.

It provides an opportunity to witness visible change in real time. The evolution is only partially complete. While the Communist push to modernise China dramatically marks cities like Beijing, Shanghai and Guangzhou, a half day of travel, by any means of transportation, will put you hundreds of years back in time to slow villages with dirt-floored houses, chickens striding confidently around compounds, and old women sitting quietly by the front door doing handiwork and ready for a chat.

With its vast size, multiple ethnic groups and long history, China is an onion that takes a lifetime to peel. In this chapter, the authors will highlight the main influences of philosophy, religion and political movements to give the reader enough context to begin to understand the perspective and influences that shape modern culture in China. The only real way to understand China is to experience her land and people yourself.

Chinese Dynasties	Period
Xia Dynasty	21st–16th century BC
Shang Dynasty	16th–11th century BC
Zhou Dynasty —Spring and Autumn Period —Warring States Period	11th century BC–771 BC 770 BC–476 BC 476 BC–221 BC
Qin Dynasty	221 BC–206 BC
Han Dynasty —Western Han —Eastern Han	 206 BC–AD 24 AD 25–220
Three Kingdoms Period	220–280
Jin Dynasty —Western Jin —Eastern Jin	 265–316 317–420

Chinese Dynasties	Period
Northern & Southern	
—Northern Dynasties	386–581
—Southern Dynasties	420–589
Sui Dynasty	581–618
Tang Dynasty	618–907
Five Dynasties & Ten States	
—Later Liang	907–923
—Later Tang	923–936
—Later Jin	936–946
—Later Han	947–951
—Later Zhou	951–960
—Ten States	902–979
Northern Song Dynasty	960–1127
Southern Song Dynasty	1127–1279
Liao Dynasty	916–1125
Jin Dynasty	1125–1234
Yuan Dynasty	1271–1368
Ming Dynasty	1368–1644
Qing Dynasty	1644–1911

BELIEFS AND CULTURE

Confucianism, Daoism (Taoism), and Buddhism form the three main pillars of historic Chinese thought. Much of Chinese tradition and culture is shaped by the influence of these three philosophies, from the way a child cares for his or her parents, to how to approach one's career.

In the past 50 years, Communism has overlaid another set of attitudes, beliefs and actions over these traditions, adding a discipline and focus that has allowed China to quickly reshape itself into a force in the modern world.

Confucius

Confucius (551–479 BC) was a thinker, political figure, educator and founder of the *Ru* School of Chinese thought. His teachings, preserved in the *Lunyu* or *Analects*, form the foundation of much of subsequent Chinese speculation on the education and comportment of the ideal man, how such an individual should live his life and interact with others, and the forms of society and government in which he should participate. Fung Yu-lan, one of the great 20th-century authorities on the history of Chinese thought, compares Confucius' influence in Chinese history with that of Socrates in the West.

A book called the *Analects*, a haphazard collage of thoughts, became the sacred book of Confucius' teachings. It is still studied by the well educated in modern Chinese society. It has influenced the values of Chinese people for centuries, even to the extent that it has been passed to illiterate peasants in the form of common proverbs and sayings.

Two of his followers, Mencius (370–300 BC) and Xunzi (310–215 BC) can be attributed with solidifying Confucius' ideas into teachings that set the thread of thought that has run through more than 2,000 years of civilisation. Each laid his hand to writing tomes that extended Confucian thinking. *The Mencius*, a book drafted by the author of the same name, had less impact than essays written by Xunzi. Mencius followed Confucius footsteps in travelling the land appealing to rulers of various states to embrace Confucian values in their rule. He thought that only through benevolent government would any ruler be able to unify China. He went beyond this to propose concrete political and financial measures to ease tax burdens and improve the lives of Chinese people. One of his unique views was around the innate goodness of human nature. It was around this last point that Xunzi had a dramatic departure from Mencius' thinking. In his writing and sermons, he disagreed with Mencius' argument that humans are innately good, arguing that men are born bad and therefore education essential.

Quick dips into the *Analects* gives us four themes that we see carried into modern Chinese society. The first concerns the proper way a person should behave. The Analects says, 'The gentleman concerns himself with the way; he does not worry about his salary. Hunger may be found in plowing; wealth may be found in studying.'

'When he eats, the gentleman does not seek to stuff himself. In his home he does not seek luxury. He is diligent in his work and cautious in his speech. He associates with those who possess the Way, and thereby rectifies himself. He may be considered a lover of learning. First he behaves properly and then he speaks, so that his words follow his actions.'

In conclusion, 'If the gentleman is not dignified, he will not command respect and his teachings will not be considered solid. He emphasises sincerity and honesty. He has no friends who are not his equals. If he finds a fault in himself, he does not shirk from reforming himself.'

The second speaks of humanity. Confucius said, 'If an individual can practice five things anywhere in the world, he is a man of humanity.' These things are 'reverence, generosity, truthfulness, diligence and kindness'.

'If a person acts with reverence, he will not be insulted. If he is generous, he will win over the people. If he is truthful, he will be trusted by people. If he is diligent, he will have great achievements. If he is kind, he will be able to influence others.'

The third is of filial piety—the ability to care for one's parents. To this Confucius said, 'When your father is alive observe his intentions. When he is deceased, model yourself on the memory of his behaviour. If in three years after his death you have not deviated from your father's ways, then you may be considered a filial child.'

'Do not offend your parents. When your parents are alive, serve them according to the rules of ritual and decorum. When they are deceased, give them a funeral and offer sacrifices to them according to the rules of ritual and decorum. When your father and mother are alive, do not go rambling around far away.'

'If you must travel, make sure you have a set destination. It is unacceptable not to be aware of your parents' ages. Their advancing years are a cause for joy and at the same time a cause for sorrow.'

Confucius concluded, 'You can be of service to your father and mother by remonstrating with them tactfully. If you perceive that they do not wish to follow your advice, then continue to be reverent toward them without offending or disobeying them; work hard and do not murmur against them.'

The final main theme of Confucius' teachings has to do with governing. Confucius suggests that virtue in government will bring out the best in people. He said, 'Lead them by means of government policies and regulate them through punishments, and the people will be evasive and have no sense of shame. Lead them by means of virtue and regulate them through rituals and they will have a sense of shame and moreover have standards.'

Daoism (Taoism)

The core concept of Daoism is *dao*, which means the Way. The Way is the order of things, the path of life, the life force, the driving power in nature, the harmony of the universe, and the eternal spirit which cannot be exhausted. Daoism

is said to have originated with Laozi, the old philosopher. It is commonly believed that Laozi was a mythical figure, the last he is rumored to have been seen was riding his ox into the sunset toward Tibet. Laozi is attributed with producing the *Tao Te Ching*, 'The Way and Its Power'.

Two others played a more significant role in shaping Daoism into a religion, Zhuangzi (4th century BC) and Zhang Daoling (143 BC). Zhaungzi, regarded as one of the greatest Daoist writers, produced *The Book of Zhuangzi*, which practically addresses the proper way to approach ethical disputes. Though practical, describing something as a *dao* or a way need not be to recommend it. The Zhuangzi tells us that every act, even thievery has a *dao*. The terms *dao* and 'way' can be used to describe a course of action—as when a person says "I saw the way you did that."

Zhang Daoling turned Daoism into a religion. He formed the Celestial Masters movement in 143 BC, which later split into two divisions: 'The Cult of the Immortals' and 'The Way of the Heavenly Teacher'. Through 'The Cult of the Immortals', one could achieve immortality through use of alchemy, meditation and exercise. 'The Way of the Heavenly Teacher' relied more upon divine intervention, asking the favour of gods and saints to enhance life.

There are five main ethical concepts put forward by Daoism. The first is *dao*, the way. The second is *de*, which can be described as the power or virtue to transform something. A common example would be the ability of an actor to bring a story to life through a character. The third is *ming*, which means name. What something is called is as important as what it is not called—it is defining the reality of something. The fourth is *chang*, or what is eternal and true, regardless of situation. For example, something that should be applied equally to all people of all cultures, times and levels of social development. The fourth is *wei* or *wu-wei*, intended or non-intended action. The fifth is *pu*, purity.

One of the most dramatic ways that Daoism continues to influence modern life in China is through the belief in *qi*. Pronounced 'chee', this is the Chinese term for vital energy or life force. It is a core concept in traditional Chinese medicine, as well as in some forms of Chinese martial arts. For example, the popular form of excercise, *tai chi,* originates from this concept.

Feng Shui

A popular concept driven from Daoist thought is *feng shui*—the Chinese art of positioning objects in buildings, homes and gardens based upon the belief in the positive and negative effects of balance and *qi*. Composed of the Chinese words for wind and water, *feng shui* (pronounced '*fung shway*') is the ancient Chinese art of recognising and utilising the relationship between one's harmony, health and prosperity, and the physical placement and layout of objects within a space.

Buddhism

Non-native to China, Buddhism is modern China's main religion. It is generally believed to have come to China during the Han Dynasty in AD 67, and that its entry point was Xinjiang. There are three different forms of Buddhism practised in China today: Han, Tibetan and Southern Buddhism.

Han Buddhism

Buddhism during the Han Dynasty was regarded as having its basis in magic in much the same way as Daoism, and it first took root among members of the royal family and aristocracy. During the Jin Dyansty, Buddhism became popularised among ordinary people. This lead to the emergence of a new social class, the scholar-bureaucrat, who brought together the established, popular metaphysics and Buddhist doctrines. The art and writings of that time can still be observed when visiting Longmen Grottoes and Yungang Caves.

At about this time, Bodhidharma, the originator of Zen Buddhism, spent time in the Shaolin Temple, famous in modern time for its fighting monks. Many of the temples, pagodas and sacred mountains that can be visited across China trace their origin to this time. Buddhism permeated through daily life and had a profound impact on architecture, painting, sculpture, music and literature. It also is the root of many colloquial phrases and parables.

Zen Buddhism, China's own form, was introduced to Korea in the 8th century and to Japan at the end of the 12th century. Subsequent political events caused Buddhism to be forbidden in China, both in 845 for social and economic reasons, as well as with the advent of Communism, where all religions were banned. Zen Buddhism eventually became known as Han Buddhism.

Tibetan Buddhism

Tibet's Buddhist history dates back to the 7th century, when King Songtsen Gampo (617–650) married Nepalese and Chinese princesses who were Buddhists. The earliest influences were the scriptures and statues that these ladies brought with them to Tibet. Buddhism has had fits and starts in Tibet—it was banned and then restored in the 10th century. The modern form of Tibetan Buddhism, called Lamaism, ws established then.

Tibetan Buddhism belongs to the Mahayana school. It utilises symbolic ritual practices of Tantric Buddhism (Vajrayana) and incorporates features of the indigenous Tibetan Bon Religion. Tibetan Buddhism is more mystical than other forms of Buddhism due to Tantric and Bon influences, relying strongly on mudras (ritual postures), mantras (sacred speech), yantras (sacred art) and other initiation rites which are performed in secrecy. Tibetan Buddhism has many sects and sub-sects. The most popular known in the world today is Gelugpa, the order of the Dalai Lama and Panchen Lama— this is also known as the yellow sect because they wear yellow hats. The sect began with Tsong Khapa, a great Buddhist reformer, in 1407. It stresses strict discipline and study of scriptures.

Southern Buddhism

Southern Buddhsim is unique to the Dai people of Xishuangbanna. It came to this region from Burma and Thailand after the wars of the 11th century. Based upon a combination of religion and politics, and its influence by Thai culture, monks can eat meat and live among normal people. Women do not become nuns because if they did so, they

Buddhism is China's main religion and many Chinese have a great respect for the Buddhist monks and the lifestyle that they lead.

The older generation of Chinese are usually religious and strongly adhere to the customs and beliefs of their religion.

would break their ancestral line. In Southern Buddhism, all young boys must go to the temples and spend some time there in training and learning. Some remain and become monks while others return to secular life.

Other Religions

There are three other religions commonly practised in China: Islam, Judaism and Christianity. The origin of these religions can be traced to trade and exposure to other countries along the Silk Road. The Uyghurs of Xinjiang are followers of the Muslim faith. They came to China during the Tang Dynasty and are of Turkish descent.

The largest community of Chinese Jews can be found in Kaifeng, in the Henan Province. Although little of their original religious beliefs and customs remain, they consider themselves Jewish. At one time, Kaifeng was the capital of China, and it is thought that these Jews came as merchants and traders to Kaifeng along the Silk Road.

About 1 per cent of Chinese are Christians. The earliest traces of Chrstianity date back to a 7th-century visit by a Syrian named Raban, who presented Christian scriptures to the imperial court. Later, the Jesuits visited in the 1580s. Christianity didn't really become embedded in the country until the early 1900s, when a number of missionaries established themselves in China during the Western colonisation. Occasionally, you will meet a Caucasian who can claim that four or five generations of their family were born in China, and these are the descendents of the earliest missionaries in China.

COMMUNISM

Religion was banned with the advent of communism in China, and only atheists were allowed to be Communist Party members. In 1982, the Chinese government amended its constitution to allow freedom of religion. This legislation was a high point for religion in Communist China—during the Cultural Revolution, there was an extreme backlash against religion that involved temples being destroyed and monks being killed by the Red Guards.

Influenced by the Russian school of political thought, an idealistic group of young men sought to overthrow a government in China that gave privilege to an elite group of the wealthy and powerful. If you ask any Chinese person what the role of the Chinese government is in their life, they will tell you it is to 'improve my quality of life'.

Communism brought a single-minded determination to this goal that had immense societal cost. The effect on modern culture can still be seen, as the educated and skilled who were 'sent' to the countryside, rural areas or borderlands, maneuver to gain their children entry into the better schools in China so that they may be successful enough in their careers to support their return to the cities of their birth.

The negative cultural effect of communism in China can be seen in how families, historically a cohesive social network, were shattered by deporting educated parents to farms and encouraging red-book waving youths to turn on their family and friends. It is not uncommon for there to be a disconnection between some 30 and 40-year-olds and their parents. Many children were raised by grandparents or in state-run boarding schools while their parents served time in the countryside.

It can also be seen in a whole generation who lost an opportunity at an education, a career and a chance to better their family situation as the universities were shut down across China during the Cultural Revolution.

Another bi-product of communist-instituted change is the one-child policy, which has created a generation referred to as 'the little emperors'—a group of 'only child in the family' who are the hope of three generations and are often considered pampered, spoiled and lacking consideration toward others. This policy has changed the view of the nuclear family in China, and you will often hear a single child referring to their cousins as their sisters or brothers.

Another policy implemented that has had ill social effect is that of the identity card, which historically designated where one could work and live. At present in major cities, there are millions of transient labourers who are the backbone of the construction industry. Most of these are illegal workers, who are routinely rounded up and returned to the countryside.

Although communism has done much to modernise China, over 60 per cent of China's citizens are still peasant farmers, living at a level that would be considered far below poverty in most developed countries of the world. While the citizens of China's major cities are living an improved life, the peasant farmers are still inundated with the Deng Xiaoping and Mao thought, clinging to the government's promise of a brighter future that will not come.

Communism has created a dramatic change in the lives of women—they now have an equal chance at education and employment. As recently as the mid-80s, there was still a great deal of bias in the system. There remains a view that there are certain subjects and positions that women are more appropriate for than men. A brilliant woman with multiple degrees once told the story of having to pretend she didn't understand math as well as the boys in the rural area that she was educated, as it was frowned upon for a female to have an affinity for math.

With the opening of China has come the greatest influx of consumer choice that any country has ever known. In just 15 years, China has gone from a supply-based economy to a demand-driven economy. While as recently as ten years ago you were lucky if you had a choice of three brands of toothpaste, today major supermarkets have a whole aisle of options to choose from. This has made the Chinese the least brand-loyal nation in the world—every month there are new items to try and new products being introduced.

One last change to the social fabric brought about by communism worth mentioning is the change that has happened in marriage. Historically, families played a significant role in the choice of partner for their child, to the extent that most marriages were arranged in advance. In modern China, marriage is an independent decision, although a happy one is better ensured by receiving the blessing of the parents.

SEASONS AND CELEBRATIONS
The Chinese Lunar Calendar

The Chinese zodiac is used to reference years, in much the same way that Westerners make reference to the Gregorian calendar. It is not uncommon to have someone respond with a zodiac sign rather than an actual year when you ask how old they are. 'I am an earth pig' is a well understood answer, giving common reference not just on age, but also on character and preferences. It even influences your love life, as some signs are meant to be more compatible than others. The Chinese only began using the Gregorian calendar in 1911.

Although the actual date of the origin of Chinese astrology is unknown, legend has it that the Yellow Emperor introduced the first cycle of the zodiac in 2,600 BC to record the Chinese Lunar New Year. The basic structure of the zodiac is ten heavenly stems and 12 earthly branches, which when combined indicate a specific hour, date and year according to the Chinese traditional system. The 12 branches match the number of months in a year and hours in a day. With each of the stems and branches combining once sequentially, a complete cycle takes 60 years. Everyone who uses this calendar can experience the exact same year only once again in their lifetime.

Chinese Zodiac

- Year of the Rat—1912, 1924, 1936, 1948, 1960, 1972, 1984, 1996, 2008
- Year of the Ox—1913, 1925, 1937, 1949, 1961, 1973, 1985, 1997, 2009
- Year of the Tiger—1914, 1926, 1938, 1950, 1962, 1974, 1986, 1998, 2010
- Year of the Rabbit—1915, 1927, 1939, 1951, 1963, 1975, 1987, 1999, 2011
- Year of the Dragon—1916, 1928, 1940, 1952, 1964, 1976, 1988, 2000, 2012
- Year of the Snake—1917, 1929, 1941, 1953, 1965, 1977, 1989, 2001, 2013
- Year of the Horse—1918, 1930, 1942, 1954,1966, 1978, 1990, 2002, 2014
- Year of the Sheep—1919, 1931, 1943, 1955, 1967, 1979, 1991, 2003, 2015
- Year of the Monkey—1920, 1932, 1944, 1956, 1968, 1980, 1992, 2004
- Year of the Rooster—1921, 1933, 1945, 1957, 1969, 1981, 1993, 2005
- Year of the Dog—1922, 1934, 1946, 1958, 1970, 1982, 1994, 2006
- Year of the Pig—1923, 1935, 1947, 1959, 1971, 1983, 1995, 2007

Age

When in discussion with a Chinese over age, remember that they often reference the lunar calendar when calculating their age and so the age that they tell you does not tie to the Gregorian calendar, which typically creates a discrepancy of a year. Oftentimes, someone who tells you that they are 29 years old would be 28 by Gregorian calendar standards. Most cosmopolitan Chinese have an understanding of the difference and will automatically adjust their answer to the Western context.

Name

The changing of each year effects your fate depending on your sign. It is common for Chinese to see fortune tellers during a zodiac transition, or if they are having a run of bad luck. In addition to the use of jade, *feng shui,* and traditional remedies, another common piece of advice is to change your name. It is not unusual for a Chinese person to change their name in order to bring themselves better luck.

FESTIVALS
Spring Festival (Chun Jie)

This is the biggest holiday in China. Otherwise known as Chinese New Year, it is celebrated on the first day of the first month of the lunar calendar. A three-day public holiday, commencing on the eve of the New Year, Chinese people spend this time with their family or travelling. Food plays a significant role in the holiday with continual gatherings for eating with friends and family occuring over a four-week period.

There are prescribed days for different activities that will guarantee success for the coming year. For example, you clean your house, sweep away the bad luck of the year, buy new clothes and get your hair cut before New Year's Day. All debts should be paid off so you start the year with a clean slate. Homes are also decorated in red.

During the holiday, people visit family and friends and pass out *hong baos* (red envelopes) containing cash. Some people believe that if the new year is the ruling year of the animal that signifies the year they are born, they will be very lucky or

very unlucky. In order to assure luck, many wear jade bangles on their left wrist so that it touches the blood going to the heart. Wearing red string is also meant to ensure luck.

Lantern Festival (Yuanxiao Jie)

This occurs 15 days after the Chinese New Year. Although not a public holiday, it is a time of colourful, joyful celebration when people make or buy paper lanterns and walk around the streets in the evening holding them. This 15th day is the first night when people can see a full moon in the lunar new year. According to the Chinese tradition, at the very beginning of a new year when there is a bright full moon hanging in the sky, there should be thousands of colourful lanterns hung out for people to appreciate. It is customary at that time for people to eat *tang yuan* (glutinous rice ball) together with their families.

Guanyin's Birthday (Guan Shi Yin Sheng Ri)

The birthday of Guanyin, the Goddess of Mercy, is a good time to visit Daoist temples. Guanyin's birthday is on the 19th day of the second moon. It falls in March or April.

Tomb Sweeping Day (Qing Ming Jie)

A day for worshipping ancestors: people visit the graves of their departed relatives and clean the grave sites. They often place flowers on the tomb and burn ghost money for the departed. It usually falls on 5 April, and on 4 April in leap years.

Water Splashing Festival (Po Shui Jie)
Held in Xishuangbanna in Yunnan, and in Thailand and Vietnam, this festival is in mid-April. The purpose is to wash away the dirt, sorrow and demons of the old year and bring in the happiness of the new.

Mazu's Birthday (Ma Zu Sheng Ri)
Mazu is the goddess of the sea. Her birthday is celebrated in south China, mainly the Fujian Province. It is celebrated at Daoist temples in the coastal regions and down the cost of South China Sea all the way to Vietnam. This usually occurs in April or May.

Dragon Boat Festival (Duan Wu Jie)
A huge holiday in south China, this festival commemorates a third-century poet and statesman named Chu Yuan who despaired because he was slandered by another and lost favour with his king. He threw himself in a river to drown. Tradition has it that people will throw rice dumplings down the river for the fishes to eat so that they will not eat Chu Yuan's body. The modern festival also has teams of dragon boat oarsmen battling it out on the rivers of China. It is thought that the boat race averts misfortunes. The holiday is on the fifth day of the fifth month of the lunar calendar (around June).

Ghost Month (Gui Yue)
Not recognised by the Chinese government, this holiday is based upon an ancient belief that people who travel at this time are prone to death. During this time, the ghosts from hell walk the earth, believed to interfere with the safety of the living. Superstition dictates that people who die during this month (usually August) are not buried until the following month. The Ghost Month is the seventh lunar month.

Mid-Autumn Festival (Zhong Qiu Jie)

Known in China as the Full Moon Festival, it falls on the 15th day of the eigth lunar month, usually in October in the Gregorian calendar. This is a traditional holiday for lovers and rebels. Celebrated outdoors under the moonlight, people eat mooncakes, gaze at the moon and light fireworks. Many businesses and individuals give gifts of mooncakes to one another. In the 4th centruy, mooncakes came in handy to overthrow the Mongolian-led Yuan Dyansty. Messages coordinating the time of the rebellion were passed inside mooncakes, a flaked pastry stuffed with fillings.

Birthday of Confucius (Kong Zi Sheng Ri)

28 September of the Gregorian calendar is the birthday of Confucius, one of China's most influential philosophers. He was born in Qufu in Shandong, which celebrates his birthday by hosting a huge party on his birthdate each year.

Public Holidays	
New Year's Day	1 January
*Spring Festival (Chun Jie)	Follows the lunar calendar, usually falls between late January and mid February. (3 days: New Year's Eve, 1st and 2nd day of the first lunar month)
International Labor Day	1 May
National Day	1 October (3 days: 1st, 2nd and 3rd October)
Tomb Sweeping Day (Qing Ming Jie)	5 April (4 April in leap years)
Dragon Boat Festival (Duan Wu Jie	The 5th day of the 5th lunar month
Mid-Autumn Festival (Zhong Qiu Jie)	The 15th day of the 8th lunar moth

ENTERTAINMENT AND THE ARTS
Poetry and Writing

China is the only country in the world with a literature written in one language for more than 3,000 consecutive years. China

> One of China's most famous novels is *Dream of the Red Chamber*, which—typical of many early novels—was written anonymously. Many authors felt it was beneath their station to be associated with this type of writing.

has a very old and rich tradition in literature and the dramatic and visual arts. Early writings generally derived from philosophical or religious essays such as the works of Confucius (551–479 BC) and Lao-tzu (probably 4th century BC). These writings were often about how people should act and how the society and political system should be organised.

China had a strong tradition of historical writing. One of the earliest historians, still published today, is Sima Qian, the historian for the Qin Dyansty of 221 BC. His *Historical Records* have been an honoured classic, read around the world since AD 8.

China's most famous 20th century writer was poet Lu Xun. His poetry, essays and novels focused on China's need to modernise through revolution. Although held up as a hero in modern-day China, his counterparts that write of change in China's social fabric are often banned from being published in China. Recent examples are Gao Xingjian who wrote *Soul Mountain* and *One Man's Bible*. There is also the self-absorbed, decadent child of modern China, Wei Hui, who wrote *Shanghai Baby*.

Opera

Chinese opera together with Greece tragic-comedy and Indian Sanskrit Opera are the three oldest dramatic art forms in the world. During the Tang Dynasty (618–907), the Emperor Taizong established the first official opera school. Since the Yuan Dynasty (1271–1368), Chinese opera has been encouraged by court officials and emperors and has become a traditional art form. During the Qing Dynasty (1644–1911), Chinese opera became fashionable among ordinary people. Performances were watched in tea-rooms, restaurants and even around makeshift stages.

Chinese opera has a rich history in China and is one of the gems of Chinese culture, featuring beautiful music, dialogue, costumes and movements.

Chinese opera evolved from folk songs, dances, talking, antimasque, and especially distinctive dialectical music. Gradually, it combined music, art and literature into one performance on the stage. These operas are accompanied by traditional musical instruments like the lute, the gong and the erhu. During the opera, actors present unique melodies and dialogues which are beautifully written and of high literary value. Combining the music, dialogue, costumes and symbolic head and body movements, Chinese opera has layers of meaning that enthusiasts delight in.

For example, designs are painted on the performer's face to symbolise personality, role and fate. A red face generally represents loyalty and bravery, a black face represents valor, yellow and white faces represent duplicity, and golden and silver faces represent mystery.

There are over 300 regional opera styles practised in China today. Kun opera, which originated around Jiangsu Province, is a typical ancient opera style and features gentleness and clearness. Qinqiang opera from Shaanxi is loud, aggressive and wild. Probably the best known is Beijing opera, which combines many regional styles. It has been designated the national opera of China.

Music

If you visit the Shanghai Museum, there are a set of bells on display that date back to the Bronze Age. Each bell is forged to make a single note, played together the musician could express in chords of melody. China has a range of unique traditional instruments, including the *erhu*, a two-stringed fiddle; the *huqin*, a two-stringed viola; a four-stringed banjo called the *yueqin*; and a variety of flutes called *sanxian*, *dongxiao* and *dizi*. It also has a ceremonial trumpet called the *suona* and gongs called *daluo*.

Taiwan and Hong Kong rock stars are well followed in mainland China. The most-loved stars are always featured on Chinese MTV and Channel V.

Adoption of modern musical instruments has happened in China as with the rest of the world. The Chinese are great lovers of classical music and it is common for visiting symphonies or the national symphony to be playing on a weekly basis. In addition, China has a blossoming rock industry, revolutionised by China's father of rock, Cui Jian. Most original music is recorded in Beijing, although many local bands can be heard on stages across China as they forge their own sound. It is typical for students of China's music schools to form their own bands and play in local pubs and bars. They create a unique blend of traditional Chinese music and modern rock.

HOBBIES AND INTERESTS

The Chinese have great energy to pursue self-improvement. Pursuits outside of work are generally viewed as creating a more well-rounded and intelligent person.

Collecting items of value is a popular hobby in China. At one time in the early 1990s, one of the largest hobbies among youths in east China was stamp collecting—there was an entire street in downtown Shanghai where you could trade or purchase stamps. More elite collections include traditional Chinese stones, jades, porcelains, traditional paintings and calligraphy. Although illegal, collecting dinasoaur eggs, which can still be unearthed in the Gobi Desert, is a popular hobby. More participatory hobbies include dance, various forms of martial arts, calligraphy and a form of stand-up comedy called cross-talk.

Probably the most popular pastime in China is massage. It is not unusual for an enthusiast to spend two or three hours a week receiving a massage. The most common form of massage to be found in China is foot massage. It is believed that each part of the body is connected to a section on the foot. A foot massage helps adjust those parts that are out of alignment.

Sports

Football (or soccer) has to be the national sport of China. Regardless of age or sex, the Chinese love football. Each major city has a team. University fields are never empty, as there are adult leagues that play on weekends. China comes to a standstill during every World Cup. In Shanghai, a city of approximately 16.6 million people, during a lazy Sunday afternoon of the 2002 World Cup, every major play was announced with an eruption of cries echoing through every street of the city as people were glued to their television screens. In the late 1990s, before air-conditioning was common in Shanghai, people used to take to the streets in their pajamas, huddled around a shared television. Taxi drivers would stop their cars in the streets to watch football, grinding traffic to a complete halt.

Yao Ming has done much to make basketball one of the favourite sports in China. The NBA now has a solid presence in the country. There are city teams and university teams. It is easy to play a pick-up game of basketball at any university court.

Tennis is viewed as a sport played by the elite. Many senior government officials in China are tennis enthusiasts. There are a number of tennis clubs in most major cities, and most modern living compounds have tennis courts.

Playing Golf

Golf is also a sport that has taken off in recent years. A number of signature courses have been built across China. Golf tournaments in China are now included in professional tours.

Car racing has also become a craze in China, although less is known about the actual sport than about the brands involved in it. With the opening of Shangahi's Formula One Track, any red sports car has become a Ferrarri and Michael Schumacher became a household name.

Martial arts are an intricate part of Chinese heritage. Some youths still practise it today in martial arts schools. Every morning in every park and living compound, troops of elderly people will go out to practice *tai chi*.

Most young people in China enjoy badminton, ping pong and bowling. Aside from karaoke, these are the most common social activities that groups undertake. Some companies even have ping pong tables set up on premises, as well as ongoing tournaments.

Dragon boat racing teams are established in most cities of China. It is both a recreational and competitive sport, and there are national meets with serious competition during the summer months.

China took the world by surprise in 2001 when Beijing won the right to host the 2008 Summer Olympics. And she certainly did not disappoint. The Games can well go down in history for having the most memorable Games Opening Ceremony, breathtaking world-class venuesand impeccable organisation. There was also an impressive showing of athletes' achievements with more than 40 world and over 130 Olympic records broken with an unprecedented 86 countries winning at least one medal. The Chinese athletes won the most gold medals and bagged a total of 100 medals.

A tradition of northern China, horse riding is still more of a recreational activity than a sport. That said, China does have a national equestrian team which made its Olympic debut at the 2008 Olympics.

A number of health-related sports are as common in China as they are elsewhere in the world. Yoga studios have sprung up in tier-one cities across China in the last five years. There are a number of membership gyms in each city, which offer cardio equipments and aerobics, kick boxing and weight training classes.

Club sports have become popular. There are clubs for volleyball, cycling, camping, hiking, running, go-karting, sailing, skiing, off-road driving, scuba diving and rugby.

Dragon boat racing is popular in China and there are various dragon boat competitions held every summer.

EXPLORING CHINA

One of the advantages of a China assignment is the opportunity that it provides you to really dig in and explore the country, her culture and her people. There is no better way to do this than to travel. The difference between internationalised first-tier cities and smaller cities in the interior is staggering. Only hours from Shanghai, which is a neon sign, brand-draped modern metropolis with some of the world's best new architecture, you arrive in smaller cities that time forgot, greeted at the city entrance by towering billboards of Deng Xiaoping's promise for a brighter future and down main streets where every business sign is a hand-lettered brown board. Exploring China is like peeling an onion, under each skin that you penetrate is a whole new next layer to discover.

Over 90 per cent of the people that inhabit China are Han Chinese, the predominant ethnic group. The remainder are Mongolian, Uyghur, Dai, Tibetan, Korean and many other smaller groups that were preserved in remote, isolated regions or share an ethnicity with the people living across any of China's 14 shared borders. Travel in China provides a wonderful opportunity to understand the different customs, beliefs, language, food and lifestyles of these people.

Planning

With solid planning and a sense of adventure, China is readily accessible. Preparation can easily overcome not speaking the language. With 1.3 billion people, there are few parts of China that are really remote and there is always someone willing to give you a helpful push in the right direction.

Weather

Spanning 9.5 million sq km (5.9 million sq miles), China is the third largest country in the world, behind Russia and Canada. With geography that ranges from the Gobi Desert to Mount Everest, optimal travel time varies with the destination. Wintertime in nomadic Inner Mongolia brings temperatures of -40°C (-40°F), while summer at the Great Game outpost of Turpan, 'the hottest place in China', can hit 47°C (117°F).

In most of China, travel in spring or fall guarantees the most pleasant weather.

Beijing has an elevation of 54 m (177 ft) with temperatures staying near 0°C (32°F), and reaching lows of -10°C (-14°F), December to February. It gets the bulk of its rainfall in July and August and snow in winter. Summers in Beijing are hot, with the rare day hitting 38°C (100°F). It is more bearable than Shanghai or Guangzhou in the summer, as Beijing is not humid.

Shanghai is on the same parallel as the US city of Jacksonville, Florida, and has similar weather patterns. Shanghai, sitting on the South China Sea, has an elevation of 5 m (16 ft). Summers in Shanghai are quite humid, from May to September temperatures are around 20°C (68°F), June through August is both the rainy season and the hottest time of year in Shanghai. Temperatures above 30°C (86°F) coupled with the rain make Shanghai a steamy sauna during the summer. The coldest days of winter in Shanghai hover around 0°C (32°F). Every three years, Shanghai gets a good sprinkle of snow that lasts long enough to cause chaos on the roads as fair-weather taxi drivers slide through intersections and onto sidewalks in Keystone Cop fashion. Shanghai gets the tail end of a few seasonal typhoons, which

Xitang, an ancient town near Shanghai where several scenes from *Mission Impossible III* were filmed, is one of the many gems in China that are worth exploring.

typically blow in from Taiwan between July and September and leaves sparkling blue skies and fat white clouds in the sky.

Guangzhou is in south China, close enough to Hong Kong that they have parallel weather patterns. Also at sea-level, it receives far more rainfall than Shanghai and has consistently higher temperatures. Guangzhou is steamy humid a majority of the year. The rainy, hot and humid periods run from April to September, during which time the temperatures can rise as high as 38°C (100°F). Guangzhou winters stay a pleasant 10°C (50°F) to 20°C (68°F), and are three short months: December to February. Guangzhou is in a typhoon corridor from July to September, during which time one can experience forceful rains.

In recent years, torrential downpours during the rainy and typhoon periods caused massive flooding and landslides in numerous provinces. The Chinese government have since spared no effort in putting up measures to minimise and curb the aftermath of the downpours.

Temperatures in Lhasa, elevation 3,658 m (12,001 ft), range from -10°C (14°F) to highs at or barely above 20°C (68°F), May to September. Its rainy season is June to August. It is suggested that the best time to trek in the Himalayas is October or November, when the rainy season is finished and before the winter cold sets in. Sandstorms are more common than rainstorms in Tibet. It is an arid place where the mid-day sun suggests short sleeves, while within eight hours you can be in a harsh cold well below freezing.

Travelling During National Holidays

People working in China receive a full week off for Chinese New Year, National Day and May Day. In the late 1990s, the government implemented extended holidays in an effort to stimulate the domestic economy through tourism and shopping, both well-loved holiday activities. What began as an attempt to stimulate the domestic economy has turned into a regular extended holiday schedule.

Traveling during any of the three week-long holidays requires allowing additional generous advance time in booking airplanes and hotels. Train and bus stations are automatically packed during this time and difficult to maneuver as many Chinese find it the most economical way to return home to see their family or sightsee.

Travel during this time provides a unique opportunity to interact with many local Chinese whose holiday destinations match your own. It is best appreciated with good preparation, an abundance of patience and a sense of humour. You will be required to wait in long lines to see sights, sit elbow to elbow at restaurants, and put up with the Chinese habit of constant snacking and dumping the packaging at some of China's most scenic nature spots. That said, the added element of seeing how enthusiastically the Chinese travel and enjoy their country adds a unique dimension to understanding the culture.

Logistics

Maps

Current maps of China can be purchased at any airport, bookstore, train or bus station kiosk or hotel. Most maps are in Chinese, which provides the most use if you ask local people at anchor spots in your travels to circle on the map where you are. To travel comfortably, you should always have the attendant at the hotel's front desk provide you with a business card and to circle the hotel's location on the map, as well as the location of any spots that you are aiming to travel to throughout the day. With a hotel business card, you can jump into any taxi if you are lost, provide them with the card, and comfortably arrive back at the hotel with minimal hassle.

Personal Documents

Anyone traveling within China is required to carry valid identification at all times. A visitor must provide his or her passport whenever checking onto a flight, checking into a hotel, changing money or purchasing tickets. It is required that anyone staying in a private residence register with the local police within days. To be safe, do it within the second day if you intend a stay of more than a week. When you check into a hotel, it automatically registers you with the police.

Accessing Money

The Chinese currency is called the reminbi (Rmb). It is not yet a convertible currency so you should exchange when entering and leaving the country to assure you do not get stuck with excess. Most hotels and every Bank of China have posted currency conversion rates. You can check online for an idea of current rates. The website http://www.xe.com gives a fairly accurate picture.

You can exchange cash or travellers checks at the airport, at hotels and at the Bank of China. Other banks may exchange cash for you, but the Bank of China offers the greatest breadth of service and is the only bank you can find in any city in the country. You may also take an advance on a major credit card at the Bank of China, as well as cash a personal check using an American Express card as a guarantee. ATM cards that have designations on them for international systems can also be used in China. The most hassle-free domestic ATM machines to use are HSBC and Bank of China. In some remote areas like Xinjiang, the switches are not yet in place to connect international data, and as of 2006, you still cannot use an ATM card in major cities there.

China is a cash-based society. Only businesses use checks and debit cards are a fairly current phenomena. Because there is such significant circulation of fake money in China, it is best not to use black market money changers. You will note that in most stores, there are money counting machines that check the authenticity of each bill while counting. Newly circulated notes have a black strip threaded through them, as well as a watermark image of Mao. That is what the taxi driver or shopkeeper is closely scrutinising when holding your note up to the light before accepting it.

The most-used notes in China are 5 Rmb, 10 Rmb, 20 Rmb, 50 Rmb, and 100 Rmb notes. Some parts of China use 1 Rmb and 2 Rmb notes, but other parts use coins for smaller denominations. Strangely enough, people in Beijing are hesitant to take coins, while they are commonly used in Shanghai. Regardless of their attitude, money is money and it is all valid. They are obligated to take it in fair payment.

If you are stuck without Chinese currency, local people will usually be willing to take US dollars. They will be aware of the value of the money, although you should carefully negotiate how much change you will receive back before handing over your money, so that the person you are exchanging it with doesn't end up holding your cash and theirs while you fight to get a fair amount returned.

Credit Cards
Most four and five-star international hotels will take credit cards in China, as will better restaurants in major cities and major department stores. Be sure and confirm this with the hotel, restaurant or store in advance. The most widely accepted cards are Visa and Mastercard. American Express charges higher usage rates and some outlets will add an additional charge to cover this expense.

Airlines and Airports
Most decently-sized cities in China have new airports. China has invested much in infrastructure, including airports and airlines. The largest airlines in China are Air China and China Eastern Airlines, hubbed out of Beijing and Shanghai respectively. In China, an airticket price is determined by the distance flown, rather than on a sliding scale according to availability and whether it is booked one-way or round trip, as is the case in much of the West. There are some discounted tickets available, based upon the airline and

seating. Discounted tickets cannot usually be changed, so be careful purchasing them if you want any flexibility. Standard tickets can be changed, both in advance and on the day itself if you miss your flight. They are also refundable with a small penalty fee.

Tickets are easily purchased through the hotel concierge or a travel office that is usually housed in or near most major hotels. There is an online service called Ctrip that allows you to book flights online. China's main airlines have also just begun issuing e-tickets.

It is critical that you allow adequate time to check in at the airport. Chinese airlines stop check-in service 30 minutes before departure time for domestic flights and 45 minutes before departure time at international airports. Be sure and check with the reception desk at the hotel to confirm the exact time that counters close at the airport in their city. In some more remote parts of China, it may be 45 minutes rather than 30 minutes as everything is done by hand. At exactly the cut-off time designated, regardless of how long the line was that you were waiting in, they will no longer issue boarding passes. It isn't the end of the world—if you have a ticket that can be changed, you can usually have a ticket issued on the next available flight, which if you are flying a common domestic route, is within the next three hours. If you don't, you will have to purchase a new ticket.

If you have a seat preference, be sure to mention it when you hand your ticket over to the agent. They will not automatically ask your preference and have a tendency to pack people into small sections of the plane. It is possible to change seats when you are on the plane, but it requires some finesse as you need to wait to move until the doors are closed and many will have the same aim, which creates a quick rush for the better available seats. They fill most flights front to back, and so if it looks as if the flight is not full, you are fairly safe moving to one of the seats in the very back of the plane before the doors are shut.

Some major airports like Shanghai and Beijing now have express check-in lines for people travelling with only carry-on luggage. The counters are well marked and easily identifiable.

Farmer tending to the rice padi fields. China is the world's largest producer of rice which comes as no surprise since rice is the staple food of the Chinese and is eaten at most meals.

Considered one of the Seven Wonders of the World, the Great Wall of China is the world's longest man-made structure. It is estimated that more than 1 million people died in the construction of the wall.

This woman is from the Yi ethnic minority. Some ethnic minority groups in China still continue to wear their vibrant and colourful traditional dress which are handmade by the women.

Xiangqi or Chinese chess is a popular game in China. Just like international chess, this game is played by two people and is both engaging and mentally stimulating. Spectators usually gather when they see people playing.

Nanjing Road in Shanghai is one of the country's busiest shopping districts. At night, the streets take on a new life of their own as the neon lights attract and bedazzle visitors.

Once you have your boarding pass, you will need to pass through both document inspection and metal detectors. In China, you are not allowed to carry on any alcoholic beverages; they should have been put into your check-in luggage. If you are carrying a bottle of wine, beer or a bottle of spirits, it will be confiscated. On occasion, some hard bargaining has led to a quick detour into a small nearby room where the bottle is returned, but don't count on it. You will be asked to open any bottles or cans that you are carrying on so that the airport security agents can smell what is in them. There is very little concern over carrying fruit or food, although within recent years if you are buying Shanghai hairy crabs to transport, they must be properly bound and packaged. In the early days, it wasn't unusual to see a box of upended crabs scurrying across the airport or find an upended box of them loose in the overhead luggage compartment.

If you are flying domestically, there is no need to fill in forms. Customs will merely require your passport. If you are flying international out of China, you need to fill in two forms for submission: one is a customs declaration form and the other an exit form.

Once through customs, your gate should be easy to identify. There are usually small restaurants that serve local food and kiosks that sell snacks and drinks within the airport terminal. Domestic flights usually start boarding 15 to 20 minutes before departure time, international flight 30 to 45 minutes before departure time.

There are some unique phenomena that you will experience flying in China. One of the first is the preference mainland Chinese have for carrying on as much luggage as possible. Do not plan to receive a fair share of luggage space in overhead compartments as many people will carry multiple boxes, bags and suitcases onto the flight. If you get stuck without an overhead area to put your carry-on luggage, pass it to the airline steward or stewardess and they will normally either find a place to put it, store it in the serving area in the back, or strap it into an empty seat near the back.

The second phenomena, which is experienced throughout China, is a need to rush and be first. On almost every flight, as soon as the airplane lands and is still taxiing, someone will pop out of their seat and open the luggage compartment to make sure that they have their bags and are ready to get off first. Inevitably, the airline steward or stewardess will have to unbuckle themselves and stagger down the aisle holding onto the backs of seats to chastise the person, close the luggage compartment and restore order.

As soon as the wheels touch the ground, you will hear beeps and chirps as phones are turned on and people begin sms-ing and calling others to let them know that they have arrived. Immediately after the plane stops at the gate, people will jump up and rush to collect their luggage with lots of pushing and shoving to gain the best position to be the first off the plane. If you are someone bothered by this kind of behaviour, the best strategy is to accept you will be one of the last off the plane, stay seated, and wait until the masses have cleared before getting your luggage and disembarking.

Hotels

In China, it is possible to find a number of unique beds to sleep in, from ancient monasteries nestled in the shadow of a sacred mountain like Sichuan's *Emei Shan*, to a recliner in Shanghai's *Xiao Nan Guo* spa. The sophistication of hotels in China has grown with its appeal as an international business and tourism destination. Most of the global five-star hotel brands are found in China's major cities. There are additional regional groups like the Shangri-la and Banyan Tree which offer the finest in Asian hospitality.

A Variety of Hotels

In the past, staying in anything less than an international five-star hotel meant staying at an over-rated state-run hotel. That is no longer the case. There are a number of modern budget chains that have built a national presence across China, including the Jin Jiang Inn, Motel 168, Motel 268 and Home Inn. There are also a number of boutique hotels which have opened on the top end of the scale, and youth hostels and independently run backpacker lodges on the other end.

Bookings

It is easy to find China hotel information online. One of the more popular websites that allows you to shop for availability is http://www.english.ctrip.com. Another easy way to find a hotel in advance is through travel agents. Both China International Travel Service and China Travel Service are large organisations.

There are also a number of agents available at airports and at or near main hotels. In addition to booking hotel rooms for you, they can arrange airport pickup and local guides at your destination. International hotels will take credit cards as deposits; domestic hotels may require pre-purchase through the agent, who will provide you a receipt to be presented at the hotel when you check in. Room rates usually include breakfast. Be sure and ask the agent when booking the room; there are usually packages and deals available but they are not proactive in offering them to you.

Travel Preparation
Immunisation

Check with your doctor to understand your country's immunisation recommendations for China. At a minimum, you should be current with courses of diphtheria and tetanus, hepatitis A, hepatitis B, Japanese B encephalitis and polio.

Packing

Although better hotels have minor medical supplies available, Western medicine is difficult to get in China. It is better to carry a small amount of your own. You should prepare a kit which includes aspirin or other pain reliever, antihistamine, antibiotics (which are available over the counter at major cities in China), an anti-diarrhoeal medicine like Immodium, cold and flu tablets, insect repellent and eye care products for contact lens wearers.

Women should also bring their preferred hygienic products as those available in more remote places are quite basic. It is best to carry your own supply.

Many hotels in China provide small containers of shampoo and conditioner, soap and a toothbrush and toothpaste. All of these items, as well as razors, fingernail files, condoms and other small items, can usually be found in the hotel's lobby store.

Pack clothes that layer easily. Few restaurants in China require formal wear, and in general, dressing requirements are lax. Avoid travelling in China wearing white; it is impossible to avoid rubbing against something that will get you dirty. Umbrellas and rain ponchos can easily be found in any China city—if there is only a remote chance you will need them, buy them locally. Better hotels provide umbrellas at the concierge desk.

It is common for hotels to have laundry service, a massage parlor, a beauty salon and a gym. Male travellers may find themselves hounded by calls through the night offering erotic massage services and companionship. Opportunistic prostitution is common in China—local hotels and bars view it as commonplace and it comes as part of the standard offering.

TOP TRIPS
Beijing: Pop Culture Meets the Great Wall

Must-sees in Beijing include the Forbidden City, the Temple of Heaven, the Summer Palace, Tienaman Square, the Great Wall and the Olympic Park.

It is worth taking the time to drive out to Simatai to see the Great Wall. There is no other man-made place in the world that inspires you with the feeling that you are steps away from heaven. If you are fortunate, the sky will be clear and the heavens within reach from the highest points of the Wall.

The best way to get a close sense of old Beijing is to take a bicycle tour of its traditional alleys, called *hutongs*. Two unique experiences not to be missed in Beijing are eating Beijing duck at Lichun Roast Duck Restaurant in the Beixiangfeng Hutong [Tel: (10) 6702-5681/6705 5578] and attending a Beijing Opera performance at Zhengyici Theatre [Tel: (10) 8315-1649].

A visit to Olympic Green—Beijing's new iconic site—is a must. Take in the spectacular sights of awe-inspiring architecture such as the National Stadium (nicknamed Bird's Nest) which hosted the opening and closing ceremonies of the 2008 Summer Olympics and the Paralympics Games, and the transparent 'Water Cube' National Aquatics Center. Since the opening, the park has seen more than 60 million visitors and is expected to become new landmarks of Beijing after the Forbidden City and Great Wall of China.

Shanghai: Waterways and Westernisation

You don't really see Shanghai, you experience it. There are two special things to experience in Shanghai which are seasonal—eating hairy crabs in the autumn and watching the entire Shanghai skyline erupt with fireworks on the first night of Spring Festival.

Additional experiences to have include strolling the Bund, visiting the top of the spaceship-like Shanghai TV Tower for a panoramic view of the city, and taking long walks through the old French Concession.

After the Olympic Games in Beijing, the World Exposition 2010 in Shanghai is probably the biggest international event to have taken place in China. With spectacular fireworks, vibrant cultural performances and other attractions, the Expo delivers more than just a 'trade fair'. Held on both

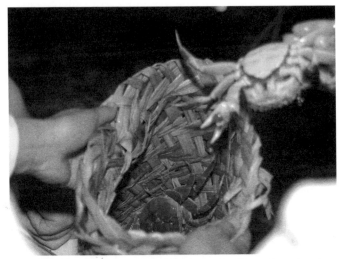

Hairy crabs are a delicacy in Shanghai, and one should not miss eating them when they are in season.

banks of the Huangpu River, the expo site was crowded with architecturally stunning pavilions and the key attraction—the Expo Axis (the main building at the Expo), has one of the world's largest membrane roofs spanning the entrance and boulevard building. Besides the China-Pavilion, the Expo Axis is the largest and most impressive building on the site. A record of more than 73 million visitors attended the Expo over six months. As of end of 2010, after a month long renovation, the Expo Park featuring the China-Pavilion is still open to visitors daily from 8 am to 8 pm. Plans are also in the pipeline to open a Expo Museum in Puxi.

The best combination for a week-long trip to Shanghai is to spend a few days experiencing Shanghai, and the rest visiting the nearby ancient cities of Hangzhou and Suzhou.

Sichuan: Grand Buddha and Monkeys

One of the best adventure trips begins with a flight to Chengdu, the capital of Sichuan and the home of the spiciest street hotpot in the world, for those brave of heart and strong of stomach.

From Chengdu, head to Leshan, near Emei Shan, and visit the Grand Buddha, a 71-metre-high Buddha carved into a cliff at the confluence of two rivers. After receiving the Buddha's blessing, continue on to Emei Shan to climb one of China's oldest sacred mountains. It is a two to three-day trek, which involves visiting monasteries that date back to the beginning of Buddhism in China, as well as an onslaught of greedy monkeys that live near the top of the mountain.

Xinjiang: Conquerors and Traders

Contrary to popular belief, it is possible to turn back time. Going to Xinjiang is like turning back the clock to a time when goods crossed the world in camel caravans over the Silk Road. Fly into Urumqi, which despite its exotic name is a modern Chinese city. From there book a car to Turpan, home to the amazing UNESCO-protected ancient city of Jiaohe, where Genghis Khan and his hordes last inhabited.

At the local museum, you can visit near-perfectly preserved Caucasian mummies discovered nearby that changed the global view of the distance travelled by nomadic herdsman from the West. An early dinner at Grape Valley provides excellent food, entertainment and shopping.

Return to Urumqi and fly to Kashgar. Some of the best things to do in Kashgar include visiting the ancient Bazaar, which is still the most active shopping area in all of Kashgar. You can visit the old Russian and British consulates, which were central to the intrigue of the Great Game.

Take a day or two to drive up the Karakorum Highway to near the Pakistan border, and you can see parts of the original Silk Road threading across the cliff face above the modern highway. Just recently, Shipton's Arch, a huge 336-metre (1,200 feet) natural arch, has been rediscovered. After Eric Shipton submitted an initial record of it to the National Geographic Society, they were unable to locate it a second time to substantiate it.

Yunnan: Dancing Tribes and Snowy Mountains

Yunnan really requires multiple trips. There are three main areas to visit: Xishuangbanna on the Myanmar border, the central region of Lijiang, Dali and Tiger Leaping Gorge, and the northern Zhongdian, also referred to as Shangri-la.

Exploring Yunnan is really about experiencing a symphony of the minority cultures of China. Northern Yunnan is ethnically Tibetan. A number of towering sacred mountain peaks are within the area and yearly treks are made by the devout.

Zhongdian is the home of the China Exploration and Research Society run by retired National Geographic journalist Wong How Man, who recently discovered a new source of the Yangtze River. A number of his preservation projects are in the area, including preservation of a Lisu Hunting Tribe village and restoration of a Buddhist nunnery by Italian fresco artists.

In central Yunnan, old Lijiang is a delightful stroll to a simpler time in life. You can take day trips outside of the city to visit the home of Joe Rock, How Man's National Geographic predecessor, who used to hitch rides with the Flying Tigers. On evenings in Lijiang, you can join hands and dance a local jig with Naxi minority women, while during the day you can wander the streets lined with rickety wooden huts along bubbling canals, colourfully decorated with plants and birds, and full of shops, restaurants and fun-loving people.

Tibet: Saddhus and Lamas

One of the most exciting ways to get to Tibet is by ttrain on the Qinghai-Tibet railway from Beijing. One of the better known experiences is visiting the Portala Palace, historically the winter home of the Dalai Lama. Also on the list should be Barkhor, a pilgrim circuit that is followed clockwise around the 1300 year-old Jokhang Temple, which is one of Tibet's holiest shrines, and the Norbu Lingka, which was the summer home of the Dalai Lama.

One of the less-known Tibetan adventures is visiting Mount Kailash in western Tibet. Kailash is the mythical home of the Hindu Lord Shiva, and is the source of the Ganges, the Indus, the Sutlej and the Brahamaputra rivers. Each year, Indian Saddhus, Buddhists and others make the high-altitude trek around the peak in search of enlightenment.

Xiamen: Pianos and Old Painted Ladies

Historically known as Amoy, Xiamen is the closest city to Taiwan in China. It is said on a clear day, you can see part of the islands that make up Taiwan. Occupied by the Portuguese, French, British and Dutch, it became an important trading port. Strolling through the old part of Xiamen city, you can still see hints of European-influenced architecture.

The most fun to be had in Xiamen is on Gulang Island. Reported to have the most pianos per capita, the island is covered with attractions, distractions and the remnants of grand old estates that must have elegantly dotted the garden-strewn island in the 18th and 19th century. One of the better attractions on the island is the Piano Museum, a private donated collection of antique pianos. Xiamen is also a golf destination—there are a number of courses outside the city, including the Greg Norman-designed Kai Kou Xiamen Golf Club.

Harbin: Ice, Fur and Vodka

If you have only one chance to visit the old Russian city of Harbin, make it during the winter when the Ice Festival is in full swing. There are a number of ice parks in the city, but the biggest is across the river that borders the city. A night spent there includes seeing swimwear-clad men flexing their muscles in -25°C (-13°F) weather, skidding down long ice slides, riding bucking bronco barrels and wandering through castles made entirely of ice. During the day, visit the old Russian church, try on furs at any number of shops along the main street and haggle in the markets.

Xian: Soldiers, False Teeth and Mosques

Xian is so old that wherever you put your shovel in the dirt, you hit something ancient—just ask the farmer that discovered the Terracotta Warriors. No matter how many times you see the Warriors, you can't help but be overwhelmed by a sense of reverence when you walk through the earth cells that is home to their military formation frozen in clay for eternity.

Other must-dos in Xian include visiting the Great Mosque in the centre of town, haggling in the markets that surround it and eating bread baked on the sides of the coal-flamed ovens that line the street. Much of the old city wall of Xian still stands, and there are many discoveries to be made walking through the streets and alleys near the Wall, from billiards games played in the open-air to beautiful carved doorways in tiny alleys that lead into large courtyards.

A great day trip from Xian is out to the Huaqing pool, a Tang dynasty bath-house set on top of natural hot springs. It was near here that Chiang Kaishek was supposed to have been caught by the Communists. In the urgency of his attempt to escape, he jumped out of the window and was captured soon after while still in his pajamas and without false teeth.

The Three Gorges: Hanging Tombs and Kite Flying

Even after the dams have been flooded, a trip down the Yangtze through the Three Gorges is a fun and exciting way to spend three days. You depart from Chongqing on a five-star cruiser just before nightfall, so by the time you wake up the next day, there is no city in sight. Highlights of the trip include the hanging tombs, taking a side trip up the dramatic Little Three Gorges, and going through the dramatic drops as you are moved from one portion of the dam to the next through the rocks.

Magic Mountains

Ancient monks were onto something when they designated some of China's most beautiful peaks as sacred mountains. A number of mountains have been designated as sacred by Buddhists and Daoists, some separately, some shared. The Chinese make religious pilgrimages to these mountains, with

There are many beautiful mountains in China and some of them are designated as sacred mountains.

the more devout prostrating themselves every few steps as they approach the peak. The trek to the top is meant to fill one with a sense of the frailty of human existence and build a sense of unity with nature.

Sacred Mountains to Visit in China

- Tai Shan (Shandong)
- Heng Shan (Hunan)
- Putuoshan (Zhejaing)
- Emei Shan (Sichuan)
- Song Shan (Henan)
- Wutai Shan (Shanxi)
- Huang Shan (Anhui)
- Jiuhua Shan (Anhui)

In addition to being able to appreciate jaw-dropping views, ancient temples, poems and inscriptions along the way, one of the most enjoyable parts of the experience is meeting hearty grandmothers trotting up the mountainsides with their temple bag draped over their shoulder, as well as being passed by ill-equipped high-heeled city dwellers tackling nature for the first time.

A great resource for more remote China adventures is http://www.wildchina.com. If nothing else, frequent visits will ignite your imagination and fuel your knowledge of the less-worn trail that one can walk when discovering one of the largest countries in the world.

LEARNING THE LANGUAGE

CHAPTER 8

'Mandarin Chinese has a reputation for being a difficult
language—some experts say it takes four times
as long to learn as Spanish or French...'
—Peter Hessler, *River Town*, 2001

THE ORIGINS OF CHINESE

Ah, the mysteries of the Orient!

For many Westerners through much of history, the alleged inscrutability of China has been perhaps best symbolised by the sing-song lilt of spoken Chinese, so unfamiliar to speakers of non-tonal languages; and by those densely complex squiggles we call 'Chinese characters' (the Chinese themselves call them 字 *zi*).

Every Chinese 101 student has at some point 'hit the wall' with those squiggles and sing-song. We have stared at pages of characters, perhaps at classical texts without even punctuation, feeling them to be impossibly unreadable, not so much a language as a mysterious code. We have sat on the edge of conversations wondering whether the topic was football, weather or the latest crisis in the Middle East. Let's face it: not many people describe something incomprehensible by saying they 'may as well have been speaking French'.

Yes, the Chinese language is difficult, different, downright alien from the perspective of English speakers. Chinese is its own linguistic group, with no underlying connection to English. Unlike English, it is also a language that (due to historical and geographic separation as well as to local pride) has borrowed remarkably few words from other languages. Learners therefore have few cognates (familiar-sounding words) to help along the way.

In major cities in China, there may be English translations for Chinese characters on signboards, but not usually in smaller cities and in small towns and villages.

True fluency, especially in written Chinese, is rare among people not raised to it. Many have observed that one measure of a language's difficulty is how many non-native speakers have become great poets in that language. In Chinese, the answer is: none. There have been great poets in Chinese who grew up speaking Japanese or Korean, but (as we'll see) those languages in written form share many Chinese characters. In all the 4,000 plus years that Chinese has, in some form or another, been in more-or-less continuous use, no native speaker of a non-character-based language has yet earned wide recognition as a poet in Chinese.

But don't despair: unlike alphabetic languages like English, Chinese has a tremendous split between its written and spoken forms, and there is no need whatsoever to learn the written forms to be able to speak. Many expatriates in China, including many who have lived in China for years or even decades, who are successful in business, who have many Chinese friends, who in short function extremely well in Chinese society, are in fact functionally illiterate in written Chinese. It gives a new appreciation for those who are illiterate in our home societies.

Meanwhile spoken Chinese, especially at a basic survival level, may be far easier to learn than you think. And there are many reasons to learn it. Chinese friends, colleagues and acquaintances (even taxi drivers and waitresses) will appreciate the gesture, and that fact alone will make your time in China more effective. Speaking even a little Chinese will also help you feel more confident in your daily life in China, better access a society in which English-speakers are still a distinct minority, and overall enjoy your stay.

This chapter doesn't pretend to offer a mini-course in the language, but we hope it will give you enough of an overview to understand at least a bit how the Chinese understand their own language, and help you feel prepared to learn at least some of it. We also include a pronunciation guide, some basic vocabulary and lists of resources for further learning, as well as notes on non-verbal communication.

THE DIALECTS

The first thing to understand about spoken Chinese is that it comes in many flavours. English-speakers tend to think of dialects as relatively minor differences in pronunciation: Yankee accents, Southern accents, a bit of Blarney or Brogue. But even today, some local English accents (e.g. Cockney, Cotswolds, Mumbai or Mamba) are extremely difficult for even other native speakers of English to understand. A hundred years ago, before TV and constant travel, there were many more distinctive local dialects of English, many of them not mutually comprehensible.

The local dialects of Chinese remain more or less distinct today. Whether globalisation, the Internet or increasing mobility for China's population will change that over time remains to be seen—at least for now, native speakers from one part of China generally cannot understand native speakers from other areas when speaking their local dialects. As we shall see, they can always communicate in writing. Mandarin Chinese, the dialect group native to north-central China (including Beijing), has been the official state dialect, officially required for schoolteachers since 1949. Thus, anyone younger than about 60 will be able to communicate in Mandarin, though perhaps with a heavy accent. Still, it is worth being aware that dialects exist so you aren't frustrated when you learn to say 'hello' in Mandarin ('*ni hao*'), only to hear '*nonghoe*' in Shanghai, '*lei ho*' in Guangdong, and so on.

For those who like to know details, the Chinese break their language into seven major dialect groups, each with further sub-groups and variations. The Mandarin group is the largest. Numbers are disputed, but by many estimates nearly 700 million Chinese speak Mandarin as their mother dialect, and some 1.1 billion speak it in some form. Since 1949, Mandarin has been called officially in Chinese '*Putonghua*', or the 'common language'. Because Mandarin is the most common dialect, except where otherwise noted, all Chinese words listed throughout this book are written as pronounced in Mandarin.

The next-largest dialect group is Wu, which includes Shanghainese and several other sub-dialects from the Yangtze River delta region in East China. Wu is mother dialect to some 100 million Chinese. Next Yue (Cantonese), native to China's South-eastern coastal areas centred in Guangdong (Canton), is mother dialect for some 70 million people in China and, due to historical emigration patterns, for most overseas Chinese. Next is the Xiang (Hunanese), dialect group of South-central China and mother dialect for some 65 million speakers. Next comes Min, native to Fujian and Hainan and parts of Taiwan, mother dialect for some 60 million. Next come the Hakka (Kejia) dialects, spoken by scattered groups across Guangxi and Fujian Provinces, but also (due to historical in-migration patterns—'Hakka' means 'guest people') in Taiwan and in Yunnan and Sichuan in China's South-west. Hakka is mother dialect for some 50 million Chinese. Finally, Gan is mother dialect for some 30 million Chinese in Jiangxi, Hubei and parts of Hunan. Mandarin, Wu and Gan are somewhat mutually intelligible with patient listening, but the other groups are not.

Note that these seven dialect systems (Mandarin, Wu, Yue, Xiang, Min, Hakka and Gan) are all considered subcategories of Chinese, the native language of the Han people who constitute some 92 per cent of China's population. Some linguists have argued that some Chinese dialects are far apart enough that they should really be considered separate languages; Mandarin and Cantonese, for instance, differ more than, say, French and Spanish. These linguists argue that it is a political decision by China's leaders to emphasise unity by speaking of 'dialects' rather than to emphasise local autonomy by speaking of 'languages'. Be that as it may, China certainly also recognises that in addition to the seven dialect groups, a number of other languages are also spoken in China. Some non-Han minority peoples in China speak languages which come from wholly other linguistic groups than Chinese. Tibetan, for instance, descends from Sanskrit and is closer to Hindi than to Chinese. The Uighur language of far North-western China is closer to Arabic than to Chinese, and so on. These are, by anyone's definition, separate languages, and should not be confused with the Chinese dialects.

Most expatriates will find it most useful to focus their learning on Mandarin, which is used across China. However, if you know you will spend most of your time in a particular region, especially in a city with deep pride in local traditions such as Shanghai or Guangzhou, you may want to consider learning at least a few words in the local dialect to sprinkle into your conversation. Doing so will earn you extra kudos and goodwill from local Chinese, and offer endless opportunities for one-upsmanship among expats.

From a broader business standpoint, foreign managers must also understand the importance of dialects, and how strongly they can affect business success for the local Chinese. Salespeople, negotiators, HR personnel, government relations experts and others will be most effective when operating in the local dialect. Chinese who speak multiple dialects are at a strong advantage when dealing with other Chinese; it is quite common for teams of negotiators and others to move back and forth between their local dialect and Mandarin, effectively excluding non-local dialect speakers from parts of the conversation. This is not to say a native of Beijing can't succeed in Shanghai, or a Cantonese in Yunnan, but it adds a layer of complication. In key positions, it may be necessary to pair a non-local who otherwise has the skills for the job with a speaker of the local dialect to assist as 'guide'. When hiring or making domestic transfers, this needs to be kept in mind.

PRONOUNCING CHINESE: ROMANISATION

Whichever dialect you choose to learn, unless you want to jump straight into learning written Chinese characters (unwise), you will need to have a way to note down the pronunciation of the spoken language using English letters.

Some businesspeople invent their own idiosyncratic notations, and there are advantages to that. But there are also advantages (in consistency and ability to communicate with other learners and teachers) in using one of the systems developed over years by foreigners studying Chinese. These are called Romanisation systems—ways of writing down the sounds of spoken Chinese using the letters of the English (Roman) alphabet.

For many years, there were seemingly as many ways of Romanising Chinese characters as there were students of Chinese, and some of their spellings differed surprisingly widely. For instance, the character 壮, meaning 'strong', can be spelled in various Romanisation systems: *zhuang*, *jhuang*, *jwang*, *chuang*, *jwang*, *joang* or *juang*. All these spellings refer to the same character—they are all simply different ways that different Westerners have devised to help them come closer to the sound represented by the character 壮. Similarly, when Peking became Beijing in Western newspapers, the characters were not changed and remained 北京. The difference was a political choice on the part of Western newspapers to switch from the Romanisation system popular in Taiwan to the one popular in Beijing.

Today, two Romanisation systems have become more-or-less standard: the Wade-Giles system, invented by two 19th century British missionaries (yes, Mr Wade and Mr Giles) is the system of choice in Taiwan and among many overseas Chinese learners. And the Hanyu Pinyin system, developed largely by Russian sinologists in the 20th century, is standard in mainland China and increasingly throughout the Chinese-speaking world.

Hanyu Pinyin, often called just Pinyin, is a relatively straightforward system, but like all forms of Romanisation has its drawbacks. There are oddities to Pinyin from the perspective of native English speakers, such as the letter 'c' at the start of a word making a sound that to English ears is closer to 'ts'. These oddities stem from how many phonemes (basic building-block sounds) in Chinese simply don't exist in English, but are also explained partly when one remembers that the system was developed by Russians. Pinyin is in some senses a double-Romanisation, from Chinese characters to the Russian Cyrillic alphabet, and from there to English equivalents of Cyrillic letters.

Despite these drawbacks, Hanyu Pinyin is the most common system today, so we have adopted it throughout this book; the pronunciation guide and vocabulary guides below all follow Hanyu Pinyin Romanisation.

A SURVIVAL GUIDE TO THE BASICS
Pronunciation

Again, most expats will become most familiar with the pronunciation of characters in Mandarin dialect, as expressed in Pinyin Romanisation. It is worth taking some time to learn the basic pronunciations and how they are spelled in Pinyin. Following is a brief guide:

Pinyin	Wade-Giles	Equivalent English Phoneme
a	a	'a' as in 'mama'
b	P	'b' as in 'bop till you drop'
C	Ts	'ts' as in 'cats'
D	T	'd' as in 'radar'
E	Er	no English equivalent, but much like 'oe' as in French 'oevre'
F	F	'f' as in 'father'
G	K	'g' as in 'got'

Pinyin	Wade-Giles	Equivalent English Phoneme
H	H	'h' as in 'hot'
I (before 'n')	I or ih	'I' as in 'pin'
I (after 'sh')	Ih	'ur' as in 'cur'
I (after other consonants)	I or ee	'ee' as in 'week'
J	Ch	'j' as in 'jump'
K	K'	'k' as in 'kite'
L	L	'l' as in 'light'
M	M	'm' as in 'mama'
N	N	'n' as in 'banana'
O	Aw	'o' as in 'dog'
P	P'	'p' as in 'pig'
Q	Ch'	'ch' as in 'chicken'
R (when followed by 'u' or sometimes by 'a')	J	'r' as in 'groove'
R (other times)	Jh	no English equivalent
S	S	's' as in 'sat'
T	T'	't' as in 'toy'
U	Eu	'oo' as in 'loon'
W	W	'w' as in 'watch'
X	Hs	'sh' as in 'harsh'
Y	Io	'y' as in 'young'
Z	Tx	'dz' as in 'adze'
Ai	I	'y' as in 'fly'
Ao	Au	'ou' as in 'loud'
Ei	Ay or ai	'ay' as in 'pay'
Ia	Ya or ia	'ya' as in 'yard'
Iao	Yao or iao	'eow' as in 'meow'
Iu	Iu	'yo' as in 'yo-yo'

Pinyin	Wade-Giles	Equivalent English Phoneme
Ui	Uay or uai	'way' as in 'way'
Uo	Aw	'aw' as in 'pshaw'
Ng	Ng	'ng' as in 'hang'
Sh	Shr	'shr' as in 'shroud'
Zh	Dz, tz, or dh	no English equivalent; halfway between 'dr' as in 'drop' and 'dz' as in 'adze'

Tones

In addition to the basic phonemes (building-block sounds) of Chinese, learners will also have to come to grips with the tones sooner or later. These are the actual musical tones used when speaking each word. Mandarin has five tones: level, rising, dipping, falling and neutral; Cantonese has nine. How much the tones are emphasised varies between dialects and between speakers. Some Chinese almost sound like they're singing arias every time they speak, while others have only a slight inflection of the voice.

Tones become really important only in the relatively rare cases where two near-homonyms (words with identical basic pronunciation) are distinguishable only by tone, and where the context doesn't allow a distinction between them. The phoneme 'ma', for instance, can famously—depending on the tone—mean mother, horse, hemp, a scolding or a question, but these meanings are unlikely to be confused even if you leave all tones off altogether. Most businesspeople won't need to bother with the tones, unless they plan to get beyond survival-level in the language.

That said, it's worth being aware that if you've proudly thrown out one of your survival phrases and all you get is a blank look back, the problem may well be in the tones. For instance, let's say you're browsing a dim shop and want to ask the owner for more light to better see an object: "*Keyi jia deng* (1st level tone) *ma*?". If he simply nods and walks away, you can be pretty sure he thought you were asking if you could wait there: "*Keyi zher deng* (3rd dipping tone) *ma*?". At that point, consider body-language; it will usually work until you get better with the tones.

Grammar

Once familiar with the sounds of Chinese, learning to speak, at least at a basic level, can be surprisingly simple. For one thing, the grammar of spoken Chinese is extremely easy. Verbs do not conjugate in Chinese, and nouns do not decline. Putting sentences in the past tense, future tense, conditional tense and so on is largely a matter of word order and the addition of certain standard participles: 了 (*le*) for the past tense, 将 (*jiang*) for the future tense, and so on.

Word-order and correct use of participles (as well as other idiosyncrasies like naming participles and counting participles) will become important if you ever decide to make a serious effort to learn Chinese. But most businesspeople operating at a survival level in the language can easily afford to ignore the whole question of grammar.

Cognates

As noted above, Chinese tends to have fewer cognates (borrowed, linked or otherwise related words) with English than many other languages. Most that exist are words in English originally borrowed from Chinese. Sometimes, you can 'guesstimate' the Chinese word by moving backward from the English, but it isn't always obvious. The English word 'tea', for instance, comes from the Cantonese pronunciation of the character 茶, which in Cantonese is '*te*'. In the days of the clipper ships, most tea traded to England (and to America, often via Boston harbour) came from Canton, hence '*te*' became 'tea'. The Mandarin pronunciation, by the way, is '*cha*', which became '*chai*' in Hindi after the Indians learned tea culture from the Chinese, which in turn inspired that sweet drink now so favoured in Western coffee shops.

Some other English words are more obviously Chinese in origin, but they are by and large words you will have relatively little need for these days: 'kowtow' (*ketou*), 'coolie' (*kuli*) and the like are relics of a long-gone and unlamented period in

Chinese-Western relations. Businesspeople do at times find themselves speaking of the need to kowtow to this or that Chinese official, but describing the situation that way in Chinese would not likely help.

The one area where useful cognates are common is food.In many cases, you can easily work backward from borrowed English words to find the correct Chinese words: tofu (*dofu*), chow mein (*chao mian*), lo mein (*lao mian*) and chop suey (*chao sui*—literally 'stir-fried leftover bits') are just a few examples.

There are also in today's spoken Chinese a few cognates borrowed from English phonetically using sound-alike characters, again often involving foods. For instance, 咖啡 (*kafei*) is a fairly recognisable sound for 'coffee', and 汉堡包 (*hanbaobao*), with a little imagination, is recognisable as 'hamburger'. The aid these cognates will give you in learning the language is limited, but they are fun.

Following is a list of a few simple basic phrases in Chinese, and any decent phrase book will get you talking more.

Forms of Address	
I	*wo*
you	*ni*
he/ she/ it	*ta*
we	*wo men*
you guys	*ni men*
they	*ta men*
father	*ba ba*
mother	*ma ma*
kids	*xiao hai*

Timing	
time	*shi jian*
today	*jing tian*
tomorrow	*ming tian*
Monday	*li bai yi*

Timing	
Tuesday	*li bai er*
Wednesday	*li bai san*
Thursday	*li bai si*
Friday	*li bai wu*
Saturday	*li bai liu*
Sunday	*li bai tian*
Today is Monday	*jing tian shi li bai yi*
January	*yi yue*
February	*er yue*
March	*san yue*
April	*si yue*
May	*wu yue*
June	*liu yue*
July	*qi yue*
August	*ba yue*
September	*jiu yue*
October	*shi yue*
November	*shi yi yue*
December	*shi er yue*

Introductions and Greetings	
My name is David.	*wo jiao David.*
Hello, Ms Chen.	*ni hao, Zeng xiao jie.*
Hello, Mr Lin.	*ni hao, Ling xian shen.*
Hello, everybody.	*da jia hao.*
How are you?	*ni hao ma?*
Good morning.	*zhao an.*
Welcome!	*huan ying!*
Good bye!	*zai jian!*
See you tomorrow!	*ming tian jian!*

FOR FURTHER LEARNING

There are many, many resources available today for native English-speakers seeking to learn Chinese: books, tapes, videos, DVDs and websites abound. There are classes and tutors available in every Chinese city (and most good-sized US and EU cities, should you want to prepare a little before you go).

In every issue of every English-language expat-oriented publication in China (Beijing's *Beijing Scene*, Shanghai's *City Talk* and so forth), you will find ads for classes and tutors, and from individual Chinese people looking to exchange language learning with native speakers of English. Some of these ads are for people seeking romance as much as language, but many are straightforward, and finding a language buddy can be an excellent way to gain insight into the local culture that goes beyond language. A few of our favourite resources include:

Books and Tapes Combos

- *Spoken Standard Chinese.* Hugh M Stimson and Parker Po Fei Huang. New Haven, CT: Yale Far Eastern Publications, 1976.
- *Chinese for Today.* Beijing Language Institute. San Francisco: China Books and Periodicals Inc, 1996.
- *Chinese Language Learning for Beginners.* Sinolingua, 1993.

Software, Video and DVD Packages

- The Rosetta Stone series (http://www.rosettastone.com)
- The China Horizon series (http://www.chinesehorizon.com)
- Clavisinica (http://www.clavisinica.com)

Useful Websites

- For general information and sale of many Chinese language and cultural or educational products: http://www.chinasprout.com
- A great on-line audio resource for spoken Chinese, plus many fun features: http://people.wku.edu/haiwang.yuan/AudioChinese/index.html
- A book-website combo for conversational Chinese that is worth looking at: http://www.csulb.edu/ ~ txie/ccol/content.htm

- Excellent background readings on Chinese poetry, linguistics, etc. plus one of the best guides we've seen to Romanisation: http://www.pinyin.info
- Daily podcasts in Chinese: http://www.chinesepod.com
- For introductions to Chinese characters, on-line dictionaries, Pinyin chat and more: http://www.zhongwen.com
- For in-depth, hard-core character etymologies: http://www.internationalscientific.org/
- Useful links: http://www.uni.edu/becker/chinese2.html

Our best advice is to not bother with written Chinese beyond 'survival characters' (as below) unless you plan to make it a subject of years of study. But we strongly urge anyone who will spend any length of time in China to try to learn to speak Chinese. The above will get you started.

WRITTEN CHINESE
The Basics

Most businesspeople will learn only a few Chinese characters. The written language is simply too complex and difficult to learn much of as a part-time or occasional endeavour, even in its simplified modern form. Classical Chinese, originally written without punctuation, is even more difficult. Most expats learn just a few 'survival characters'. These will likely include 男 and 女 ('male' and 'female', needed to distinguish between restroom doors), the characters on the street signs or a few other landmarks near the expat's apartment, and perhaps the names of a few basic foods, as follows:

- 牛肉 (*niurou*): beef
- 鸡 (*ji*): chicken
- 肉 (*rou*): meat in general, but by itself it usually means pork.
- 豆腐 (*doufu*): tofu
- 菜 (*cai*): vegetables, but it can also mean a dish of food.
- 素 (*su*): vegetarian
- 面条 (*miantiao*): noodles
- 米 (*mi*): rice

That said, it is worth the while of businesspeople to understand a little about how written Chinese works, if only to better appreciate the pride Chinese people take in their language. The following sections offer an overview.

Written Chinese: A 'Pictographic' History

Written Chinese is one of the world's oldest languages, perhaps the oldest in more-or-less continuous use. Chinese people date the use of characters from the 'oracle bone' scripts found on burnt ox-bones and other shamanistic religious objects dating from as early as 1800 BC, then later from bronze seal-script characters. Those early, primitive characters were in fact often pictographs. For example, this was an oracle bone character for 'rain': 雨 (we can see the drops falling from the clouds).

But as with Egyptian hieroglyphs, over the centuries the language evolved tremendously. First, the pictographs became more stylised as writing became more common—first on carved jade seals, then bronzes, then written with brush and ink on paper (a Chinese invention).

Orthography (basic character shapes) were standardised and fixed in about 200 BC. This was known as the 'rectification of writing', one of the great accomplishments of that great over-achiever the Emperor Qinshihuang (also known for starting construction on the Great Wall and the Grand Canal, and for the army of terra-cotta warriors who accompanied him to his grave). But by that time, characters were quite stylised relative to their original forms. The modern character for 'rain' is 雨; already, the pictographic origin is less obvious.

Then, and crucially, pictographs began to be combined to create more complex characters that had new and more abstract meanings. In some cases, these more abstract meanings can be guessed from the combination of pictographs. For instance, rain with lightning streaking from the clouds to the ground is 電 (but in modern script, it is 電), traditionally meant 'lightning storm'. In modern usage, it has come to mean 'electricity'. But the combinations are far from always being as obvious as that. For instance, the combination of a person (人) passing a door (门) became the character 閃 (in modern script 闪, which also means 'lightning'.) One traditional etymology explains that lightning happens 'in a flash', just as a person moves quickly through a door. This explanation is wonderful, but hardly intuitive; 'person in doorway' does not automatically suggest 'lightning'.

Additionally, as we now know also about Egyptian hieroglyphs, in many cases Chinese combinations are based on sound as much as or more than they are on pictographic content. For instance, the character that means 'meat' or 'flesh' (肉) is often combined with other characters to suggest parts of the human body. The characters it combines with generally suggest the sound of the body part, at least the sound that was in use at the time the character was created.

Bird's Nest and Brain

The flesh character combines with the top part of the character that means 'bird's nest' (巢) (today pronounced '*chao*', and in Middle Chinese closer to '*nao*') to make the character 脑 (also pronounced '*nao*'), which means 'brain'. The etymology is simply phonetic: this, the components tell us, is the character for that body part which sounds like 'nao'. We defy anyone, using any logic other than phonetics, to explain why a fleshy bird's nest should otherwise suggest 'brain'.

The Complexity of Chinese Writing—the Learner's Bane and Joy

Eventually, these various sorts of combinations came to far, far outnumber primitive 'pure' pictographs in Chinese. When Chalmers Johnson, a leading scholar of classical Chinese, made an exhaustive analysis of more than 10,000 Chinese characters in 1882, he found just 300 which he considered to be true pictographs. Even more telling, a famous Chinese etymological dictionary compiled around AD 100 analyses 9,353 characters, finding that just 364 (3.9 per cent) could be clearly traced to a specific pictographic origin.

This process of character creation via ever-more complex combinations of pictographs, increasingly impossible to guess the meaning of based on their component parts, each thus needing to be individually memorised, continued over centuries. In many cases, the changes made were minor variants of existing characters made for the sake of literary flourishes by Chinese scholars long past. Eventually, the growing weight of Chinese tradition (and the growing burden of memorising the existing characters) squelched such inventiveness. New characters have not been created in recent centuries—which is just as well. Perhaps the most complete modern Chinese dictionary, the *Xiandai Hanyu Dacidian*, includes some 56,000 characters. Most are obscure and archaic.

Less is More

One study done in Beijing estimated that 80 per cent of all written Chinese documents can be read using just the 500 most common characters, 91 per cent with the 1,000 most common, and 99 per cent with the 2,500 most common. That said, for the learner, it always seems that whatever you are currently reading necessarily includes some of the most obscure characters.

Meantime, even though character creation has halted, word creation has of course continued, for unlike Egyptian hieroglyphs, Chinese remains very much a living language. Today, Chinese create new words by stringing together existing characters in creative ways. For instance, the most common modern translation for 'computer' is 电脑 (*diannao*): literally 'electric or lightning brain'.

If these sorts of character combinations are considered, the total standard Chinese lexicon runs to well over 200,000 words—an awful lot for a non-native speaker (or even a native speaker) to memorise. And that's not even beginning to touch on slang, or jargon specific to different academic or business fields, or the new phrases constantly being created to translate new words from other languages.

The Beauty of Chengyu

There are the wonderfully poetic idioms called *chengyu*, combinations of characters which can often be understood only in context of the myth or legend they refer to. Many educated Chinese seed their writing with *chengyu*, just as many educated Westerners seed their writing with literary and other allusions. But the *chengyu* provide allusions in highly compressed form. The classic *chengyu* is just four characters long, but many pack meanings that take paragraphs of English to explain.

Add in all that, and it starts to become clear why Chinese 101 students always, sooner or later, run into that seemingly unreadable wall. All the richness of Chinese etymology and slang and *chengyu* makes for a language that can be a great deal of fun to learn, but which is also a constant challenge —even for native speakers. The average age of independent reading in native speakers of English is between five and six; among native speakers of Chinese, it is between seven and eight, with the additional time required to learn so many symbols the commonly cited reason for this difference. And before the age of computers, typing or printing anything in Chinese required racks and racks of fonts, which traditionally had to be switched by hand. While skilled typists in English can often type 120 words per minute (wpm), skilled Chinese typists on traditional typewriters rarely hit 30 wpm.

Even looking up words is a challenge without an alphabet. A set of 214 stylised versions of early pictographs, commonly called in English the 'radicals', form underlying components of most of the 50,000 plus characters in the total Chinese lexicon. Traditional Chinese dictionaries and encyclopaedias were organised around a commonly agreed order of these radicals, with individual characters under each radical listed in 'stroke order' (the number of brush or pen strokes required to write the character). Still, the radicals do not function like an English alphabet, since they rarely offer clues to pronunciation. And though they do provide a way of organising dictionaries, looking up words is still hardly as straightforward as A-B-C.

So, Why Do They Do It?

With all these complications, many a Western learner has wondered why the Chinese bother. Why not give up characters, which must be memorised individually by the thousands, for an alphabetic system like ours, where only 26 shapes are enough to arrange and rearrange into all the nearly one million words of the English lexicon? Why not at least add alphabetic components to the language, as have the Japanese and Koreans? Many Chinese have raised this suggestion, and it was seriously debated at the time of the 1949 revolution, prior to which an estimated under 10 per cent of China's population was literate, in large part due to the difficulties of written Chinese.

The answer, of course, is: tradition. It is not just that Chinese people are attached to the character system because their ancestors used it for thousands of years so there is sentimental value (though in a Confucian culture that sort of sentiment is significant). Even more importantly, the fact that Chinese ancestors wrote in characters makes the writing of the ancestors relatively accessible to their more literate descendents.

All spoken languages, like oral traditions, change significantly over time. In alphabetic systems like English, where the written form of words is tied (at least to some degree) to their pronunciation, writing evolves nearly as quickly as speaking. That is why students of English literature often need special training even to read an author as relatively recent as Shakespeare, let alone Chaucer or Beowulf.

A character-based system is different. Of course, grammar shifts over time, nuances of words evolve, and popular word choices come and go. But the basic meaning of most characters remains pretty much unchanged through the centuries. And of course, many texts still require special study. Anything dating from before the 20th century will be written in the dense grammar of Classical Chinese; even native speakers of modern Chinese must read closely and carefully to understand these earlier texts, and in many cases will need special training. For Western language students, Classical Chinese presents an even higher wall to scale than do modern texts. But with relatively little help, any reasonably well-educated native speaker of Chinese is able to read many ancient texts in the original. This provides a degree of connection to the ancient past almost unimaginable in the West. It would be like a smart high school student in England being able to pick up and read—incompletely perhaps, haltingly certainly, but read—a text from centuries before Beowulf, perhaps from ancient Greece, or Mesopotamia.

For instance, spoken Chinese has changed drastically since the Tang Dynasty (AD 618–906). The justly famous poetry of the Tang was, in Tang times, pronounced far differently from today. Ezra Pound and other Western poets, not realising this, looked to Tang poetry as an early model for free verse. The irony is that when pronounced in Middle Chinese, as they would have been when they were written, the Tang poems not only rhyme, but generally follow rhythmic schemes at least as strict as any sonnet.

But here's the thing: while modern Chinese readers likely won't know how the Tang poems were originally pronounced, they can, by and large, still read them. Many famous Tang poems are memorised in their original written form by elementary school students across Greater China. That would be like modern American third-graders memorising, in their original, odes by late Roman poets written shortly after the fall of Rome.

In fact, this connection goes beyond the texts of Chinese history to the texts and peoples of all the nations which in ancient times adapted the Chinese character system as part of their own writing. Many other Asian cultures later added alphabetic overlays over their use of the character system, but still use the characters to some degree. And so it is that, for instance, a Chinese person, a Japanese person, and a Korean, who do not to any degree speak each other's languages (which fall in their spoken forms into wholly different linguistic systems), can struggle through reading each other's historical texts, and even today can hold at least a basic conversation in writing.

Thus, those frustratingly difficult, intriguingly mysterious Chinese characters serve to give Chinese people broad connections across time and space to their own history, and to the past and present lives of their neighbours.

Pound's Interpretation

The famous English poet Ezra Pound famously loved the 'mystery' of Chinese characters. He declared them to be word-signs, pictographs like the Egyptian hieroglyphs were then still widely understood to be, not so much words to be read as suggestive imagery to be 'deciphered'. He developed a theory of 'visual interpretation of Chinese poetry', based in part on the quasi-linguistic theories of Ernest Fenellosa, and made his own 'translations' (other have called them 'translucences') of many classical Chinese poems, even of the entire Analects of the philosopher Confucius.

Pound was a brilliant poet and his 'translucences' are brilliant poetry, well worth reading in their own right. But he was no scholar of Chinese. His versions of Chinese poetry were inspired by the classical texts, but often depart widely from them (and in his later work, make no pretext of even being connected to them). A fine analysis by George A Kennedy of Pound's use of Chinese characters as springboard for his own poetry, originally published in the Yale Literary Magazine in 1958, is now available online at: http://www.pinyin.info/readings/texts/ezra_pound_chinese.html, and is also well worth reading. The bottom line is that in terms of his understanding of how written Chinese works, Pound was more wrong than he was right.

Making Written Chinese Simpler

As noted above, Chinese writing has evolved somewhat over the centuries, although far less than the spoken language. There were however two major breaks in the Chinese writing system in the 20th century worth being aware of. The first, leading into the 1911 revolution that toppled the last Qing

Dynasty, was the so-called 'Vernacular Movement' (*baihua yundong*). This movement, led by the writer Hu Shi and others, sought to abolish Classical Chinese grammar, in favour of writing that was structurally and grammatically closer to spoken Chinese, as an aid to literacy and toward shaking off the shackles of 'imperial thinking'.

The second major break, following the 1949 revolution that created the People's Republic, was to create simpler versions of the traditional characters as an aid to popular literacy. These so-called 'simplified characters' (jiantizi) require memorising significantly fewer strokes to write than their 'traditional character' (fantizi) equivalents. For instance, the traditional character 髒 (zang), which means 'dirty', requires 22 strokes to write. The simplified version is 脏, which takes just ten strokes. To further aid literacy, China's post-revolution Communist government established a 'National Standard' set of the 'most crucial characters' (6,766 of them, according to the latest standards), and required that all official documents, including government-funded newspapers, confine themselves to this character set.

Many traditionalists deplore the simplified characters and the National Standard character set as cutting the Chinese people off from their traditions. This is especially true in Taiwan—partly for political reasons—which has steadfastly continued to teach traditional characters and has no limitations on the number of characters that can be used in official documents. In Taiwan, an island with a population of some 23 million which now has first-world per-capita incomes, these decisions to hold to tradition have not come at a significant cost to literacy: today, literacy on Taiwan is over 96 per cent, one of the world's highest rates. But when the Nationalist (KMT) government, which built up those literacy rates on the island, instead ruled China's vast and densely populated mainland, literacy was estimated to be below 10 per cent.

The effectiveness of the simplified characters and the National Standard character set as aids to literacy is pretty hard to deny. Between these, vernacular writing and better rural education, China current mainland government skyrocketed literacy rates within a generation after the revolution. Specific numbers are hotly debated, but almost all observers agree China's literacy rate today is well over 85 per cent nationwide, and in urban areas well over 90 per cent, probably higher than for urban areas in the United States. In this book, except where otherwise indicated, all printed characters are in simplified form.

Meantime, throughout Mainland China and in much of the Chinese-speaking world, Pinyin spellings have increasingly become the standard way of organising Chinese characters, replacing the 214 radicals in dictionaries and encyclopaedias and, crucially, for purposes of entry into word-processing software. Today, typing in English letters using Pinyin spelling, working with intelligent software that helps auto-select the specific character combinations wanted from lists of characters with similar spelling, Chinese typists can enter words just about as quickly as their English-speaking equivalents. This is undoubtedly an important part of the very rapid rise in Chinese-language content available on the Internet—some observers believe Chinese may in the coming years replace English as the majority language of online content.

All this, of course, raises the question (often raised in Taiwan) of whether or not younger generation mainland Chinese, raised on Pinyin-based software, simplified writing and the 6,766 characters of the National Standard set, still to any meaningful degree have that connection with the writings of their ancestors so valued by traditional Chinese.

To some extent, this is of course an unanswerable question, being dependent on individual abilities, interests and exposure. Certainly a mainland high school student would have more trouble than a Taiwanese high school student with ancient texts. That said, our impression, based wholly on unscientific and anecdotal observation, is that whenever mainlanders put their minds to learning to read classical Chinese, they are able to learn it very quickly; certainly far more easily than native speakers of English. The rules of character simplification are, after all, standard, and can be learned in reverse to go back to the traditional characters, just as the rules of classical Chinese grammar are fairly predictable. Crucially, even the most modernised Chinese, when looking at ancient texts, understand how characters work, know quite a few of them, and thus are unlikely to hit that infamous wall foreign students hit. Once nearly 7,000 characters have been learned, even in simplified form, adding a few thousand more and learning to read their complex equivalents seems to be, if not a trivial task, at least a relatively manageable one.

UNSPOKEN CHINESE

One final area of language which is important to be aware of in any country is non-verbal communication. Gestures, pacing, pausing and the like are of course individual, but there are also general trends that run across any culture and help define it from other cultures. It is important to be aware of these non-verbal differences.

In the case of China, from the perspective of people from an Anglo-American background, most non-verbal communications will be relatively familiar. An up-and-down head shake means 'yes', a side-to-side head shake means 'no', smiles and frowns, looks of surprise and looks of blank incomprehension generally mean exactly the same things they would mean in your home country.

There are some key points of difference worth being aware of, however. First, non-verbal cues in China are often more subtle than in the West. While individuals of course vary, Chinese on the whole are less comfortable with 'wearing emotions on their sleeves' than are Westerners. The smiles and frowns, surprise or anger, joy or incomprehension, will be there on their faces, but you may need to watch closely to catch it. This is particularly important for expatriates to be aware of in the case of frowns or incomprehension. This topic will be explored further in Chapter Nine. The basic idea is that if you are the new Western boss, and you say things that your new team-mates are upset by or simply don't understand, it may very well be that no one will go out of their way to tell you. This may be part of the Chinese reputation for being inscrutable, but the truth is, no one is trying to hide anything; there is simply a cultural tendency in China toward measured response, at least in public. It is up to you to watch for those measured responses, and adjust your style as needed. Otherwise, you may well watch your new relationships crumble for reasons you may never understand.

Second, and similarly, Chinese people also tend on the whole to be a little more reserved than Westerners about physical contact. Handshakes are more common than hugs or kisses on the cheek, even among friends. Chinese people you have known a long time may enjoy the novelty of a Western hug, but it's best to wait till you know people well. A back-slapping style is generally not well-received. Even handshakes among Chinese tend to be a little softer and more tentative than the Western equivalents—though you may well encounter Chinese who have heard that Westerners like firm handshakes, and may respond with all the best intentions by giving you a bone-crusher.

Third, Chinese people on the whole are significantly more comfortable with silence than are Westerners, and tend to leave longer pauses in their conversations, often deliberately delaying responses to show respect to the speaker (i.e. "I must consider how I respond to such a thought-provoking question or comment.") This fact probably explains more instances of Sino-foreign miscommunication than any other. From the Western perspective, the pregnant silence of a Chinese person politely considering a response may feel uncomfortable, and the Westerner tends to rush in and say something, anything, to fill the silence.

From the Chinese perspective meantime, the Western tendency to interrupt, talk all the time and never stop for a moment to think about what to say or what has been said makes it next to impossible to get a word in edgewise. Often, therefore, in

Silent Business

Tales abound of negotiations where Westerners have made an offer, and Chinese counterparts remained silent. The Chinese may have been merely considering their response, but Westerners, taking silence to mean anger, may jump in offering immediately to amend their own offer, effectively negotiating against themselves. Indeed, many experienced Chinese negotiators have found that with Westerners, simple silence is their best negotiating tool!

mixed situations, the Chinese say nothing. This explains much of the famous 'quietness' of Chinese students in Western colleges, of Chinese team-mates in cross-cultural business situations, and of Chinese journalists in mixed press conferences dominated by their garrulous Western colleagues. Westerners who seek to benefit from the wisdom and deep local knowledge of their Chinese colleagues, friends, students or teachers need to be aware of this and adjust accordingly. In the case of the press conference, it may be necessary to segregate and have separate events for Chinese and Western media. In the case of the students or the colleagues, it may be necessary for whoever is leading the discussion to deliberately hold off acknowledging some comments or follow-up questions from Western participants in order to encourage Chinese participants to speak.

Outside the Courtyard

Not all aspects of Chinese non-verbal communication have to do with Chinese tending to be quieter and more tentative than Westerners. In crowd situations, with strangers toward whom they have no social obligations, Chinese can be, from the Western perspective, surprisingly loud, pushy and lacking in manners. The great Cambridge Sinologist Dr Joseph Needham wrote about what he called the Chinese 'courtyard vision of the world': inside the courtyards of their lives (at home, school or work), Chinese tend to be models of tact, care and attention. Outside the courtyard with strangers, there are generally no holds barred. If you want to get to a ticket window, get on a bus, make your way through a crowded entrance or otherwise negotiate in situations with large numbers of Chinese strangers, you too may need to sharpen your elbows. Many an expat has found a need to re-learn culturally appropriate 'crowd manners' once they returned home.

It is also worth noting that Chinese people, used to small and crowded spaces, tend to stand closer to other speakers than do Westerners. And finally, in terms of what the non-verbal communications experts call 'olfactics', it is worth noting that Chinese tend to judge cleanliness by sight more than by smell. We sniff armpits to see if a shirt can be worn again; Chinese peer closely for stains. So, be careful about judging that Chinese businessman you just met as slovenly because his suit smelled a little less than fresh; he may be thinking the same about you because your pants-cuffs had a small stain.

WORKING IN CHINA

CHAPTER 9

'When people have just arrived, they want to change things.
But making quick moves in the wrong way isn't the right
thing to do. You need to have patience, patience, patience.
It is one of the clichés you hear in China, but it is true.
You need to make a long-term strategy and stick to it.'
(Guy McLeod, President, Airbus China)
—Juan Antonio Fernandez and Laurie Underwood, *China CEO*

1.3 BILLION CUSTOMERS

In the 1930s when he wrote the book *400 Million Customers*, Carl Crow, journalist and China business pioneer, opened the imagination of the world to the potential of China. His book encouraged the first wave of foreign business into modern China. Seventy plus years later, Carl Crow would be staggered by the amount of foreign direct investment (FDI) into China and the rate of her development.

In 2010, FDI in China hit an unprecedented high of $105.7 billion, driving economic growth to 10.3 per cent. Economic growth fuelled output from the country's millions of factories as it rose 15.7 per cent to meet the growing demand for Chinese-made goods.

Consumer Paradise

The development of China and the related deployment of her peasant farmers as skilled labourers has been driven by creating preferential treatment to incoming business in the coastal region. In the early 1980s, China opened herself to business through the establishment of special areas that foreign companies could invest. These were called special economic zones and offered tax breaks and simplified permit and licensing regulations for foreign businesses to establish a China presence.

Companies came with the intent of establishing a foothold in China to tap the market potential of the 1.3 billion

of Shanghai
7

China has developed in leaps and bounds and is one
of the fastest-growing economies in the world today.

customers. The illusion lasted only a short period of time. Two things worked against this aim. The first was that most licences were issued for companies to export, rather than produce goods for the domestic market. The second, most of those 1.3 billion people had neither the discretionary income to buy nor the access to choose foreign branded products.

China was focused on attracting investment that would prime her economic engine, providing foreign exchange for her coffers and jobs for her people. Deng Xiaoping, the architect of China's opening, was attempting to follow the model laid out by Taiwan, Singapore and Hong Kong, which had lifted their economic position on the back of export.

As a Chinese Kennedy School graduate explained, Deng created a few special areas along the coastal region where the best talent and infrastructure was placed to support the growth of modern manufacturing practices in China. As these areas became successful, they began to absorb workers, converting unskilled labour into skilled labour, building reserves of foreign currency and delivering on China's promise to her people to improve quality of life.

This is fundamentally why China will remain the manufacturing centre of the world for the next 70 years. She has laid the transportation and supply infrastructure to reproduce those silos through the undeveloped interior of the country and has 60 per cent of her population waiting for their turn to become skilled labourers. While the promise to improve quality of life has been met in the coastal region and provincial capitals, much of China still clings to the promise rather than the experience.

With the growth of discretionary income of her skilled workers, China has slowly opened up her market to foreign goods. The giant posters of Deng Xiaoping thought lining highways have been replaced with Coca Cola and Mercedes billboards. You can purchase a bar of Dove soap just as easily in the Grand Bazaar of Kashgar as you can at Wal-Mart in New York.

As barriers to entry have fallen, there has been a mad scramble of business to China. Every company has equal opportunity to take a lead position in a virgin consumer market where there are no quality legacy brands. Unilever, the manufacturer of Dove soap, goes head to head with most of its global competitors in China. Companies that wouldn't imagine taking Unilever on in Europe or the United States because the cost of entry is far too high to gain market share view China as fair game. The brand battlefield in China contains more players than almost any other country in the world.

Too Many Choices

Because they have so many choices, Chinese are fickle consumers. There is no brand loyalty. Historically, goods were so scarce and the choice so limited that almost no one would consider using their grandmother's brand of laundry detergent. It is likely that granny didn't even have a washing machine. She was lucky if she had a bar of soap to wash her clothes with, rather than just plain water. If every two months when you go to the market there is a brand new product to try, why just stick to one?

CREATING YOUR PERSONAL CHINA MAP

One of the biggest challenges for a newcomer in China is to map the business environment. It is hoped that before sending you to an overseas posting, your company has done its business due diligence, established a legitimate presence in China, and is handing you a business to add value to and grow. If all of these minor details have been well attended, to the important thing for you to do is to orient yourself as quickly as possible.

One of the best ways to do this is through expatriate business organisations. There are a number of business organisations and clubs that provide a forum for you to share and compare views with your contemporaries from your home country and other parts of the world. In a rapidly changing business environment where information comes at a premium and is neither transparent nor easy to pinpoint, belonging to the right organisations is a great way to stay abreast of China business.

Some of the better business organisations to plug yourself into are your home-country chamber of commerce. Contact your nearest consulate for details. Those that are most active in China include:

- The American Chamber of Commerce
- Australian Trade Commission (Austrade)
- British Chamber of Commerce
- Canada China Business Council
- China Australia Chamber of Commerce
- European Union Chamber of Commerce
- Finland Trade Centre (Finpro) China
- French Chamber of Commerce and Industry in China
- French Trade Commission
- Delegation of German Industry and Commerce (AHK)
- Hong Kong Chamber of Commerce
- Italian Trade Commission
- Japanese Chamber of Commerce
- Korean Chamber of Commerce
- Swiss Chamber of Commerce

There are additional business resources that are not focused on citizens of a specific country or anchored to a single geography. The most useful of them are:

- The Asia Pacific Council of American Chambers of Commerce (APCAC)
  Website: http://www.apcac.org
- China Council for the Promotion of International Trade (CCPIT)
  Website: http://www.ccpit.org
- The Economist Group
  Website: http://www.economistgroup.com
- Quality Brands Protection Committee
  Website: http://www.qbpc.org.cn
- The United States Chamber of Commerce
  Website: http://www.uschamber.com
- The United States-China Business Council
  Website: http://www.uschina.org

In addition, almost every key industry in China has a local industry association that supervises it. These groups are quasi-government organisations which collect views and implement business regulations to guide their business sectors within China.

Keeping Up To Date

To keep abreast of current events and business trends while in China, many expats subscribe to the *International Herald Tribune*, *The Asian Wall Street Journal* and the *Financial Times*. The latter two are available by Internet subscription.

WHO MATTERS?

In China, there are a number of critical stakeholders that you must keep in consideration when you are doing business. First and foremost is the Chinese government. There is not any business action that you take in China that does not somehow include the government. From licence approvals to taxation to labour unions and party cells, the government has reach into and authority over your China business.

The most benevolent link between government and business are the industry associations. They are meant to be the communication conduit between business and government. It is within the industry associations that early drafts of regulations get floated for feedback and comment. The industry association provides a platform to voice your views. It also has the obligation to keep members informed of change through briefings and information distribution.

Another link between government and business is the media. Still heavily regulated in China, the media continues to be the mouthpiece of the Chinese government. Although increasingly liberalised to create financial self-sufficiency, good journalists know where the line is and not to cross it. If the government wants to deliver a message to a company or industry, the media is a useful platform. Your relationships with the media are important in providing your side of the story to create a balanced image should you be under scrutiny by government, competitors or the public. It is also an important partner in telling your China story.

China creates unusual bedfellows in that your competitors are also a stakeholder in your business. The approvals and setbacks that you encounter in China provide a precedent for your competitors, either to be restricted or to make forward movement.

Wal-Mart and Carrefour

When Wal-Mart made its China play, it leveraged on the precedent created by Carrefour, which had already established an aggressive national presence in China. Carrefour had expanded well beyond national guidelines by creating a number of favourable regional deals. In the end, the Chinese government revisited the regulation forcing Carrefour to restructure its business and providing the same structure for Wal-Mart to build its China presence.

With hopes running high about the upside in China, headquarters is also a critical stakeholder. There is a balance to be achieved between managing and delivering on expectations. An added responsibility of a China posting that is seldom mentioned is the amount of entertaining that is required. China has become such an attractive destination for board meetings, executive visits and due diligence trips by related businesses that each senior executive in China spends a good part of their time briefing and entertaining visitors.

The stakeholder group that you have the most interaction with in China are your employees and customers. The following section will address guidelines to consider when interacting with the people that make up the core of your China experience.

BEING GLOCAL

One of Deng Xiaoping's most famous sayings was 'it doesn't matter if it is a black cat or a white cat, as long as it catches the mouse'. The success formula for companies in China melds the best of China and Western business practices, being neither global nor local, but rather 'glocal'.

When explaining why they would like to work for a glocal company, many Chinese professionals cite their preference for transparency, merit-based promotion, opportunities to train or work overseas and formal development programmes as their major attraction. In addition, professionals pursue careers in MNCs (multi-national corporations) with aggressive localisation policies as they find this provides better opportunity to move quickly up the corporate ladder into senior leadership positions.

Being a manager in a glocal company means setting high business standards but being pragmatic about how they are implemented. One of the first challenges for non-Chinese speakers will be to create systems and processes that provide the management information that you need without creating unnecessary administrative burden.

Working in a new culture, where you have limited ability to speak the language, poses a challenge. The business language of China is Mandarin. Financial records must be kept in Chinese. The Chinese version of a contract is the one that is enforceable. Your colleagues will find it most comfortable to communicate clearly with one another in Chinese.

There are two important steps to take when arriving to address the challenge. The first is to secure a savvy, intelligent assistant who can act as your conduit to employees and clients who are non-English speakers. The second is to find a trusted local mentor to act as a guide. If you choose well, both of these people will guide you to better understand the intent and actions of people around you, providing valuable advice about how you are perceived and what you can better do to be effective.

MAKING A GOOD IMPRESSION

First impressions are as critical in China as they are anywhere in the world. But impressions on what? There are additional ways that you are judged in China that you may not be in other parts of the world.

People like to dress up: China is on the more formal side of the global business attire spectrum. It is customary to see people in suits tromping through half-constructed building sites and touring countryside factories. While the rest of the world was going through a dot-com dress down, China was shedding Mao suits and hitting her formal business stride. Many companies do follow a casual Friday dress code in China.

For men, proper business attire means suit and tie. For women, a nice dress suit or pants suit is appropriate. It is important to wear practical shoes in China as many floors are marble and leather soles tend to send you sliding across the floor in an uncouth fashion that does little to make a good impression

One of the first ways to create a good first impression when meeting others is to give adequate attention to exchanging business cards. The proper way to exchange cards in China is to present the card with two hands, with the text in the language of the person you are presenting the card to facing up and toward them. For example, the right way to present to a Chinese person would be with the Chinese side of the card on top and the text facing toward the person so that they can read it immediately upon receiving it.

When you sit down to meet with a group of people, you keep all business cards that have been given to you arranged on the table in front of you. Some people arrange them to reflect seating order around the table so that they can properly refer to people when addressing them.

You receive a card in the same fashion. Once cards have been exchanged, you give proper consideration to the other person by studying the card intently, looking at their name, their title and the location of their office. To demonstrate that you have given the card proper consideration, you may make a remark on any of these details.

Another consideration in China that has far less importance in the West is attention to where people are seated, particularly if meeting with local partners or government agencies. Title and degree importance need to be properly matched around a room when organising seating.

If invited to a government office, traditional seating is large soft chairs arranged in a U-shape. The most important people will be seated in the centre of the U. You will usually be served a cup of tea as you are seated.

The cadence of speech is also important. If relying on a translator, be sure and pause often to allow the message to be passed accurately. If you speak too long and the translator is not strong enough, they will miss a majority of the nuance that you expressed and just hold onto the detail.

Chinese people do not get directly to the point. A first meeting is to get to know you and lay the groundwork for future discussions. Chinese-speaking style is less direct than

Western style. When speaking, you should be clear in the points that you are making but non-confrontational. If you need to deal with confrontational issues, it is best to float subject points in advance of the meeting to understand positioning and begin initial negotiations, rather than to spring it on meeting attendees for the first time in a public forum where they could suffer a loss of 'face'.

One other important courtesy to be extended is offering drinks. Chinese will view it as a slight if they are invited to be seated for a meeting and are not politely offered a beverage. The usual preference is green tea or hot water. Ideally guests are offered drinks by the person that brings them into the room and seats them. You must also pay attention to refilling water in glasses throughout the meeting.

Finally, it is important to accompany guests when leaving the building. At a minimum, take them to the elevator bank or door. If they are very important or very senior, accompany them to the car.

BUILDING A SOLID TEAM

The expectation that local employees will have of you is that you will provide adequate support in their career development. The single most important way to assure solid team performance is to create a clear path to success and provide the tools needed to travel that path. An often overlooked factor mentioned in *China CEO: Voices of Experience from 20 International Business Leaders* is the degree to which loyalty assures retention. Loyalty is built by acting as guide and mentor to Chinese within your organisation, creating the success for them that enables them to improve their quality of life, and that of their extended family.

A consistent finding in Hudson's quarterly survey (http://china.hudson.com) is that limited career advancement is one of the primary reasons that Chinese consider changing jobs. Personal reasons such as taking a career break, furthering education, caring for family or starting a private business are also often cited for reasons to leave a job. Salary is often a third or fourth reason that someone would consider changing jobs.

The term 'glass ceiling' has become a buzzword in China, to the extent that recent university graduates are referring to 'glass ceiling' limitations in their potential career path. To address concerns, employers must have transparent hiring and promotion criteria, build strong training and advancement opportunities, and lay clear career paths that let Chinese employees feel confident in their future.

One of the most important elements to building a solid team is assuring effective communication. Chinese employees prefer Western companies because of merit-based promotion and transparency. It is important to establish a vision supported by actionable milestones so that employees

Do's and Don'ts at Work

- Do maintain global ethical standards in China, once you consider compromising because 'that is how things are done locally', it is a slippery slope that is difficult to reverse.
- Don't ignore the advice of local colleagues on obstacles or barriers that will exist when trying to accomplish something. Oftentimes, this view is based on China idiosyncrasies that they have a difficult time explaining but have often experienced. There is an adage in China that anything is possible and nothing is possible. You need the insight of your local colleagues to accomplish the 'anything is possible'.
- Do be clear on the business goal you want to accomplish and link it to the personal success of your team.
- Don't be so strategic and macro that they do not have a clear roadmap to implement from. Break down expectations into incremental tasks that are clearly defined and achievable. You are unlikely to hear that someone didn't understand or have the skills to accomplish something until well past a critical delivery date.
- Do give clear feedback to individuals on performance issues and actions to be undertaken to better accomplish the job.

understand direction, their role in it, and how to achieve success. On an interpersonal level, this involves active, patient listening, with regards to a person's entire life: work, family, aspirations and frustrations.

The best expatriate executives in China play an important role in the 'glo' part of glocal. Their task is to bring global business knowledge and practices to strengthen the professional competence of their team. The most sought after competence to gain from an expatriate executive is the judgment and credibility required to be a global businessperson. If you deliver this to your team, you have given both them and their families a ticket to the world.

- Don't give that feedback in a front of their peers where they will lose face. Make sure that you have important conversations in private, ask a number of questions to begin to make sure you clearly understood the situation, and clearly lay out actions to be taken that create improved job performance. Typically when chastised publicly, a Chinese person will not defend themselves, but will be deeply hurt and remember long after you do.

- Do have a clear outcome in mind when negotiating. Make sure that you negotiate from a point that leaves room for win-win solutions that give all parties credibility when they are reporting back to their superiors.

- Don't squeeze so much from a deal that the other side feels unfairly treated, whether business partners, customers or employees. Chinese have a way of continuing to negotiate past a signed agreement or agreed conclusion if they didn't get terms they fundamentally want. You need to assure the deal you have struck is one that everyone is comfortable with and committed to in order to comfortably draw a line and move forward.

VOLUNTEERING

One of the most rewarding ways to become involved in the community in China is through helping with a worthwhile cause. There is an immense amount of good that can be done merely through taking an interest and putting time, money, or both, into charities in China.

Once living in China, you will note that most business and social organisations have at least one annual charity event. If you want to passively participate, attend a ball or auction where the proceeds go to charities that the organisation has vetted.

More active participation requires more due diligence as some organisations that have deemed as 'legitimate' by the Chinese government have been fraught with scandal and corruption, while other organisations that have not been allowed to register in China have demonstrated integrity and transparency.

Part of this discrepancy stems from the fact that the only 'legitimate' charities in China historically had to be registered through the government and funds filtered through an official government body which, in the not so distant past, had a way of diluting the amount of money that ended up in the chosen charity.

Because charity has to do with taking care of Chinese people, it is a sensitive point with the government. Remember that the purpose of the Chinese government, according to her citizens, is to improve their quality of life. The issue with this is that there are such a vast number to care for in China, and with very limited resources.

Another factor that contributed to government scepticism toward NGOs may have to do with the fact that during colonial times, much charity came with a caveat of religion as missionaries made their way into China to convert her people. Under the guise of doing good, many were furthering their own purpose, either to persuade others to throw away tradition or using the guise of charitable action to penetrate the interior and report back to government as spies. Many of the historical challenges to China's government have come packaged in religion.

Positive interaction with foreign NGOs in recent years has softened the government's posture toward foreign entities doing charity work in China. What used to be viewed as interference is now viewed as a legitimate constructive channel for taking care of groups of people with special needs.

In the late 1970s and early 1980s, foreigners had to do good works in China informally and discreetly through personal contacts. Today, reputable organisations and committed volunteers have regained the trust of China's people and leaders. Early entrants into China included the Red Cross and Amity. China's first modern charitable foundation was started in 1981. Since that time, nearly 2,000 have come into being.

Challenging the China belief that, as one NGO report puts it, 'an individual citizen's responsibilities stop at their front gate; and that it is up to the government to solve problems not the citizens', is an immense undertaking. Individual involvement in charity is growing rapidly in China. Some organisations, like Care for Children which chooses families to provide foster care for children, have a natural affinity with Chinese. In a country where you are usually allowed only one child, the opportunity to bring a second child into the home has great appeal.

Giving Back to the Community

Corporations like Intel are providing a worthwhile model to create citizen involvement in the community. At Intel's manufacturing plant in Shanghai, an employee group is given an amount of money to allocate for charitable contribution each year. Because of Intel's commitment of giving back to the communities that its facilities are located in, employees are guided to put money where they can see a visible return. It is easier for many to give when they see the benefit firsthand.

Many groups have found that once a new cause has been properly introduced, Chinese will embrace and support it. A good example of this is the Special Olympics. In China, it was viewed as shameful to have an intellectually challenged family member. One of the reasons that having an intellectually handicapped child creates challenge for the family is that in a one child world, your child is meant to be your retirement insurance.

Their ability to support carrying forward the family line through marriage, as well as creating financial success, assures the parent a serene, enjoyable old age. An intellectually challenged child is able to do neither. He or she is a guarantee that the parents will have to work until old age and that the family line will be broken.

Special Olympics has come to China providing a support network for parents and a platform for the intellectually challenged to achieve personal success, greater confidence and value. After being awarded a chance to host the Special Olympics World Summer Games in Shanghai in 2007, the Chinese government has dedicated itself to identifying and involving intellectually challenged citizens nationally. It has gone from a handful of athletes and their families being involved in Special Olympics, to more than a half a million.

In addition to the message that the Games brings to China about the potential of the intellectually challenged, those involved with the Games will undergo screening by a team of doctors that attends the Games and be provided with glasses, hearing aids, nutritional information and special athletic gear.

Special Olympics is a good example of the Chinese government's evolution in embracing charities. It has taken to heart the intent of Special Olympics, involved citizens and corporations, and created a seminal change in the way society views the intellectually challenged.

China law still considers social and environmental welfare to be the domain of the government. It is immensely difficult to set up a registered charitable organisation in China. Many that exist at present are better described as GONGOs, 'government organised non-government organisations'. This process is so cumbersome that many charitable organisations and non-profit business groups operate in China without being officially registered, although they are recognised by the government. This conditional tolerance leaves charitable organisations in a precarious position, and many are careful to steer clear of sensitive issues. It is yet another intricate China dance.

Charitable Organisations

- **Care for Children** (http://www.caringforchildren.org)
  Provides foster care for children.
- **Rotary Club** (http://www.rotary.org)
  Offers humanitarian assistance and encourages high ethical standards.
- **Junior Achievement** (http://www.jachina.org)
  Pairs business professionals with high school and college students to act as career mentors.
- **Operation Smile** (http://www.operationsmilechina.org)
  Organises international doctors to team with local surgeons to provide cleft palate surgery to children.
- **Project HOPE** (Health Opportunities for People Everywhere) (http://www.projecthope.org/where-we-work/china)
  Provides health education and humanitarian assistance.
- **Roots and Shoots** (http://www.janegoodall.org/youths)
  Part of the Jane Goodall Institute, it encourages children to take action to make the world a better place.
- **Shanghai Sunrise** (http://www.shanghaisunrise.com)
  Funds education for underprivileged children in Shanghai and surrounding regions.
- **Special Olympics** (http://www.specialolympics.org)
  Assists the intellectually challenged to become physically fit, respected community members through participation in sports competitions.
- **Terry Fox Run** (http://www.terryfoxrun.org)
  Raises money for cancer research in the name of Terry Fox, a Canadian who died at the age of 22 of cancer after raising awareness and money by running 5,000 km.
- **The Smile Train** (http://www.smiletrain.org)
  Provides medical equipment, training and financial assistance to enable local surgeons to perform cleft palate surgeries.

Choosing Your Charity

The American Chamber of Commerce has created a vetting procedure for NGOs based upon guidelines used by the Council of Better Business Bureaus (CBBB) in the United States. Their website (http://www.amcham-shanghai.org) gives an evaluation of the charities that have passed through their vetting procedure.

An additional resource is China Development Brief (http://www.chinadevelopmentbrief.com) which provides a guide of over 300 NGOs in China. It is the best single source of information on local agencies, and lists nearly as many global NGOs with China operations. It is also a platform to advertise full-time and part-time paid NGO postings in China.

Two additional resources are GuideStar (http://www.guidestar.com), which lists over 500 charities with some focus on China, and Charity Navigator (http://www.charitynavigator.com), which provides evaluation of a few China charities.

If conducting your own due diligence on charities, some points to consider include:

- What percentage of funds raised by the organisation are used to support core functions of the programme?
- How much accountability is there? What are the reporting processes? Can donors designate what funds are used for?
- Are the organisation's finances independently audited? Are the audit records available for review?
- Is the organisation officially recognised in China? If not, is it recognised in another country? What is the legal umbrella the organisation operates under? Can it provide proof?

'China is big enough to permit many views.
Precisely because the country eludes generalization,
some observers have tended to grasp at straws,
too willing to convert a trend into a prophecy—
many people are buying cars,
so eventually half a billion will own cars;
some groups want democracy, soon everyone will.'
—Jasper Becker, *The Chinese*

Official Name
People's Republic of China

Capital
Beijing

Flag
Red with a large yellow five-pointed star and four smaller yellow five-pointed stars (arranged in a vertical arc toward the middle of the flag) in the upper left-hand corner

Time Difference
Greenwich Mean Time plus 8 hours (GMT + 0800). There is one official time zone in the country, although for practical purposes, Xinjiang runs on an unofficial time two hours behind Beijing time. In Xinajiang, all government services run on Beijing time, while other business operate according to local time.

Telephone Country Code for China
86

Climate
Covering 9.5 million sq km (5.9 million sq miles), China is the third largest country in the world, behind Russia and Canada. With geography that ranges from the Gobi Desert to Mount

Everest, weather patterns vary with region. In general, the south of China is semi-tropical with hot, humid summers. Eastern China has hot and humid summers, with winters near freezing. Northern China is dry, hot in the summer and extremely cold in the winter. Inner Mongolia winter temperatures can reach lows of −40°C (−40°F). Much of North-west China is desert and mountains.

Population
1,330,141,295 (July 2010 est.)

Language and Dialects
The official language is Mandarin, however there are a variety of regional dialects spoken across China. Major dialects spoken include Cantonese, Shanghainese, Fuzhou, Hokkien-Taiwanese, Xiang, Gan and Hakka dialects. English is not commonly spoken in China, although it is a newly required subject for schoolchildren.

Religion
China's main religions are Buddhism and Taoism. Secondary religions are Islam, Christianity and Judaism. Must Muslims are found in Xinjiang. China's largest Jewish population is in Kaifeng, Henan Province. Christians form 1 per cent of the Chinese.

Government Type
Communist State

Currency
The Renminbi (Rmb), also referred to as the *yuan* (Cny), is the official currency in China.

Industries
China's main industries are mining and ore processing, iron, steel, aluminum and other metals, coal; machine building; armaments; textiles and apparel; petroleum; cement; chemicals; fertilizers; consumer products, including footwear, toys and electronics; food processing; transportation

equipment, including automobiles, rail cars and locomotives; ships and aircraft; telecommunications equipment, commercial space launch vehicles and satellites.

Exports
Main exports are machinery and equipment, plastics, optical and medical equipment, iron and steel.

Ethnic Groups
China consists of Han Chinese, which make up 91.9 per cent of all Chinese. The remaining 8.1 per cent is made up of Zhuang, Uygur, Hui, Yi, Tibetan, Miao, Manchu, Mongol, Buyi and Korean.

Airports
China has 502 airports (as at 2010)

Electricity
220 volts

FAMOUS PEOPLE
Sun Yat-sen
Famous for leading the republican forces which overthrew the Manchu Empire in 1912, he is the only person who remains a hero in both mainland China and Taiwan. Known as 'The Father of the Revolution', Sun Yat-sen was an idealistic leader who sought to unite China under one stable government.

Chiang Kai-shek
Chiang Kai-shek was the leader of the Chinese Nationalist Party which eventually become know as the Kuomintang Party. Promoted by Sun Yat-sen, he rose to leadership of the Nationalist Party shortly after Sun Yat-sen's death in 1925. Chiang Kai-shek was best known for the defeat of his Kuomintang party by the communists in 1949. Chiang Kai-shek and his party were driven from the mainland and set up an government in exile in Taiwan with its capital in Taipei. He then became the leader of the government in exile until his death in 1975.

Soong Qingling

Wife of Sun Yat-sen, and one of the three famous Soong sisters, she was the first lady of modern China. After the establishment of the People's Republic of China in 1949, Soong remained on the mainland, where she was revered by the communists because she provided a symbolic link between the People's Republic and the older revolutionary movement of Sun Yat-sen. She became an important official within the new government, focusing on the welfare of women and children. In 1951, she was awarded the Stalin Peace Prize for her work on welfare and peace committees. She was named honorary Chairman of the People's Republic in 1981, shortly before her death.

Mao Zedong

Mao Zedong was the preeminent leader of the People's Republic of China and first secretary of the Chinese Communist Party (CCP) from 1943 until his death. Heavily influenced by Marxist thinking, Mao was a leader in the Communist Revolution that overthrew Chiang Kai-shek's forces, defeated the Japanese and forged modern China. A keen strategist, capable poet, avid swimmer and charismatic politician, Mao sought to remake China into a modern and industrial power using unorthodox means. His role in the Cultural Revolution, coupled with the damage inflicted by The Great Leap Forward, have diminished his status in modern Chinese society.

Zhou Enlai

An early labour organiser, in 1949, with the establishment of the People's Republic of China at Beijing, Zhou became premier and foreign minister. He headed the Chinese Communist delegation to the Geneva Conference of 1954. In 1958, he relinquished the foreign ministry but retained the premiership. A practical-minded administrator, Zhou maintained his position through all of Communist China's ideological upheavals, including the Great Leap Forward and the Cultural Revolution. Although supportive of government initiatives, Zhou was reputed to be a voice of reason behind the scenes and helped restrain extremists. As a result, he was attacked by Red Guards for attempting to shelter its victims. He is credited with arranging the historic meeting between US President Nixon and Chairman Mao. Zhou initiated contact with the West that eventually led to the US recognition of the communist government in China.

Deng Xiaoping

One of the original founders of the Chinese Communist Party with Mao, Deng Xiaoping became the party's Secretary General in 1954. He was subsequently purged by Mao in 1966 for his strong objections to the destructive excesses of the Great Leap Forward. By 1974, Deng had been 'rehabilitated' and returned to power. After Mao's death, Deng was the de facto leader of China until he finally died in 1997. Deng is thought to be the father of modern China as the reform programmes he initiated opened China's economy to the rest of the world.

The Gang of Four

Composed of Mao's wife Jiang Qing, as well as Zhang Chunqiao, Wang Hongwen and Yao Wenyuan, this group played a major role in implementing the destructive measures of the Cultural Revolution. Upon Mao's death, the Gang of Four made a play to take over the leadership of China. The play backfired and they were all arrested. When publicly announced, news of their arrest was celebrated across China.

Li Ka Shing

Considered China's most successful businessman, Li is the richest person of Chinese descent in the world, the richest person in Asia and the 10th richest man in the world. The Hutchison Whampoa Limited Chairman was named 'Asia's Most Powerful Man' by Asiaweek in 2000, as well as being recognised by the Forbes Family with the 'Malcolm S. Forbes Lifetime Achieve Award' in 2006.

Hu Jintao

Current president of the People's Republic of China (CPC) and chairman of the Central Military Commission. Hu, a native of Anhui Province, joined the Communist Party of China in December of 1942. He forged his political career in Guizhou and Tibet. In 1992, he became an elected member of the Standing Committee of the Political Bureau of the CPC Central Committee, his first step toward a role in the central leadership of the CPC.

Zhang Yimou

China's best-known movie director was born in Xian, to a newly-formed communist nation. Zhang Yimou's family background made him a target of the Cultural Revolution. He was sent to the countryside to work with the peasants and was later transferred to a textile factory. He is rumoured to have sold his own blood to buy his first camera. Globally renowned and having received numerous awards, some of his best-known works are *Raise the Red Lantern*, *The Story of Qiu Ju* and *Ju Dou*. He was also the chief director of the opening ceremony of the Beijing Summer Olympics in 2008, which reportedly cost more than US$ 100 million to produce.

Chow Yun-Fat

One of the most recognised Chinese male actor, Chow made his mark in action films in the late 1980s. He also co-starred with Michelle Yeoh in the acclaimed *Crouching Tiger, Hidden Dragon*. A Hong Kong native, Chow started as a professional actor in his teens after being selected by Hong Kong TV station TVB to attend a young actors training programme.

Gong Li

China's most famous actress was born in the northern industrial city of Shenyang, and her father was an economics professor. Gong Li had her first big break while still in acting school when she secured the lead role of the 1988 film *Red Sorghum*. Her collaboration, both onscreen and offscreen, with director Zhong Yimou established her as China's leading lady. Noteworthy movies include *Farewell My Concubine* (1993) and *Memoirs of a Geisha* (2005).

Yao Ming

Drafted into the NBA's Houston Rockets in 2002, Yao is China's best-known basketballer. The Shanghai native's parents both played for the national basketball teams of China. His mother is 6 feet 3 inches tall, his father is 6 feet 7 inches tall, and he is 7 feet 5 inches (2.26 meters) tall. He is the third Chinese national to play in the NBA and has been part of the China Olympic team since 2000. At the Beijing Summer Olympics 2008, he had the honour of carrying the Chinese flag and leading the delegation during the opening ceremony.

CULTURE QUIZ

SITUATION 1

At a morning language lesson, you ask your Chinese tutor for help correctly pronouncing the name of a Hong Kong client. You hand him the piece of paper on which you have carefully copied the client's name: Chan Tai Man. But the tutor shakes his head, saying that he's not sure how to pronounce the name. You decide:

Ⓐ The teacher is a bit dim.

Ⓑ There is something you don't understand about Chinese names; better bring the business card to your next lesson, or at a minimum have someone write the name in characters.

Ⓒ Hong Kong Chinese is different than Mainland Chinese.

Ⓓ The teacher's sister is actually married to Chan Tai Man and he is angry with him for winning at mahjong last week and so thinks you shouldn't associate with him.

Comments

Chinese names are traditionally written with the family name first (almost always one character) and the given name second (usually two characters). When writing in Chinese characters, whether traditional complex characters (as in Hong Kong) or simplified characters (as in the Mainland), family name is always first. When writing a Romanised version of the name using English letters, Westernised Chinese sometimes reverse order and put given name first 'for the convenience of Western friends'. This can cause confusion, especially with two-character names.

The correct answer is **Ⓒ**. Hong Kong Chinese speak Cantonese while Mainland Chinese speak Mandarin, so a word in Pinyin that appears the same could have a completely different pronunciation. For example, in Cantonese the word for big is *tai*, while in Mandarin it is *da*. His name would actually be pronounced Chan Da Man in Mandarin. It will help your teacher to see the characters, at a minimum he can give you the pronunciation in Mandarin.

SITUATION 2

After eight grueling months in your new China job, you have decided to take your first R&R trip, a holiday at a friend's condo on the French Riviera. You have one week to relax and enjoy sun, food and no obligations. Better yet, it is one of the perks that is provided you in an overseas assignment so you are travelling at the company's expense.

Your secretary takes note of what you want to do and makes all travel arrangements. She notes in your diary that you will be picked up at 3:00 pm by the driver to be taken to the airport. Thus begins the worst holiday you have ever had in your entire life. The driver promptly drops you at the airport at 3:45 pm, only to have you discover that your flight doesn't leave until 7:00 pm. When you check in at the counter, because they have not been given your airline mileage number upon booking, you have been overlooked for the five free upgrades that were given to people with less miles than you. Not only that, but when you further check your ticket, you realise that what should have been a direct nine-hour flight has 16 hours of travel time because of a connection through Narita and a layover in Frankfurt.

Because your mileage number had not been recorded, your seating preference was not noted and so you are stuck in the middle seat of the centre row, in the middle of a red-cap wearing tour group that is intent on making the most of their holiday from the time the plane takes off until it returns to Beijing airport. They are boisterously shouting and laughing across you. Mid-way through the flight when they finally begin to wear out, the man to your left falls asleep and you discover that his snoring is probably going to cause you permanent hearing loss.

During the long sleepless hours on the airplane, you ponder why your assistant arranged your travel the way she did. Is it because:

A She was saving the company money by booking you on the cheapest flights available.

B She is getting even with you for making her work until midnight three nights in a row preparing next year's budget.

❸ She has never travelled outside of China and so has no idea the wear and tear that multiple long-haul flights can cause.

❹ She relied on an incompetent travel agent.

Comments

The answer is **❸**. Most Mainland Chinese people who are in administrative positions have had no opportunity to travel beyond Mainland China because it is difficult to secure a passport and they do not have the financial means to travel. Because of this, their decision-making criteria may be far different than that of a person who has weathered long-haul flights, layover and time zone changes. It is likely the secretary's primary decision making criteria, without further instruction, is to save money for the company. She was probably relying on the advice of a travel agent that has also never travelled outside of the country and is on a promotional perk scheme.

It is important when you are asking your administrative staff to undertake tasks to give clear direction, lay out decision-making criteria and set up a review process before final confirmation.

SITUATION 3

The first three days of your new *ayi's* work have gone smoothly. The house is clean, refrigerator well stocked, her cooking is fabulous, and your bed so tightly made that you have to peel back the sheets each night to crawl in. On the fourth day when you return home, you are absolutely horrified to see your favourite Irish wool sweater laid out to dry shrunk to a size most appropriate for a two-year-old. To assure that this situation will not happen again, you:

❹ Fire your *ayi* on the spot and call the service to find you a new one.

❸ Dock your *ayi's* salary the cost of the sweater to teach her a lesson so that she will never make that mistake again.

❻ Explain to your *ayi* that from now on, she must read the care instruction labels and show her where to find them in your clothes.

ⓓ Redesign your system so that she only washes clothes when you place them in the blue clothes hamper and only sends clothes in the red clothes hamper to the dry cleaners.

Comments

The answer is **ⓓ**. You can assume that most new *ayis* have limited experience with both electronic appliances and with clothes that require special care. It is highly likely that the care that they give to their own clothes is to wash them in cold water by hand with bar soap and hang them outside to dry.

Chances are if you sacked your *ayi*, you would run into the exact same situation again with her replacement. The only way to assure things will be handled properly is to create a fool-proof system that does not require judgment calls. This is best done in the case of clothes by designating different hampers for different kinds of care and sorting the clothes into these hampers yourself to assure they are handled properly. The same logic applies to other kinds of decisions in the house, for example you may need to code different kind of cleaners for different surfaces, different cleaning cloths for dishes versus floor, different soaps for hand washing and washing the dog, etc. The more specific you are, the less chance you leave for mistakes.

SITUATION 4

You have been invited by the local government to attend a banquet encouraging foreign investment in the local economy. Upon arrival at the event, you are escorted from the door and seated at a table in the centre front. It occurs to you as others are being seated at the table that you are in the company of the senior-most people of the 60 in attendance. The young man who has shown you to your seat advises you that it would be appreciated if you could make a VIP speech in just a few minutes. You note photographers and video cameras being set up. How should you respond to him?

ⓐ Gracefully agree to give the speech and ask what the most appropriate subject would be.

ⓑ Politely decline saying that in addition to not having had time to prepare remarks, your language skills are inadequate to make the speech in Chinese.

ⓒ Offer one of your more junior colleagues sitting at a nearby table to make the speech in your place.

ⓓ Pretend your mobile phone has just vibrated, have an animated discussion with a non-existent assistant, and excuse yourself from the banquet saying that you have an urgent emergency to attend to.

Comments

The appropriate response would be to gracefully accept to give the speech, answer **ⓐ**. Your host has invited you to sit at the head table and give a speech not for the content that you would provide, but because your presence will give him 'face', demonstrating his ties and support to key members of the foreign investment community. Your remarks can be brief but should give generous credit to the local government entity and the support they have given you. Being adaptable in this type of situation will earn you credit with the government and build a stronger relationship that will be to your advantage in the future.

SITUATION 5

You have been asked by your future landlord to put down a deposit of US$ 1,000 in order to hold the gorgeous new apartment that you have just identified after three months of searching. Confident that you can have the money for her tomorrow, you promise to deliver it in person at 4:00 pm. You have withdrawn this amount of foreign currency from your bank two other times and think that it will be a simple transaction. When you show up at the bank the next day, the clerk tells you that the regulations changed the first of last month and that you are no longer allowed to withdraw more than US$ 500 in any one day. Your future landlady has been insistent that the only way you will get the apartment is to give her the money by 4:00 pm tomorrow. She has someone else interested that can have the money to her the day after. After 15 minutes of heated debate about why you were allowed to change money previously and not now, the teller pulls out the regulations in Chinese and insists you read them. She tells you there is absolutely nothing she can do to give you more than US$ 500 today. What should you do?

Ⓐ Throw a fit and ask to speak to the manager in the hopes that they can override the regulations on your behalf.

Ⓑ Call your landlady and negotiate with her to allow you to give her US$ 500 today and US$ 500 the following day.

Ⓒ Explain the situation to the teller and ask her to advise you on any other ways you may be able to secure the extra US$ 500 before 4:00 pm.

Ⓓ Call your best friend and casually ask if they have US$ 500 on hand to loan you for the day.

Comments

Although **Ⓐ**, **Ⓑ** and **Ⓓ** may be viable options as fallbacks, the best way to approach the situation is **Ⓒ**. Unless you ask someone in China to help you solve your problem, they will not consider giving you options. Many times, people, especially those working for government entities, are very linear in their thinking and do not want to take responsibility for anything that could get them into trouble with superiors or cause them an inconvenience. In addition, Chinese are very pragmatic after living for 50 years under a system that is often dysfunctional. They can quickly find practical solutions to impractical situations. Should you get the bank teller to help you problem solve, you would find that there are at least three different ways you can get the additional US$ 500 in one day.

The first would be to bring in your employment contract and receipts demonstrating you have paid tax, which would give you the right to withdraw funds in USD. The second is to withdraw the money in RMB and go to a currency exchange centre at an international airport to change the RMB into USD. The third, and least attractive, would be to use a black market moneychanger. The degree of transparency and risk in using a moneychanger depends upon the city you are in. For example, at China World in Beijing, at least five of them are permanently stationed outside of the local bank in the basement.

SITUATION 6

You have moved into a beautiful neighbourhood full of local charm. Every morning, the older people in the community are out in the garden doing *tai chi*, in the late afternoon the garden is full of parents out playing with their children. The guards in your compound are courteous and helpful. After the first week in the apartment, you notice that the kitchen sink is leaking so you ask the management to have a maintenance man come repair. After an initial review, he says that it will require additional parts and he will have to come back in the afternoon. He appears in the afternoon and repairs it, and then says he needs to come back later to check it. Thus begins a series of spontaneous visits by the repairman day and night to look at sink, which continues to leak. He interrupts dinner parties, shows up at 11:00 pm at night, and comes by while you are in the shower. You have finally had it when he rings the doorbell at 7:00 am on Saturday to change the part to another that he believes will finally repair the sink. You respond by:

Ⓐ Seeing him outside the door, not answering in the hopes he will take a hint and go away until a decent time (which causes him to stand there and ring the doorbell another 30 times until all of your neighbours are in the hallway wondering what is going on).

Ⓑ Answer the door, tell him to come back at a reasonable hour, and then slam it shut in anger.

Ⓒ Deciding it is time to set some boundaries, you get dressed and go down to the management office with him to remind them that he needs to make an appointment in advance to come to your apartment for repairs, and that unless agreed otherwise, those repairs must take place at an agreed time between 9:00 am and 7:00 pm.

Ⓓ Putting on your best 'I didn't just wake up' smile, open the door and invite him in to repair the sink again, in the hopes that it will be the final time.

Comments

Because people in China have become accustomed to living so closely with others, they have a more relaxed set of social boundaries when it comes to personal space. It is likely that the repairman has the good intention of demonstrating his dedication to fixing your problem and it would not occur to him that his frequent, unannounced and untimely visits to your home would cause you discomfort. He likes you and wants to help you fix your problem, he is a little embarrassed that it has gone on so long without being solved and so is making up for lack of progress by showing great enthusiasm. The appropriate answer is **❻**, because you live in two different social contexts, you need to sit down with him and his manager and while thanking him for his dedication to fixing your problem, explain that there are rules that you would like him to observe when helping you. You can explain that you have a very busy life and require private time to prepare for it and to relax. You need to do it in a way that gives him 'face' for his efforts, but provides the outcome that you require for your own sanity.

SITUATION 7

It is 2:00 pm and you are sitting at your desk in the office putting the finishing touches on next year's budget, which is due to your regional headquarters in an hour. Your receptionist calls to inform you that a delegation from the district government is at the reception and would like to meet now. You tell her that she should inform them that you are unavailable right now, but if they would like to make an appointment, you would be happy to meet them later. She calls back and says that they insist on meeting you because they are in the building now. They are explaining the changes in the labour laws to building tenants and need to inform you of the new regulation that requires your company to form a labour union within the week. You quickly email your boss saying you will be an hour late getting the budget to her and agree to meet them. During the meeting, they pointedly explain to you the regulation change and tell you that you will need to nominate a labour union leader within the week, making subtle threats that if you don't nominate a labour union representative, they have the right to insert their own person into your company as the labour union representative. You respond by:

Ⓐ Refusing to assign a labour union representative and thank them for their time.

Ⓑ Ask them to provide you a written copy of the regulations and give you two weeks to explain this to your headquarters so that you can properly comply with the support of your head office.

Ⓒ Call in your HR person and ask them to handle the situation.

Ⓓ Tell them you will get back to them in a week with the name of the appropriate person.

Comments

Government agencies often act as bullies in China, using scare tactics to gain your cooperation. Oftentimes, they take the local interpretation of a provincial or national charter and implement it without understanding intent or outcome. They may be under direction to test a regulation in advance of it being implemented in order to determine whether there will be easy compliance. The best response to this situation is **Ⓑ**. You should create enough time and collect enough facts to allow you to do full due diligence, before responding to the directive. Two weeks would allow you enough time to check with your industry association, your attorney, the commercial section of your consulate, your chamber of commerce and competitors to understand the real requirements and how they are being translated. In this instance, it so happens that the regulation had not been passed and was only being tested. The government official in question was trying to win kudos with his boss by signing up multi-nationals in his district in advance of implementation. He had no ability to enforce the threats he was making.

SITUATION 8

You had a big Friday night out with guests in town from overseas and had intended a lovely sleep in on Saturday morning. That is cut short when a high-pitched noise and rattling wall wake you up at 6:30 am. The construction crew renovating the upstairs apartment seem to have decided to get an early start at it today. You respond by:

A Calling the management office and asking them to make the crew stop drilling.
B Personally going upstairs to ask the crew to stop drilling.
C Covering your head with a pillow and hoping you are tired enough to sleep through the noise for a few more hours.
D Personally going upstairs to not only ask the crew to stop drilling, but when they laugh at you, to take their drill away from them and bring it back to your apartment, lock the door behind you and go back to sleep.

Comments

Although **D** is a response that was deployed by a person who had been doing battle with a construction crew for two weeks, the appropriate response is **A**. In the last five years in China, regulations have been passed at a city level and within compounds about the hours that construction is allowed. It is the obligation of the building management to enforce these regulations. If they don't, in many cities you can call a citizen complaint line and the police will follow up. Most construction crews are made up of peasants who come from the countryside and live in the apartment while they are doing construction. Typically they are sleeping on the floor and are paid upon completion of the project, so it is in their interest to finish quickly. They are up with the sun, have no interest in being your neighbour, and come from a place where there are no rules. They will find a hundred ways around the rules, which have little relevance to them, to get the job done.

SITUATION 9

The kindly Chinese family living next to you shows up one evening en masse, explaining to you that Junior in the corner has been accepted to Harvard but is unable to get a visa. Since you are an American, they would appreciate it if you could pull some strings at the consulate to help him get a visa. He has applied once but has been declined. The future of their family is at stake. You think about how nice this family has been to you. They invited you over for Spring Festival dinner, shared their fireworks with you, and helped you the day you got locked out of your apartment. They bring treats like fragrant tea and special snacks by every other week. You respond by:

A Promising to go down to the visa office with Junior and discuss his situation with the visa officer.

B Suggest that they call Harvard and ask for it to try to work with the Consulate to get a visa issued.

C Offer to act as a personal referee for Junior and write a letter to that effect that can be presented at the Consulate.

D Explain that the visa approval system is a transparent process and that although you would like to help their family, you have no influence over the process and that Junior needs to follow the advise the visa officer gave him.

Comments

Because relationships, or *guanxi*, is so prevalent in influencing outcomes in China it is difficult for Chinese people to understand that foreign country visa processes cannot be influenced through connections. Chances are if Junior was turned down for a visa once, he is unlikely to do any better a second time. The correct answer is **D**. Unless you are frank upfront, in a very constructive way, there will be expectations that you will be able to pull strings and get Junior a visa, which is highly unlikely. The family has been carefully building the relationship with you since you first moved in because they knew that they may need your support in this situation. The relationship is sincere, but they expect some kind of return. The best that you can do to help Junior is something which is within your control, like arrange for him to get an internship with your company if he is unable to find a way to get approval on his visa. You are demonstrating goodwill while keeping it to something reasonable and within your authority.

SITUATION 10

You have decided to have a first dinner out in your new city with your six-month-old son. You sit down in a restaurant and the waitress swoops over, coos at your child in Chinese, then picks him up and trots off to show him to a gaggle of other waitresses. You should:

Ⓐ Scream for the police.

Ⓑ Step in front of the waitress, explain politely but firmly that you don't want your child touched by strangers, and take your son back.

Ⓒ Relax and let the waitress babysit your son while you enjoy your meal.

Ⓓ Smile, stand and follow the waitress, letting her understand that you're happy she shares your joy in your son, and that you are also available to keep an eye on him.

Comments

This common situation is one of the most jarring for new parents in China, whose instinct often tells them to do **Ⓐ**. The trouble is, of course, that the waitress intended no harm, **Ⓑ** is less damaging, but will still brand you as rather cold and untrusting. **Ⓓ** is probably the best balance, at least at first—although in time, if you have a good view of him just in case he becomes upset, particularly on repeat visits to the same restaurant, you may well find you can relax into **Ⓒ**!

DO'S AND DON'TS

DO'S

- Do explore and get to know China.
- Do try to learn Mandarin Chinese.
- Do be persistent in experimenting with the Chinese words you have learned, repeat yourself if necessary, changing tones and adding context until the other person understands your intent.
- Do be as adventurous as you feel able to in trying new foods and other experiences.
- Do treat guests to your home or office in proper Chinese fashion by offering them something to drink.
- Do become comfortable greeting people and being greeted with, "Have you eaten?"
- Do learn how to 'give face' and how to avoid making people 'lose face'.
- Do prepare business cards in Chinese and English, and always carry a stack with you.
- Do always carry tissue, bottled water and medicines like antihistamines and immodium with you when travelling outside of central areas of large cities.
- Do exercise caution when crossing streets, especially motorcycles and bicycles travelling the wrong way on a one-way street.
- Do wear a helmet when riding bicycles and motorcycles, regardless of local regulation.
- Do politely ignore strangers, unless you want to invite interaction with them.
- Do shake hands when introduced.
- Do reciprocate hospitality and acts of generosity.
- Do bring small gifts when invited to someone's home: wine, chocolates or a nice fruit arrangement are appreciated.
- Do be generous in praise and compliments that you mean as it breaks down barriers and builds rapport.
- Do clarify expectations for household and business staff, to the best of your ability demonstrating what you intend as well as saying it.

- Do observe and provide appropriate token gifts for Chinese holidays like Mid-Autumn Festival.
- Do accept that 'business is personal' in China, and encourage friendly relations among staff and clients.
- Do fee free to share your perspective on Chinese culture, cities and other experiences with Chinese people in a way that is constructive and respectful.

DON'TS

- Don't take offense at invasive questions like how much money do you make or how much do you weigh; they are asked out of genuine naïve interest.
- Don't be one of those expats that lives in an expat enclave and never tries to enjoy China.
- Don't constantly compare what is good at home and lacking in China.
- Don't feel uneasy about people staring or being far more invasive than you are used to with personal space; there is a different sense of privacy in China than other places.
- Don't give up on learning Mandarin Chinese; you can learn at least enough to get around if you try.
- Don't feel you must eat something you find repugnant; you can politely push it around on your plate while continuing to eat other things.
- Don't be impatient with small talk—it is often a prelude to more important things.
- Don't interpret a token gift as implying anything.
- Don't accept anything more than a token gift without considering clearly what is being implicitly 'asked for' in return.
- Don't give a clock as a gift: it is considered unlucky. The Chinese for 'to give a clock' sounds the same as 'to wish someone death'.
- Don't crumble to repeated offers of food or drink; if you decline more than three times, it will be accepted.
- Don't fail to offer someone food, drink or paying the bill multiple times as Chinese people may be declining so that they will not seem greedy.

- Don't wear white to a wedding; it is unlucky.
- Don't make a negative comment about China or raise sensitive issues such as religion or political issues.

GLOSSARY

THE BASICS

English	Mandarin Pinyin	Simplified Characters
hello	*ni hao*	你好
thank you	*xie xie*	谢谢
goodbye	*zai jian*	再见
man	*nan ren*	男人
woman	*nu ren*	女人
no problem	*mei wen ti*	没问答
take care	*xiao xin*	小心
Is that right?	*shi bu shi*	是不是
Do you want it?	*yao bu yao*	要不要
sorry	*bao qian*	抱歉
not bad	*hai ke yi*	还可以

NUMBERS

English	Mandarin Pinyin	Simplified Characters
zero	*ling*	零
one	*yi*	一
two	*er*	二
three	*san*	三
four	*si*	四
five	*wu*	五
six	*liu*	六
seven	*qi*	七
eight	*ba*	八
nine	*jiu*	九
ten	*shi*	十

PLACE NAMES AND TERMS

English	Mandarin Pinyin	Simplified Characters
Australia	*ao da li ya*	澳大利亚
Canada	*jia na da*	加拿大
China	*zhong guo*	中国
Denmark	*dan mai*	丹麦
England	*ying guo*	英国
Europe	*ou zhou*	欧洲
France	*fa guo*	法国
Germany	*de guo*	德国
Holland	*he lan*	荷兰
Hong Kong	*xiang gang*	香港
Ireland	*ai er lan*	爱尔兰
Italy	*yi da li*	意大利
Japan	*ri ben*	日本
Korea	*han guo*	韩国
Mongolia	*meng gu*	蒙古
Scotland	*su ge lan*	苏格兰
Singapore	*xin jia po*	新加坡
South Africa	*nan fei*	南非
Sweden	*rui dian*	瑞典
Switzerland	*rui shi*	瑞士
Tibet	*xi zhang*	西藏
United States	*mei guo*	美国
gate	*men*	门
outside	*wai mian*	外面
inside	*li mian*	里面
east	*dong*	东
west	*xi*	西
north	*bei*	北
south	*nan*	南

NAMES AND TITLES

English	Mandarin Pinyin	Simplified Characters
Mister (Mr)	*xian sheng*	先生
Miss (Ms)	*xiao jie*	小姐
Mistress (Mrs)	*tai tai*	夫人
colleague	*tong shi*	同事

FOOD

English	Mandarin Pinyin	Simplified Characters
fish	*yu*	鱼
meat	*rou*	肉
chicken	*ji*	鸡
egg	*dan*	蛋
beef	*niu rou*	牛肉
lamb	*yang rou*	羊肉
crab	*xia*	蟹
seafood	*hai xian*	海鲜
mineral water	*kuang quan shui*	矿泉水
tea	*cha*	茶
rice	*mi*	米
tofu (bean curd)	*dou fu*	豆腐
vegetables	*shu cai*	疏菜
water	*shui*	水

MISCELLANEOUS

English	Mandarin Pinyin	Simplified Characters
close enough	*cha bu duo*	差不多
correct	*dui*	对
foreigner	*wai guo ren*	外国人
friend	*peng you*	朋友

English	Mandarin Pinyin	Simplified Characters
Mandarin	Pu tong hua	普通话
outsider	*wai di ren*	外地人
relationship	*guan xi*	关系
subway	*di tie*	地铁
work unit	*dan wei*	单位
English	*Ying wen*	英文
the day before yesterday	*qian tian*	前天
yesterday	*zuo tian*	昨天
today	*jin tian*	今天
tomorrow	*ming tian*	明天
the day after tomorrow	*hou tian*	后天
last year	*qu nian*	去年
this year	*jin nian*	今年
next year	*ming nian*	明年
morning	*zao shang*	早上
noon	*zhong wu*	中午
afternoon	*xia wu*	下午
night	*wan shang*	晚上

RESOURCE GUIDE

EMERGENCY NUMBERS
- Emergency ambulance: 120
- Police: 110
- Fire: 119
- Directory assistance: 114
- Weather forecast: 121

AIRLINE, HOTELS AND TRAVEL ARRANGEMENTS
- C-Trip: http://www.english.ctrip.com
- China Travel: http://www.travelchinaguide.com

CLUBS AND ORGANISATIONS
- Beijing: http://www.cityweekend.com.cn/beijing/listings/community/
- Guangzhou: http://www.cityweekend.com.cn/guangzhou/listings/community/
- Shanghai: http://www.cityweekend.com.cn/shanghai/listings/community/

FOREIGN EMBASSIES AND CONSULATES
- Argentinian Embassy in Beijing
  11 Dong Wu Jie, San Li Tun, 100600 Beijing
  Tel: (10) 6532-2142 / 1406 or 6532-2090 / 1852
  Fax: (10) 6532-2319
- Argentinian Consulate in Shanghai
  Suite 1202, Golden Finance Tower
  No. 58 Yan'an Road East (Corner Middle Sichuan Road)
  Huangpu District, Shanghai 200002
  Tel: (21) 6339-0322. Fax: (21) 5350-0058
  Website: http://www.consuargensh.com/
- Australian Embassy in Beijing
  21 Dongzhimenwai Dajie
  Sanlitun, Beijing 100600
  Tel: (10) 5140-4111. Fax: (10) 5140-4204
  Website: http://www.china.embassy.gov.au/

- Australian Consulate-General in Shanghai
  Level 22, Citic Square
  1168 Nanjing West Road
  Shanghai 200041
  Tel: (21) 5292-5500. Fax: (21) 2215-5252
  Website: http://www.shanghai.china.embassy.gov.au/
- Australian Consulate-General in Guangzhou
  12th Floor, Development Centre
  No. 3 Linjiang Road
  Zhujiang New City, Guangzhou 510623
  Tel: (20) 3814-0111. Fax: (20) 3814-0112
  Website: http://www.guangzhou.china.embassy.gov.au
- Embassy of Austria in Beijing
  No. 5, Xiushui Nanjie
  Jianguomenwai, Beijing 100600
  Tel: (10) 6532-2061. Fax: (10) 6532-1505
  Website: http://www.bmeia.gv.at/botschaft/peking.html
- Bangladeshi Embassy in Beijing
  42 Guang Hua Lu
  Chao Yang District, Beijing 100600
  Tel: (10) 6532-2521 / 6532-3706. Fax: (10) 6532-4346
  Website: www.bangladeshembassy.com.cn
- Belgian Consulate in Shanghai
  127 Wu Yi Road, Shanghai 200050
  Tel: (21) 6437-6579. Fax: (21) 6437-7041
  Website: http://www.diplobel.org/shanghai/
- Bolivian Embassy in Beijing
  2-3-2 TaYuan Office Building, Beijing 100600
  Tel: (10) 6532-4370 / 6532-3074
  Fax: (10) 6532-6657 / 6532-4686
- Brazilian Embassy in Beijing
  27, Guanghua Lu, Jianguomenwai
  Chaoyang District, Beijing 100600
  Tel: (10) 532-2881. Fax: (10) 532-2751
  Website: http://pequim.itamaraty.gov.br/en-us/
- Bulgarian Embassy in Beijing
  4 Xiushui Bei Jie
  Jian Guo Men Wai, Beijing 100600
  Tel: (10) 6532-1946 / 6532-1916. Fax: (10) 6532-4502

- Cambodian Embassy in Beijing
  No. 9 Dong Zhi Men
  Wai Dajie, 100600 Beijing
  Tel: (10) 6532-1889. Fax: (10) 6532-3507
- Cambodian Consulate in Guangzhou
  Room 811, The Garden Hotel
  Huan Shi Road East,
  Guangzhou, 5100064
  Tel: (20) 8387-9005. Fax: (20) 8387-9006
- Cambodian Consulate in Shanghai
  Huasheng Commercial Building
  9th Floor, Hankou Road 400
  Tel: (21) 636-6681 / 6360-0949. Fax: (21) 6361-1437
- Canadian Embassy in Beijing
  19 Dongzhimenwai Dajie
  Chao Yang District, Beijing 100600
  Tel: (10) 5139-4000. Fax: (10) 5139-4454
  Website: http://www.canadainternational.gc.ca/china-chine/
- Canadian Consulate in Guangzhou
  Suite 801, China Hotel Office Tower
  Liu Hua Lu, Guangzhou 510015
  Tel: (20) 8611-6100. Fax: (20) 8611-6196
  Website: http://www.canadainternational.gc.ca/china-chine/
- Canadian Consulate in Shanghai
  604, West Tower, 1376 Nanjing Road (West)
  Shanghai 200040
  Tel: (21) 3279-2800. Fax: (21) 3279-2801
  Website: http://www.canadainternational.gc.ca/china-chine/
- Czech Embassy in Beijing
  2 Ri Tan Lu
  Jian Guo Men Wai, Beijing 100600
  Tel: (10) 8532-9500. Fax: (10) 6532-5653
  Website: http://www.mzv.cz/beijing/en/index.html
- Danish Embassy in Beijing
  San Li Tun
  Dong Wu Jie 1, Beijing 100600
  Tel: (10) 8532-9900. Fax: (10) 8532-9999
  Website: http://www.ambbeijing.um.dk/en

- Danish Consulate in Guangzhou
  China Hotel Office Tower, Suite 1578
  Liu Hua Lu, Guangzhou 510015
  Tel: (20) 8666-0795. Fax: (20) 8667-0315
  Website: http://www.gkguangzhou.um.dk/en
- Danish Consulate in Shanghai
  Room 701, Shanghai International Trade Centre
  No. 2200, Yan'an Xi Lu, Shanghai 200336
  Tel: (21) 6209-0500. Fax: (21) 6209-0504
  http://www.gkshanghai.um.dk/EN
- Ecuadorian Embassy in Beijing
  2-62 San Li Tun Office Building
  Beijing 100600
  Tel: (10) 6532-3849 / 6532-0489 / 6532-3158
  Fax: (10) 6532-4371
- Egyptian Embassy in Beijing
  No. 2, Ri Tan Dong Lu, Beijing
  Tel: (10) 6532-1825.Fax: (10) 6532-5365
- Equatorial Guinean Embassy in Beijing
  No.2 Dong Si Jie, San Li tun, Beijing 100600
  Tel: (10)6532-3679. Fax: (10) 6532-0438
- Eritrean Embassy in Beijing
  Ta Yuan Office Bldg 2-10-1
  No. 14, South Liang Mahe Road
  Chao Yang District, Beijing 100600
  Tel: (10) 6532-6534 / 6532-6535
  Fax: (10) 6532-6532
- Estonian Embassy in Beijing
  Beijing Lufthansa Center
  Office Building: C-617 / C-618
  No. 50, Liangmaqiao Road
  Chaoyang District, Beijing 100125
  Tel: (10) 6463-7913. Fax: (10) 6463-7908
  Website: http://www.beijing.mfa.ee/
- Ethiopian Embassy in Beijing
  No. 3, Xiu Shui Nan Jie
  Jian Guo Men Wai, Beijing 100600
  Tel: (10) 6532-5258. Fax: (10) 6532-5591
  Website: http://www.ethiopiaemb.org.cn/index.pl

- Fijian Embassy in China
  1-15-2 Ta Yuan Diplomatic Building
  14 Liang Ma He Nan Lu
  San Li Tun, Chaoyang District, Beijing 100600
  Tel: (10) 6532-7305. Fax: (10) 6532-7253
  Website: http://www.fijiembassy.org.cn/
- Finnish Embassy in Beijing
  Beijing Kerry Centre, Level 26, South Tower
  Guanghua Lu 1, Beijing 100020
  Tel: (10) 8519-8300. Fax: (10) 10 8519-8301
  Website: http://www.finland.cn
- French Embassy in Beijing
  3 Dongsanjie, Sanlitun, Chaoyang District, Beijing 100600
  Tel: (10) 8532-8080. Fax: (10) 8532-8009
  Website: http://www.ambafrance-cn.org/
- German Embassy in Beijing
  17, Dong Zhi Men Wai Da Jie
  Chaoyang District, Beijing 100600
  Tel: (10) 8532-9000. Fax: (10) 6532-5336
  Website: http://www.peking.diplo.de
- German Consulate in Shanghai
  181 Yongfu Road, Shanghai 200031
  Tel: (21) 3401-0106. Fax: (21) 6471-4448
  Website: http://www.shanghai.diplo.de
- German Consulate in Guangzhou
  14. Floor, Teem Tower
  208 Tianhe Lu, Guangzhou 510620
  Tel: (20) 8313-0000. Fax: (20) 8516-8133
  Website: http://www.kanton.diplo.de
- Greek Embassy in Beijing
  117/Floor, The Place Tower, The Place
  No.9 Guang Hua Lu
  Chao Yang District, Beijing 100020
  Tel: (10) 6587-2838, Fax: (10) 6587-2839
  Website: http://www.grpressbeijing.com/
- Greenlandic Embassy in Beijing
  1 Dong Wu Jie, San Li Tun, Beijing 100600
  Tel: (10) 8532-9900. Fax:(10) 8532-9999
  Website: http://www.ambbeijing.um.dk

- Hungarian Embassy in Beijing
  10 Dongzhimenwai Da Jie,
  Sanlitun, Beijing 100600
  Tel: (10) 6532-1431 / 6532-1432 / 6532-1433
  Fax: (10) 6532-5053
  Website: http://www.mfa.gov.hu/kulkepviselet/CN/en/
- Icelandic Embassy in Beijing
  Landmark Tower 1 #802
  8 North Dongsanhuan Rd
  Chaoyang District, Beijing 100004
  Tel: (10) 6590-7795, Fax: (10) 6590-7801
  Website: http://www.iceland.org/cn
- Indian Embassy in Beijing
  1, Ritan Dong Lu, Beijing 100600
  Tel: (10) 6532-1908. Fax: (10) 6532-2684
  Website: http://www.indianembassy.org.cn/
- Indian Consulate in Shanghai
  Shanghai International Trade Centre 1008
  2201 Yan An (West) Road, Shanghai 200336
  Tel: (21) 6275-8882 / 6275-8885 / 6275-8886
  Fax: (21) 6275-8881 /6295-6892
  Website: http://www.indianconsulate.org.cn/site/
- Indonesian Embassy in Beijing
  No.4 Dongzhimen Wai Street
  Chaoyang District, Beijing 100600
  Tel: (10) 6532-5489 / 6532-5486/ 6532-5488
  Fax: (10) 6532-5368 /6532-5782
  Website: http://www.indonesianembassy-china.org/
- Irish Embassy in Beijing
  3 Ritan Dong Lu, Beijing 100600
  Tel: (10) 6532-2691 / 6532-2914. Fax: (10) 6532-6857
  Website: http://www.embassyofireland.cn/
- Israeli Embassy in Beijing
  No. 17 Tianzelu, Chaoyang District, Beijing 100600
  Tel: (10) 8532-0500. Fax: (10) 8532-0555
  Website: http://beijing.mfa.gov.il
- Israeli Consulate in Shanghai
  7th Floor, New Town Mansion
  55 Loushanguan Road

Changning District, Shanghai 200336
Tel: (21) 6126-4500 / 6126-4527 / 6126-4526
Fax: (21) 6126-4555
Website: http://www.isconshanghai.org

- Italian Embassy in Beijing
  2, San Li Tun Dong Er Jie, Beijing 100600
  Tel: (10) 8532-7600. Fax: (10) 6532-4676
  http://www.ambpechino.esteri.it/ambasciata_pechino

- Japanese Embassy in Beijing
  Ritan Road 7, Jian Guo Men Wai
  Chaoyang District, Beijing 100600
  Tel: (10) 6532-2361. Fax: (10) 6532-4625
  Website: http://www.cn.emb-japan.go.jp

- Japanese Consulate in Guangzhou
  368 Huangshi Dong Lu, Guangzhou 510064
  Tel: (20) 8334-3009 / 8334-3090
  Fax: (20) 8333-8972 / 8388-3583
  Website: http://www.guangzhou.cn.emb-japan.go.jp

- Japanese Consulate in Shanghai
  8 Wan Shan Road, Shanghai 200336
  Tel: (21) 5257-4766. Fax: (21) 6278-8988
  Website: http://www.shanghai.cn.emb-japan.go.jp

- Kazakhstani Embassy in Beijing
  No. 9, Dong Liu Jie, San Li Tun, Beijing 100600
  Tel: (10) 6532-6182 / 6532-4189
  Fax: (10) 6532-6183 / 6532-5386

- Korean Consulate in Shanghai
  60 Wan Shan Road, Shanghai 200336
  Tel: (21) 6295-5000. Fax: (21) 6295-5191
  Website: http://shanghai.mofat.go.kr

- Korean Embassy in Beijing
  No.20 DongfangdongLu,
  Chaoyang District, Beijing 100600
  Tel: (10) 8531-0700 / 8531-0704. Fax: (10) 8531-0726
  Website: http://china.koreanembassy.cn/

- Laotian Embassy in Beijing
  No. 11, Dong Si Jie, San Li Tun
  Beijing 100600
  Tel: (10) 532-1224. Fax: (10) 532-6748

- Latvian Embassy in Beijing
  Unit 71, Green Land Garden
  No 1A Green Land Road
  Chaoyang District, Beijing 100600
  Tel: (10) 6433-3863. Fax: (10) 6433-3810
  Website: http://www.latvianembassy.org.cn
- Lithuanian Embassy in Beijing
  B-30 King's Garden Villas
  No.18, Xiao Yun Lu, Chaoyang District, Beijing 100016
  Tel: (10) 8451-8520. Fax: (10) 8451-4442
- Luxembourg Embassy in Beijing
  Unit 1701, Tower B, Pacific Century Place
  2A Gong Ti Bei Lu, Chaoyang District
  Beijing 100027
  Tel: (10) 8588-0900. Fax: (10) 6513-7268
  Website: http://pekin.mae.lu/en
- Malaysian Embassy in Beijing
  No. 2, Liang Ma Qiao Bei Jie
  Chaoyang District, Beijing 100600
  Tel: (10) 6532-2531 / 6532-2532 (10) 6532-2533
  Website: http://www.kln.gov.my/web/chn_beijing/home
- Malaysian Consulate in Guangzhou
  Units 1912, 1913, 1915-1918
  Citic Plaza Office Tower
  233 Tian He Bei Road, Guangzhou 510610
  Tel: (20) 3877-0763 / 3877-0766. Fax: (20) 3877-0769
  Website: http://www.kln.gov.my/web/chn_guangzhou/home
- Malaysian Consulate in Shanghai
  Units 01, Block B - 9th Floor
  Dawning Centre, No. 500 Hongbaoshi Road
  Changning District, Shanghai 201103
  Tel: (21) 6090-0360 / 6090-0390
  Fax: (21) 6090-0371 / 6090-0398
  Website: http://www.kln.gov.my/web/chn_shanghai/home
- Mauritian Embassy in Beijing
  202 Dong Wai Diplomatic Office Building
  No. 2 Dongzhi Men Wai Da Jie, Beijing 100600
  Tel: (10) 6532-5695 / 6532-569596 / 6532-569598
  Fax: (10) 6532-5706 / 6532-7102

- Mexican Embassy in Beijing
  Sanlitun Dongwujie 5
  Chaoyang District, Beijing 100600
  Tel: (10) 6532-2070. Fax: (10) 6532-3744
  Website: http://www.sre.gob.mx/china/
- Moroccan Embassy in Beijing
  16 San Li Tun Lu, Beijing 100600,
  Tel: (10) 6532-1796 / 6532-1489. Fax: (10) 6532-1453
- Myanmar Embassy in Beijing
  No. 6 Dongzhi Men Wai Street
  Chao Yang District, Beijing 100600.
  Tel: (10) 6532-0351 ext. 24. Fax: (10) 6532-0408
  Website: http://www.myanmarembassy.com/
- Nepalese Embassy in Beijing
  No 1, San Li Tun Xi Liu Jie, Beijing 100600
  Tel: (10) 6532-1795 / 6532-2739
  Website: http://www.nepalembassy.org.cn/
- Dutch Embassy in Beijing
  Liangmahe Nanlu 4, Beijing 100600
  Tel: (10) 8532-0200. Fax: (10) 8532-0300
  Website: http://china.nlembassy.org/
- Dutch Consulate in Shanghai
  10/F Tower B Dawning Center, 500 Hongbaoshi Rd
  Changning district, Shanghai 201103
  Tel: (21) 2208-7288. Fax: (21) 2208-7300
  Website: http://shanghai-en.hollandinchina.org/
- Dutch Consulate in Guangzhou
  208 Tianhe Road, Teem Tower, Floor 34
  Guangzhou 510620
  Tel: (20) 3813-2200. Fax: (20) 3813-2299
  Website: http://guangzhou-en.hollandinchina.org/
- New Zealand Embassy in Beijing
  Ritan Dongerjie No. 1
  Chaoyang District, Beijing 100600
  Tel: (10) 8532-7000. Fax: (10) 6532-4317
  Website: http://www.nzembassy.com/china
- New Zealand Consulate in Guangzhou
  Room1055 China Hotel Office Tower
  Liuhua Road, Guangzhou 510015

Tel: (20) 8667-0253. Fax: (20) 8666-6420
Website: http://www.nzembassy.com/china

- New Zealand Consulate in Shanghai
  Room 1605-1607A, The Centre
  989 Chang Le Road (c)
  Tel: (21) 5407-5858. Fax: (21) 5407-5068
  Website: http://www.nzembassy.com/china
- Norwegian Embassy in Beijing
  1, Dong Yi Jie, San Li Tun, Beijing 100600
  Tel: (10) 8531-9600. Fax: (10) 6532-2392
  Website: http://www.norway.cn
- Norwegian Consulate in Shanghai
  Room 321, 12 Zhong Shan Dong Yi Lu
  Shanghai 200002
  Tel: (21) 6323-9988. Fax: (21) 6323-3938.
  Website: http://www.norway.cn/
- Norwegian Consulate in Guangzhou
  Suite 1802, Citic Plaza
  233 Tian He North Road, Guangzhou 510613
  Tel: (20) 3811- 3188. Fax: (20) 3811-3199
  Website: http://www.norway.cn/
- Peruvian Embassy in Beijing
  Sanlitun, Bangong Lou 1-91
  Diplomatic Building. Beijing 100600
  Tel: (10) 6532-3477 / 6532-2913 / 6532-2494 / 6532-3719
  Fax: (10) 6532-2178
- Philippine Consulate General in Shanghai
  Suite 301, Metrobank Plaza Building
  No. 1160 Yan'an West Road (corner Fanyu Road)
  Changning District, Shanghai 200052
  Tel: (21) 6281-8020. Fax: (21) 6281-8023
  Website: http://www.philcongenshanghai.org
- Philippine Consulate in Guangzhou
  Rm. 709-711, 7th Floor
  Guangdong International Hotel
  339 Huanshi Dong Lu, Guangzhou
  Tel: (20) 8331-1461 / 8331-0996. Fax: (20) 8333-0573
  Website: http://www.guangzhoupcg.org

- Philippine Embassy in Beijing
  No. 23 Xiu Shui Bei-jie, Jiangoumenwai, Beijing 100600
  Tel: (10) 6532-1872 / 6532-2451. Fax: (10) 6532-3761
  Website: http://www.philembassychina.org
- Portuguese Embassy in Beijing
  San Li Tun Dong Wu Jie, N 8, Beijing 100600
  Tel: (10) 6532-3242 / 6532-3220. Fax: (10) 6532-4637
- Romanian Embassy in Beijing
  Ri Tan Lu, Dong Er Jie, Beijing 100600
  Tel: (10) 6532-3442. Fax: (10) 6532-5728
- Russian Embassy in Beijing
  4 Dongzhimen, Beizhongjie, Beijing 100600
  Tel: (10) 6532-1267 / 6532-1991. Fax: (10) 6532-4853
  Website: http://www.russia.org.cn/eng/
- Singaporean Embassy in Beijing
  No. 1 Xiu Shui Bei Jie, Jian Guo Men Wai
  Chaoyang District, Beijing 100600
  Tel: (10) 6532-1115. Fax: (10) 6532-9405
  Website: http://www.mfa.gov.sg/beijing
- Singaporean Consulate in Shanghai
  89 Wan Shan Road, Shanghai 200336
  Tel: (21) 6278-5566. Fax: (21) 6295-6038
  Website: http://www.mfa.gov.sg/shanghai
- South African Embassy in Beijing
  5 Dongzhimenwai Dajie, Beijing 100600
  Tel: (10) 6532-7323 / 6532-0171. Fax: (10) 6532-7139
- Spanish Embassy in Beijing
  Sanlitun Lu, 9, Beijing 100600
  Tel: (10) 6532-3629, Fax: (10) 6532-3401
  Website: http://www.maec.es/embajadas/pekin
- Sri Lankan Embassy in Beijing
  3, Jian Hua Lu, Jian Guo Men Wai, Beijing 100600
  Tel: (10) 6532-1861 / 6532-1862. Fax: (10) 65325426
  Website: http://www.slemb.com/
- Swedish Embassy in Beijing
  3, Dongzhimenwai Dajie
  Sanlitun, Chaoyang District, Beijing 100600
  Tel: (10) 6532-9790. Fax: (10) 6532-5008
  Website: http://www.swedenabroad.com/beijing

- Swedish Consulate in Shanghai
  1521-1541 Shanghai Central Plaza
  381 Huaihai Road (Middle), Shanghai 200020
  Tel: (21) 5359-9610. Fax: (21) 5359-9633
  Website: http://www.swedenabroad.com/shanghai
- Swiss Embassy in Beijing
  Sanlitun Dongwujie 3, Beijing 100600
  Tel: (10) 8532-8888. Fax: (10) 6532-4353
  Website: http://www.eda.admin.ch/eda/en/home/reps/asia/
  vchn/embbei.html
- Swiss Consulate General in Shanghai
  22F, Building A
  Far East International Plaza
  319 Xianxia Road, Shanghai 200051
  Tel: (21) 6270-0519 / 6270-0520. Fax: (21) 6270-0522
  Website: http://www.eda.admin.ch/eda/en/home/reps/asia/
  vchn/cncgsh.html
- Swiss Consulate General in Guangzhou
  Grand Tower, 27th Floor
  228, Tianhe Lu, Tianhe District, Guangzhou 510620
  Tel: (20) 3833-0450 / 3833-0451. Fax: (20) 3833-0453
  Website: http://www.eda.admin.ch/eda/en/home/reps/asia/
  vchn/cncggh.html
- Thai Consulate in Shanghai
  15th Floor, No.567 Wei Hai Road, Jing An district
  Tel: (21) 6288-3030. Fax: (21) 6288-9072
  Website: http://www.thaishanghai.com
- Thai Embassy in Beijing
  No. 40, Guang Hua Lu
  Chaoyang District, Beijing 100600
  Tel: (10) 6532-1749. Fax: (10) 6532-1748
  Website: http://www.thaiembbeij.org
- Turkish Embassy in Beijing
  No. 9, Dong Wu Jie, San Li Tun, Beijing 100600
  Tel: (10) 6532 1715. Fax: (10) 6532 5480
  Website: http://beijing.emb.mfa.gov.tr/
- Turkish Consulate in Shanghai
  1375 Huai Hai (M) Road, 13-B, Qi Hua Tower
  Shanghai 200032

Tel: (21) 6474-6838 / 6474-6839 / 6474-7237
Fax: (21) 6471-9896
Website: http://sanghay.bk.mfa.gov.tr/

- United States Embassy in Beijing
  55 An Jia Lou Road, Beijing PRC 100600
  Tel: (10) 8531-3000. Fax: (10) 8531-4200
  Website: http://beijing.usembassy-china.org.cn/
- United States Consulate in Guangzhou
  No. 1 Shamian Street South
  Guangzhou 510133
  Tel: (20) 8121-8000. Fax: (20) 8121-9001
  Website: http://guangzhou.usembassy-china.org.cn/
- United States Consulate in Shanghai
  1469 Huai Hai Zhong Road (Near Wulumuqi Nan Lu)
  Shanghai 200031
  Tel: (21) 6433-6880. Fax: (21) 6433-4122
  Website: http://shanghai.usembassy-china.org.cn/
- Venezuela Embassy in Beijing
  14, Sanlitun Road, Beijing 100600
  Tel: (10) 6532-1295 / 6532-3654 / 6532-2694
  Fax: (10) 6532-3817
  Website: http://www.venezuela.org.cn/
- British Embassy in Beijing
  11 Guang Hua Lu
  Jian Guo Men Wai, Beijing 100600
  Tel: (10) 5192 4000. Fax: (10) 5192 4239
  Website: http://ukinchina.fco.gov.uk/en/
- British Consulate in Shanghai
  Suite 301, Shanghai Centre
  1376 Nan Jing Xi Lu, Shanghai 200040
  Tel: (21) 3279 2000.
  Website: http://ukinchina.fco.gov.uk/en/about-us/other-locations/shanghai/
- British Consulate in Guangzhou
  7/F Guangdong International Hotel
  339 Huanshi Dong Lu
  Guangzhou 510098
  Tel: (20) 8314-3000. Fax: (20) 8331 2799

Website: http://ukinchina.fco.gov.uk/en/about-us/other-locations/guangzhou/

For additional information please refer to http://embassy.goabroad.com/embassies-in/china

INTERNATIONAL SCHOOLS
Beijing:
- Beijing BISS International School
  No 17, Area 4, An Zhen Xi Li
  Chaoyang District, Beijing 100029
  Tel: (10) 6443-3151
  Fax: (10) 6443-3156
  Website: http://www.biss.com.cn
- The British School of Beijing
  - Shunyi Campus
    South Side, No.9 An Hua Street,
    Shunyi District, Beijing 101318
    Tel: (10) 8047-3588. Fax: (10) 8047-3598/8047-3599
  - Sanlitun Campus
    5 Xiliujie, Sanlitun Road
    Chaoyang District, Beijing 100027
    Tel: (10) 8532-3088. Fax: (10) 8532-3089
    Website: http://www.britishschool.org.cn
- Western Academy of Beijing (WAB)
  PO Box 8547
  #10 Lai Guang Ying Dong Lu
  Chao Yang District, Beijing 100102
  Tel: (10) 8456-4155 .Fax: (10) 6433-3974
  Website: http://www.wab.edu

Guangzhou:
- British School of Guangzhou
  983-3 Tonghe Road, Nanhu,
  Guangzhou 510515
  Tel: (20) 8709-4788 / 3430-5886
  Fax: (20) 8709-8248 / 3430-5887
  Website: http://www.bsg.org.cn

- American International School of Guangzhou
  - Ersha Island Campus (Preschool-Gr.5)
    No. 3 Yan Yu Street South
    Ersha Island, Yuexiu District, Guangzhou 510105
    Tel: (20) 8735-3392 / 8735-3393
    Fax: (20) 8735-3339
    http://www.aisgz.org/
  - Science Park Campus (Gr.6-12):
    19, Kexiang Road Luogang District
    Science Park, Guangzhou 510663
    Tel: (20) 3213-5555. Fax: (20) 3208-6477
    http://www.aisgz.org/
- Guangzhou Nanhu International School
  No. 55, Huayang Street
  Tiyu Dong Lu, Tianhe District
  Guangzhou 510620
  Tel:(20) 3886-6952 /3886-3606 / 3886-5920
  Fax:(20) 3886-3680
  Website: http://www.gnischina.com

Shanghai / Suzhou:

- British International School
  600 Cambridge Forest New Town
  2729 Hunan Road, Pudong, Shanghai 201315
  Tel: (21) 5812-7455. Fax: (21) 5812-7465
  Website: http://www.bisshanghai.com
- Shanghai American School
  258 Jin Feng Lu
  Huacao Town, Minhang District, Shanghai 201107
  Tel: (21) 6221-1445. Fax: (21) 6221-1269
  Website: http://saschina.org
- Dulwich College
  Suite 901, Aviation Centre
  1600 Nanjing West Rd, Shanghai 200040
  Tel: (21) 6248-7878. Fax: (21) 6248-6899
  Website: http://www.dulwichcollege.cn/
- Suzhou Singapore International School
  208 Zhong Nan Street
  Suzhou Industrial Park, Jiangsu 215021

Tel: (512) 6258-0388. Fax: (512) 6258-6388
Website: http://www.ssis-suzhou.net/

For more information on English-based curriculum schools, see http://www.english-schools.org/china/index.htm, or for multiple language based curriculum, see http://www. internationaleducationmedia.com/china/schools.htm.

LIFESTYLE, FOOD AND ENTERTAINMENT GUIDES

- Asia Expat
  http://www.asiaxpat.com
- City Weekend (Beijing, Guangzhou, Shanghai)
  http://www.cityweekend.com.cn
- My Beijing
  http://www.mybeijingchina.com
- Shanghai-ed, owned by SinoMedia
  http://www.shanghai-ed.com
- Shanghai Expat
  http://www.shanghaiexpat.com
- That's Beijing Magazine
  http://www.thebejinger.com
- That's Shanghai Magazine
  http://www.thatsshanghai.com

MEDICAL SERVICES
Beijing

- Bayley & Jackson Medical Center
  7 Ritan Dong Lu
  Chaoyang District, Beijing 100020
  Tel: (10) 8562-9998. Fax: (10) 8561-4866
  Website: http://www.bjhealthcare.com
- Beijing United Family Hospital
  2 Jiang Tai Lu
  Chao Yang District, Beijing 100016
  Tel: (10) 5927-7000
  Emergency hotline: (10) 5927-7120
  Website: http://www.beijingunited.com

- Beijing United Family Clinic
  Pinnacle Plaza, Unit # 818,
  Tian Zhu Real Estate Development Zone,
  Shunyi District, Beijing 101312
  Tel: (10) 8046-5432. Fax: (10) 8046-4383
- Beijing International SOS
  Suite 105, Wing 1
  Kunsha Building, No 16 Xinyuanli
  Chaoyang District, Beijing 100027
  Tel: (10) 6462-9199. Fax: (10) 6462-9117
  Website: http://www.internationalsos.com/cn/
  Beijing International SOS (24-hour Alarm Center)
  Tel: (10) 6462-9100. Fax: (10) 6462-9111
- Beijing International SOS Clinic
  Suite 105, Wing 1, Kunsha Building
  No 16 Xinyuanli, Chaoyang District, Beijing 100027
  Tel: (10) 6462-9112. Fax: (10) 6462-9188

Guangzhou:

- Global Doctor Medical Center
  Global Doctor Clinic
  Room 401-403 (3A), Morgan Business Center
  North Tower, Fuli Yingli Mansion
  No.3 Hua Qiang Road, Pearl River New City
  Tianhe District, Guangzhou, PRC
  Tel: (20) 3884-1452 (24 hours). Fax: (20) 3884-1485
  Emergency call: 13500014119
  Website: http://www.globaldoctor.com.au/
- Guangdong Concord Medical Center
  9/F of the Guangdong Provincial Hospital
  96 Dong Chuan Road, Guangzhou
  Tel: (20) 8387-4283 / 8387-4293 / 8387-4313
  Emergency: (20) 8387-4283
- Guangzhou Can Am International Medical Center
  5/F Garden Tower, Garden Hotel
  368 Huanshi Dong Lu, Guangzhou 510064
  Tel: (20) 8386-6988. Fax: (20) 8760-5276
  Website: http://www.canamhealthcare.com/

Shanghai

- Hua Shan Hospital
  15th Floor, Foreigner's Clinic
  Zong He Lou, 12 Wulumuqi Zhong Lu
  Tel: (21) 6248-3986 / 6248-9999 x 2531
- Shanghai United Family Hospital
  #1139 Xian Xia Lu
  Changning District, Shanghai 200336
  Tel: (21) 2216-3900
  24-Hour Emergency Hotline: (21) 2216-3999
  Website: http://www.unitedfamilyhospitals.com/en/sh/
- World Link Clinic
  Shanghai Center #203 W
  1376 Nanjing Xi Lu, Shanghai 200040
  Tel: (21) 6279-7688.
  For appointments: (21) 6279-8678
  Fax: (21) 6279-7698

For additional information on medical, emergency and evacuation services in Beijing, Chengdu, Guangzhou, Shanghai and Shenyang, see: http://www.usembassy-china. org.cn/us-citizen/medical.html

VETERINARY HOSPITALS

- Shanghai: http://www.scaashanghai.org/veterinarian_ services.shtml
- Beijing: http://beijing.yoolk.com/entertainment/pets/

FURTHER READING

CHINESE LANGUAGE STUDY

Barron's Chinese at a Glance. Scott D Seligman and I-Chuan Chen. Huappage, NY: Barron's Educational Series, 2001.

Business Chinese 500. Beijing Language Institute. San Francisco: China Books & Periodicals, 1982.

Chinesepod. Online Chinese language podcasts. (http://www. chinesepod.com).

A Chinese-English Dictionary and *An English-Chinese Dictionary.* Both Beijing Commercial Press, 1988.

Chinese for Today. Beijing Language Institute. San Francisco: China books & Periodicals Inc, 1982.

Continental's English-Chinese Dictionary. Hong Kong: Hong Kong Press, n.d.

English-Chinese Lexicon of Business Terms. Compiled by Andrew C Chang. Boston: Cheng & Tsui Company, 2002.

Matthew's Chinese-English Dictionary. Taipei: Dunhuang Press, 1975 (13th ed).

Rosetta Stone CD-ROM. Web-based Chinese Programme (http://www.rosettastone.com).

Spoken Standard Chinese (3 Volumes). Hugh M Stimson and Parker Po-Fei Huang. New Haven, CT: Yale Far Eastern Publications, 1976.

Xinhua Zidian. Beijing: Xinhua Press, 1975.

BUSINESS GUIDES / ECONOMIC OVERVIEWS

Back-Alley Banking: Private Entrepreneurs in China. Kellee Tsai. Ithica, NY: Cornell University Press, 2002.

China CEO: Voices of Experience from 20 International Business Leaders. Juan Antonio Fernandez and Laurie Underwood. Singapore: John Wiley and Sons (Asia) Pte Ltd, 2005.

The China Dream: The Elusive Quest for the Last Great Untapped Market on Earth. Joe Studwell. London: Profile Books, 2002.

Chinese Business Etiquette. Scott D Seligman. New York: Warner Books, 1999.

Chinese Intellectual Property Law Guide (Asia Business Law). The Hague: Klewer Law International, 2005.

Integrating China into the Global Economy. Nicolas R Lardy. Washington, DC: Brookings Institution, 2002.

Internationalizing China. David Zweig. Ithica, New York: Cornell University Press, 2002.

One Billion Customers: Lessons from the Front Lines of Doing Business in China (Wall Street Journal Book). James McGregor. Free Press, 2005.

Success Secrets to Maximize Business in China. Larry T Luah. Portland, USA: Graphic Arts; Singapore: Marshall Cavendish Business, 2001.

Strategy, Structure and Performance of MNCs in China. Luo Yadong. Westport, Connecticut: Quorum Books, 2001.

Wen and the Art of Doing Business in China. Daniel R Jospeh. Pittsburgh, PA: Cultural Dragon Publishing, 2001.

CULTURE-RELATED ISSUES
The Traveler's Guide to Asian Customs & Manners. Nancy L Braganti and Elizabeth Devine. New York: St. Martin's P ress, 1988.

Iron and Silk. Mark Salzman. New York: Vintage, 1987.

Living in China. Rebecca Weiner, Margaret Murphy and Albert Li. San Francisco: China Books & Periodicals, Inc., 1991/1997.

Two Years in the Melting Pot. Liu Zongren. San Francisco: China Books & Periodicals, Inc., 1988.

CHINESE HISTORY / CULTURE
Bird in a Cage: Legal Reform in China After Mao. Stanley B Lubman. Palo Alto, CA: Stanford University Press, 1999.

China Chic. Vivienne Tam with Martha Huang. New York: Regan Books, 2000.

Chinese Lessons: Five Classmates and the Story of the New China. John Pomfret. New York: Henry Holt and Co., 2006.

Chinese Shadows. Simon Leys. New York: Penguin Books. 1978.

Confucian China and Its Modern Fate: A Triology. Joseph R Levenson. Berkeley, CA: University of California Press. 1965.

The Gate of Heavenly Peace. Jonathan D Spence. New York: Penguin Books, 1982.

Mooncakes and Hungry Ghosts: Festivals of China. Carol Stepanchuk and Charles Wong. San Francisco: China Books & Periodicals, Inc., 1991.

Good Deeds & Gunboats. Hugh Deane. San Francisco: China Books & Periodicals, Inc., 1990.

The Private Life of Chairman Mao. Li Zhi-Sui. New York: Random House, 1996 .

Red Azalea. Anchee Min. New York: Berkley, 1995.

Riding the Iron Rooster. Paul Theroux. New York: Ivy Books, 1988.

Roses and Thorns: The Second Blooming of the Hundred Flowers in Chinese Fiction, 1979-80. Perry Link. Berkeley, CA: University of California Press, 1984.

Shanghai Baby. Zhou Wei Hui. London: Constable and Robinson, 2001.

Shark Fins and Millet. Ilona Ralf Sues. New York; Garden City Publishing, 1945.

Son of The Revolution. Liang Heng and Judith Shapiro. New York: Vintage Books, 1984.

The Soong Dynasty. Sterling Seagrave. New York: Harper & Row, 1986.

Soul Mountain. Gao Xinjiang. New York: Harper Perennial, 2001.

ABOUT THE AUTHORS

Angie, like many long-term residents, came to China 'on a three-week trip' in 1995, and has lived and worked in the country since. Deeply involved with the community, she served two years as the Chairman of the Board of the American Chamber of Commerce in Shanghai, and co-founded a charity race in Outer Mongolia (http://www. ultramongolia.org) to support sustainable tourism in Lake Hovsgul National Park. Angie is General Manager of Hudson China.

Rebecca spent 11 years in China, including five years in Shanghai. She has now returned to the United States to live with her husband Mike Rastelli and their daughter Sarah, but is always up for return visits to the land of *zongzi* and jazz.

292

INDEX

Titles in the CultureShock! series:

Argentina	France	Portugal
Australia	Germany	Russia
Austria	Great Britain	San Francisco
Bahrain	Hawaii	Saudi Arabia
Beijing	Hong Kong	Scotland
Belgium	India	Shanghai
Berlin	Ireland	Singapore
Bolivia	Italy	South Africa
Borneo	Jakarta	Spain
Brazil	Japan	Sri Lanka
Bulgaria	Korea	Sweden
Cambodia	Laos	Switzerland
Canada	London	Syria
Chicago	Malaysia	Taiwan
Chile	Mauritius	Thailand
China	Morocco	Tokyo
Costa Rica	Munich	Travel Safe
Cuba	Myanmar	Turkey
Czech Republic	Netherlands	United Arab
Denmark	New Zealand	Emirates
Ecuador	Pakistan	USA
Egypt	Paris	Vancouver
Finland	Philippines	Venezuela

For more information about any of these titles, please contact any of our Marshall Cavendish offices around the world (listed on page ii) or visit our website at:

www.marshallcavendish.com/genref